Structural change and economic growth

Structural change and economic growth

*A theoretical essay on the
dynamics of the wealth of nations*

LUIGI L. PASINETTI

CAMBRIDGE UNIVERSITY PRESS

Cambridge
London   New York   New Rochelle
Melbourne   Sydney

Published by the Press Syndicate of the University of Cambridge
The Pitt Building, Trumpington Street, Cambridge CB2 1RP
32 East 57th Street, New York, NY 10022, USA
296 Beaconsfield Parade, Middle Park, Melbourne 3206, Australia

First published 1981

Text set in 10/12 pt Linotron 202 Times, printed and bound in
Great Britain at The Pitman Press, Bath

ISBN 0 521 23607 X

British Library Cataloguing in Publication Data
Pasinetti, Luigi Lodovico
Structural change and economic growth.
1. Economics
331.1   HB75   80–41496
ISBN 0 521 23607 X

HD
75.5
P37

Contents

Part II Economic dynamics theory

Preface

The work which is here presented is a theoretical investigation into the long-term evolution of industrial economic systems. A combination of three factors – one factual and two theoretical – originally prompted this investigation. The factual element was provided by the extremely uneven development – from sector to sector, from region to region – of the environment in which I lived (post-war Europe) at the time I began my training in economics. The two theoretical factors are represented by the two types of theories – specifically the macro-dynamic models of economic growth and input–output analysis – that were offered to me when, as a research student, I came in contact with the economists of the University of Cambridge, England (1956–57 and 1958–59) and of Harvard University in the United States (1957–58).

Both the macro-dynamic growth models and input–output analysis impressed me at the time; but they left me profoundly dissatisfied when I tried to use them in order to understand what is going on in economic systems with a very high degree of dynamism, i.e. of technical progress. And I began to think that an attempt might be made to develop a theoretical scheme which, while retaining the analytical character of input–output analysis, could also deal with uneven increases in productivity, in the way the macro-dynamic models had begun to do, but only for the very simplified case of a one-commodity world. It was from this determination to look for new tools of analysis that the present work has come into being.

The basic model took shape rather rapidly, while I was at Cambridge and at Harvard, and was the subject of discussions with my supervisors. But as I engaged myself in the task of drawing all the implications it contained, I got involved into more and more fundamental problems of economic theory. Slowly, the work became a theoretical essay on the dynamics of industrial systems. It was complete enough as to be submitted (with the title 'A Multi-sector Model of Economic Growth') as a successful Ph.D. dissertation at the University of Cambridge by the summer 1962. And a year later (October 1963), the analytical part of the dissertation (five out of nine chapters) was presented at a Study Week of the Pontifical Academy of Sciences.[1] At that time, I almost reached the point of publishing the dissertation as it was, but I was held back by two problems, which account for the long time that has elapsed since.

First of all, the publication of Sraffa's book called for some reflections. The basic theoretical scheme underlying the present work was conceived and formulated before the publication, and quite independently, of Sraffa's *Production of Commodities by Means of Commodities*. Sraffa's book brought theoretical attention back to the process of production considered as a circular process. This is precisely what, on purpose, I had completely eliminated from my analysis, by adopting not only a vertically integrated conception of the production process but also sharp simplifications as to the employment of labour and capital goods in each single sector. My approach had the great advantage of leading to dynamic analysis straightaway, without that fixity of coefficients which had constrained all inter-industry analysis into a static strait-jacket. Yet it was reasonable to ask oneself whether, with my simplifications, I had eliminated something too important to be left out of consideration. Of course I did see quite soon the direction in which the relation with Sraffa's analysis could be found (see chapter VI of my Ph.D. dissertation, reproduced here with some changes). Yet, it was not until my article in *Metroeconomica*[2] that I worked out in detail all the analytical inter-connections. This was an important step for me, as it confirmed that I could stick to my original simplifications, with all their great advantages for dynamic analysis, without any loss of generality.

The second problem that arose was by far more intricate and tricky. It is a distinctive feature of the present theoretical scheme to begin by carrying out the whole analysis at a level of investigation which the Classical economists called 'natural', that is to say, at a level of investigation which is so fundamental as to be independent of the institutional set-up of society. This feature could be kept quite easily with reference to prices and physical quantities. The difficulties, which looked unsurmountable at the beginning, arose with reference to the

---

1 Published in 1965 as 'A New Theoretical Approach to the Problems of Economic Growth', *Pontificiae Academiae Scientiarum Scripta Varia*, No. 28, Vatican City 1965, pp. 571–696. (Republished in *The Econometric Approach to Development Planning*, North Holland Publ. Co., Amsterdam 1965).

2 'The Notion of Vertical Integration in Economic Analysis', *Metroeconomica*, vol. 25, 1973, pp. 1–29; reprinted in *Essays on the Theory of Joint Production*, Macmillan, London 1980.

determination of the rate(s) of profit and the rate(s) of interest. In my Ph.D. dissertation I had looked for a 'natural' rate of profit at the macro-economic level. In a subsequent article[3] I thought I had found a confirmation of the same concept in a truly Classical sense – i.e. in the sense of defining a behaviour, in terms of propensities to save, that led to natural positions. But it did not take long to realise that introducing behavioural (savings) relations did not fit consistently into a theoretical framework which was basically conceived independently of institutions.

I had to look more deeply and, in the end, I did find the new concepts I needed – not at the macro-economic, but at the sectoral, level, where, as I soon realised, there logically exists a whole series of 'natural' rates of profit. In parallel, from an investigation on inter-personal debt/credit relations, there emerged a 'natural' rate of interest, coming out of a whole series of own-rates of interest. In this way, the entire theoretical scheme was rendered logically consistent and remarkably complete.

There is a further, very neat, methodological consequence that followed, namely a sharp discrimination between those economic problems that have to be solved on the ground of logic alone – for which economic theory is entirely autonomous – and those economic problems that arise in connection with particular institutions, or with particular groups' or individuals' behaviour – for which economic theory is no longer autonomous and needs to be integrated with further hypotheses, which may well come from other social sciences. It is with the first type of problems that the present work is basically concerned. And yet, when institutional characteristics are introduced, they are explicitly pointed out. Therefore, one will indeed have to go on, from the present analysis, to more detailed investigations concerning particular institutional set-ups, if more specific conclusions are to be drawn, but with no danger of confusing the two levels of enquiry. For the first, more fundamental, stage of analysis a complete and self-contained theoretical scheme has at last clearly emerged.

As it is here finally presented, the work maintains the original structure of my Ph.D. dissertation. But the original nine chapters have been supplemented with two additional ones – on the natural rate of interest (inserted as chapter VIII) and on international economic relations (chapter XI), respectively. Some of the dissertation chapters have remained virtually unchanged (such as chapters II and III); others

3 'Rate of Profit and Income Distribution in relation to the Rate of Economic Growth', *Review of Economic Studies*, 1962, pp. 267–79, reprinted in *Growth and Income Distribution – Essays in Economic Theory*, Cambridge University Press, Cambridge 1974.

have been almost entirely re-written (such as chapters VII and IX). All of them, including the new ones, have been maintained within the simple framework and the elementary logic of the original approach, which has proved remarkably flexible *vis-à-vis* the most intricate analytical problems of economic dynamics.

As is only too natural for a theoretical work which was carried on over many years – during a time in which I moved from Milan to Cambridge, England, to Cambridge, Mass., to Oxford, to Cambridge, England, again, and finally back to Milan – I have contracted huge debts of gratitude towards a large number of scholars. First and foremost, I must thank Richard Goodwin and Richard Kahn, who were, at different stages, my Cambridge supervisors over the years I was writing my Ph.D. dissertation. It was Richard Goodwin who skilfully directed my very first timid steps into research work. And later, when I began to write a great deal, Richard Kahn very patiently read, criticised and commented every single note I submitted to him. Through Kahn I came in contact with that unique mixture of radicalism, wisdom and social concern that was the distinct mark of Keynes' environment. Through Goodwin I was stimulated to open up my intellectual curiosity and interests towards tools of analysis that came from outside. At the same time, I also benefited from long discussions, and often from daily conversations, with Nicholas Kaldor, always bubbling with new ideas, Joan Robinson, always hard as a rock on her theoretical conceptions, and Piero Sraffa, the real master of all critics. It is from them that I learnt that passionate critical attitude which has been the *conditio sine qua non* for starting and pursuing an investigation of this type.

This unique group of scholars in that unique intellectual environment that was the Cambridge of the late 1950s and early 1960s provided an ideal background for the present work. Needless to say their ideas have been absolutely essential to me and I shall never find words to thank them adequately. Yet I must also add that they may not necessarily or entirely approve of the use I have made of their theories. In the following pages, their theories are taken for granted and an analysis is developed which goes on to explore a ground (that of structural change) which has so far remained almost untrodden. I must accept for this full responsibility.

At various times and on different points, in the early stages of the work, I received helpful criticisms and comments, for which I am most grateful, from Siro Lombardini in Milan; David Champernowne, Robin Marris, Amartya Sen, Richard Stone in Cambridge; James Duesenberry, Franco Modigliani, Carl Kaysen at Harvard; John Hicks, Ian

Little in Oxford. At the very last stages, I also received useful criticisms and comments from Terenzio Cozzi and Alberto Quadrio-Curzio.

I need hardly add that responsibility for all views expressed is entirely mine.

L.L.P.

Milano, December 1979

Chapter I

Introduction

. . . if orthodox economics is at fault, the error is to be found not in the superstructure, which has been erected with great care for logical consistency, but in a lack of clearness and of generality in the premisses.

J. M. Keynes, from the Preface to the *General Theory*

1. Foreword

What follows is an essay in economic theory. Although relatively short and concise it aims at fundamental problems, and as such it perhaps reveals its main features in the nature of the approach it adopts to economic reality.

The set of premises on which the work is built is not one to which economists are nowadays accustomed, but the basic ideas behind the premises are not new – their roots can be found, at one stage or another, in the long history of economic thought. In the present investigation, however, many of these ideas are taken from the original context at their source, at a stage at which they were susceptible of being developed in different directions from those along which they actually happen to have been developed.

To clarify these concepts, I have thought it useful to devote the present introductory chapter to a rapid survey of the various approaches to economic reality which have been adopted hitherto, with the purpose of showing how I should like to consider the present work in the stream of development of economic thought.

2. The historical background of economic analysis

I shall begin with a few remarks, which may sound at first rather general and far-fetched, but which will soon turn out to have a justification.

If we consider the historical context in which economic analysis has come into being, we may say that this context is represented by the *modern* world; namely the stage of our history which is known as the age of experiment and science, because of the dominating idea that man, by using his own critical intellect, by observing nature and by experimenting, can learn in a systematic way and can pass on his improved knowledge to the following generations. The idea that man can systematically progress, simple though it may seem to-day, took a long time to emerge; but once discovered, it has, in a few centuries, revolutionised the whole prospects of humanity and has pervaded every activity involving human ingenuity.

In economic terms, the direct consequence has been a process of unprecedented increase in material wealth. The process may be divided, for analytical purposes, into two distinct phases, which we may call the phase of trade and the phase of industry. There is no clear-cut distinction between the two, as they have a common origin and are intermingled, but they appear nevertheless with very definite characteristics on the historical scene.

The phase of trade is the first to break through. It can be perceived even as early as the turn of the first millennium, with the rise of the Mediterranean maritime republics; but it can be seen more clearly later on, after the Renaissance 'opening of the minds' towards the outside world. A few basic improvements in the technique of transportation led to the discoveries of new lands and extended the horizon of the known world to include countries with climates and products previously unknown. New possibilities of trade were opened up, with a profound impact on the economic conditions of the whole world. The trading nations were suddenly better off, not because of a rise in world's production, but because of a better utilisation of the production which already took place. Each nation kept her own institutions and organisational structure of production, but could now advantageously exchange the products which were proper to her particular climate or localised resources for products which she could never produce or which she could produce only at much higher cost. The material wealth of all nations was increased just by exchange, by a better spatial allocation of existing resources and products. This is the merchant era, an era which represents perhaps the most outstanding example of how all people can gain from trade.

Much slower to manifest itself is the phase of industry, which requires the existence of, and thus presupposes, trade. Industry is a process of augmenting wealth through a material increase in the quantity and number of products, to be achieved by the practical application of the advances of science, division and specialisation of labour, better organisation, invention and utilisation of new sources of energy and new materials. Unlike trade, industry requires changes in the organisational structure of society. Therefore, it comes about slowly; but progressively. In fact, it requires long and painful social changes in the relations between men and the means of production before it can fully break out in the 'industrial revolution' that England experienced in the eighteenth century. Of course trade remains the natural and necessary complement of industry but, as a cause of *further* increases of wealth, it is bound to subside. Industry, on the other hand, is bound to remain a permanent cause of increase in wealth and to become pre-eminent as time goes on, owing to the very nature of its cumulative process.

These two aspects of the modern world seem to me very helpful in indicating the directions in which the emergence of the modern era has stimulated economic analysis.

The concept of trade is, so to speak, a *static* concept. It is associated with a situation in which a plurality of economic systems (or of individuals) are endowed with particular resources or products and try to gain advantages through exchange. The interest that such a situation arouses in an economist concerns the problem of how to reach the best allocation of given resources, namely of how to make the best use of what is already available. We may imagine a stationary situation in which a plurality of economic systems have reached equilibrium internally, but do not trade among themselves; and then another stationary situation in which the same economic systems, besides having reached an internal equilibrium, also trade with one another. It is easy to show that the passage from the first to the second situation – i.e. a once-for-all change from no trade to a new situation of trade, to be maintained thereafter – normally brings about a gain for all. The problem involved is a *problem of rationality*, which may be expressed by a mathematical function to be maximised under certain constraints.

The concept of, and the problems entailed by, industry are quite different. Industry is, so to speak, a *dynamic* concept. It implies production, i.e. the engagement and the application of man's ingenuity to make and shape the products he wants. But since by doing and experiencing man learns, it is implicit in the very nature of carrying on a production activity that new and better methods of production will be discovered. Of course, to find new methods takes time, and takes time in a persistent way. The economist is faced here no longer with a problem of rationality, but with a *process of learning*. Any mathematical formulation of it cannot but be in terms of functions of time, since the process makes short steps, and may appear quite negligible, in the short run; but as it goes on incessantly, it is inevitably bound to become the more pronounced the longer the period which is considered. The contrast with the simple concept of trade is now evident. The passage from a position of no trade to a position of trade requires a jump, which may be quite big but which is temporary, as it ends when the new equilibrium situation has been reached. The process of learning associated with industry, on the other hand, implies a persistent movement – not a once-for-all change, but a *rate of change* in time, a cumulative and indefinite movement.

Clearly, these are two distinct series of problems. A particularly important difference between the two, for theoretical analysis, is that they acquire an opposite practical relevance in relation to time, the former being relevant (in the short run) just when the latter is practically irrelevant, and the latter becoming relevant (in the long run) just when the former becomes irrelevant. This opposition carries with it profound consequences for theoretical analysis, as it normally induces the theorist to diametrically opposite attitudes to the type of hypotheses to choose. It will be argued in the following pages that both series of problems have actually been considered in the course of the development of economic thought. But the opposition between the two and the different approaches they require have not been clearly realised. From this failure, unfortunately, it is the theoretical analysis of the industrial aspects of the modern world – i.e. of those aspects which are cumulatively becoming more important – that seems to have suffered most.

3. A hint at Mercantilism and at Physiocracy

After what has been said in the previous section, it cannot be surprising to find that the immediate responses stimulated among economists by the inception of the modern world have been of a 'mercantilist' type. As is well known Mercantilism – with its central tenet that a nation, in order to increase her wealth, should aim at an excess of exports over imports – is a doctrine that dominated economic thought in the sixteenth, seventeenth and first half of the eighteenth centuries. The mercantilists' arguments and their over-enthusiasm about the merits of trade have subsequently been proved faulty but this only underlines how strong must have been the impact of the benefits from trade on the minds of the scholars who, during those centuries, tried to analyse and understand the relevant economic aspects of the commercial environment of the time.

However, the other economic aspect of the modern world – the aspect connected with industry and production – could not fail to be noticed as time went by. Already in the second half of the eighteenth century, Physiocracy, the new economic doctrine which came to submerge Mercantilism, centred the attention precisely on *production* and –

understandably enough in the eighteenth century – indicated agricultural production as the real source of wealth of a nation. It is to the Physiocrats that we owe the first table representing the circulation of commodities in an economic system (François Quesnay's celebrated *Tableau économique*). The radical change introduced by this table concerns precisely the concept of 'wealth'. No longer the accumulated stock of precious metals, but her *produit net*, her annual net production, was indicated as the real source of wealth of a nation. The economists of this school of thought were then able to go on to consider trade in the commodities which are produced, and to develop those arguments in favour of free trade which came to break the mercantilistic *récipes* after two and a half centuries of undisputed domination.

It may be interesting to make a remark here, the relevance of which will become clear in the following pages. A theorist can analyse trade without any reference to production; in fact, in order to isolate the problem, he (she) will very likely ignore production altogether. But when a theorist analyses the process of production to begin with, he (she) is bound also to go on to consider the trade in the commodities which are being produced, although he (she) may tend to ignore the goods which are not produced – the natural resources.

4. The 'Classical' approach to economic reality

The stream of economic thought – from Adam Smith to John Stuart Mill – which is now known as 'Classical' followed the physiocratic lines but under a much more powerful impact: that of the English industrial revolution. It was, not surprisingly, the industrial aspect of the modern world that impressed the Classical economists as being the most important feature of the new society. Trade, of course, was also a big topic, but it was the trade of manufactured goods. This had obvious consequences on the attitude the Classical economists adopted towards the economic reality they wanted to investigate. This attitude can be caught immediately in the very opening pages of their works, when they are outlining the subject of their inquiries.

Consider, for example, the two most prominent Classical figures – Adam Smith and David Ricardo.

Adam Smith begins his *Wealth of Nations* with an analysis of 'the causes of improvements in the productive power of labour', which are immediately singled out as the main source of the wealth of nations. At the very beginning of the work, when sketching out the plan of the whole inquiry, Smith explains that 'the proportion [of the produce] to the number of those who are to consume it' – namely per capita income, as we may say in modern terms – 'must in every nation be regulated by two different circumstances; first, by the skill, dexterity, and judgment with which its labour is generally applied; and, secondly, by the proportion between the number of those who are employed in useful labour, and that of those who are not so employed. Whatever be the soil, climate, or extent of territory of any particular nation, the abundance or scantiness of its annual supply must . . . depend upon those two circumstances.'[1] But Smith insists further. He wants to underline the pre-eminence of 'the skill, dexterity and judgment with which labour is applied' over the quality of 'the soil, climate and extent of territory' and he points out how 'the savage nations of hunters and fishers [where] every individual who is able to work is more or less employed in a useful labour . . . however, are so miserably poor . . . [while] among civilised and thriving nations, though a great number of people do not labour at all . . . yet the produce of the whole labour of the society is so great that all are often abundantly supplied'.[2]

Even today these sentences are worth meditating on. Under the compelling pressure of the striking disparities between developed and underdeveloped countries, it is with a sense of achievement that we have recently been re-discovering the same factors accounting for differences in per-capita incomes that Adam Smith had clearly singled out two centuries ago!

David Ricardo, fifty years later, by becoming more analytical, had already missed Smith's emphasis on the effects of improvements in technology. His basic approach to economic reality remained, however, the same; indeed, he centred his analysis on production in a way much more suitable for analytical elaboration, as he had a clear conviction that, when simplifications are necessary, they ought to be made in the direction of eliminating from the analysis what in practice is least important. Like Smith, he considered the phenomena connected with the commodities which are given by nature as 'by far' less important than those connected with the process of production. Therefore, when faced with a choice, he never hesitated in devising his analytical apparatus with reference to the latter, even if that sometimes implied some crude simplifications with regard to the former.

It is on the first two pages of his *Principles* that Ricardo draws a distinction which seems to me of crucial importance. It sets out, precisely in terms of types of commodities, the opposition between the trade aspect and the production aspect of modern society which has

1 Adam Smith, *An Inquiry into the Nature and Causes of the Wealth of Nations*, ed. by Edwin Cannan, London 1904, vol. I, p. 1.
2 Adam Smith, *ibid.*, p. 2.

been described above. Ricardo says that 'there are some commodities the value of which is determined by scarcity alone'.[3] We may call these the commodities of the *natural endowment* type. They are given (by nature or by particular circumstances or by peculiar skills) in a fixed quantity and they have to be accepted as they are. They become economically relevant when they are scarce, i.e. when their fixed quantity is insufficient to meet all needs (*scarce goods*). For Ricardo they have very little economic importance. 'These commodities,' he adds, 'form a very small part of the mass of commodities daily exchanged in the market.'[4] Therefore, he prefers not to consider them at all. He is interested in a different, more relevant, type of commodities. 'By far the greatest part of those goods, which are the object of desire, are procured by labour, and they may be multiplied, not in one country alone, but in many, almost without any assignable limit, if we are disposed to bestow the labour necessary to obtain them.'[5] We may call these the commodities of the production type. It is on these commodities exclusively (the produced – or reproducible – commodities) that Ricardo concentrates his analysis.

This approach presents a difficulty in the treatment of natural resources (in particular of land). Natural resources are goods which are provided by nature; they belong to the category of *scarce goods*; nevertheless they do enter the process of production. When Ricardo met the problem, he solved it by following the logic of his basic approach. It was essential for him not to blur the picture of the most important phenomena – those connected with production – with secondary complications from the existence of non-homogeneous natural resources. Therefore, he referred his analysis to that piece of land which, by being at the limit of cultivated land, yields no rent, namely to that land which is no longer scarce. All the other lands (or natural resources, in general) which have better intrinsic qualities than those at the limit of cultivation, yield a net gain or *rent* to the person who happens to own them. After deduction of this rent, all lands are put on the same footing of non-scarce land. The problems of scarcity had thereby been 'eliminated' from the analysis, and Ricardo could carry on his inquiry into the commodities which he really wanted to investigate – the produced commodities, which are 'by far the greatest part of goods, which are the object of desire'.

Another difficulty was bound to arise in connection with short-run

3 David Ricardo, *On the Principles of Political Economy and Taxation*, vol. I of 'The Works and Correspondence of David Ricardo', in 11 vols., ed. by Piero Sraffa, Cambridge 1951 (to be referred to as *Principles*), p. 12.
4 David Ricardo, *ibid.*, p. 12.
5 David Ricardo, *ibid.*, p. 12.

situations. As Ricardo says, the 'wants and wishes of mankind' may suddenly change, and the various processes of production may require some time for adaptation to the new requirements. Meanwhile, even produced goods may become *temporarily* scarce, and their market prices may diverge from what they would be on the basis of their fundamental determinants. Again Ricardo solves the difficulty within the logic of his basic approach. He simply refuses to follow 'accidental and temporary deviations', because in the long run they become irrelevant. These deviations only come to blur, without influencing, the fundamental picture which is behind them. And Ricardo is mainly interested in the fundamental picture, namely in those values of economic variable which are – as he calls them – 'primary and natural'.[6]

5. Marginal economic analysis

Classical economics was bound to come under the fire of criticism at the very moment at which – as happened in the second half of the last century – economists turned their attention to problems connected with demand. The Classical economists had neglected demand almost completely and criticism was legitimate. However, the economists who criticised them did not correct them on this point (we shall come back to this in chapter VII); they went on instead to deal with an entirely different order of problems: the problems related to those commodities – the scarce goods – which the Classical economists did not consider at all.

It was natural to expect, from this new approach, a polarisation of the whole analysis on the other aspect – the trade aspect – of the modern world. This new theoretical movement began in the 1870s with the elaboration of the concept of marginal utility and took up an approach to economic reality which appears as exactly opposite to the classical one. The Marginalists began to study the real world not with what is most important but with what is easier to begin with. An analogy taken from the field of mechanics suggested to them that they study the static aspects of reality first: not because these aspects are supposed to be more important than the dynamic, but because they seem to offer the first logical step to take. From a formal point of view, the analysis which has come out is impeccable. It starts from clear premises, and, by the use of the most elegant analytical tools, arrives at logically consistent conclusions.

Over the past hundred years, hundreds of economists have carried out an enormous amount of analytical work along these lines, and by

6 David Ricardo, *ibid.*, p. 88, and also chapter XIX.

now marginal analysis has been cleared of the sundry small traps that the original arguments contained. The analytical tools themselves have been perfected through time and have become more and more elegant. To a first generation of Marginalists using diagrams, a second generation has succeeded using calculus, and then a third generation using set theory. As was to be expected, through this long analytical process, the model has been schematised and stripped down to essentials, so that the basic approach has by now emerged most clearly.

We may say that the typical marginalist scheme of general equilibrium, as it has been called, is a model of what has become known as a *pure exchange* economy.[7] The model presupposes the existence of given natural resources in fixed quantities and of a given number of individuals, who are endowed with them. These individuals own the resources in a way which is accepted as given and they have well-defined utility preferences. The economic problem that is investigated is that of finding those prices (equilibrium prices) which bring about, through exchange, an optimum allocation of the given resources; this optimum allocation being defined as that situation at which the individuals maximise their utilities, relative to the original distribution of resources among them. This model is worked out, in its basic features, with no reference whatever to a process of production. The only type of commodities that exist are given by nature and, in equilibrium, their prices will be either zero (and they will be called *free goods*) or positive, and they will be called *scarce goods*, the only ones to be economically relevant. In such a context, the economic problem is only one of *rational choice*. The individuals of the community, if they behave rationally and act atomistically, will exchange among themselves the given commodities up to that point where the ratios of marginal utilities are equal to the corresponding ratios of prices. At this point their utilities are

---

7 Such a basic model is always the first to be worked out, independently of anything else, in the first chapters of all standard treatises of marginal economic theory. See, for example: Léon Walras, *Elements d'économie politique pure*, Lausanne 1874–78 (English translation: *Elements of Pure Economics*, ed. by W. Jaffé, London 1954); Vilfredo Pareto, *Cours d'économie politique*, Lausanne 1896, and *Manuel d'économie politique*, Paris 1909; J. R. Hicks, *Value and Capital*, Oxford 1939; Jacob L. Mosak, *General Equilibrium Theory in International Trade*, Cowles Commission Monograph No. 7, Bloomington, Indiana 1944; Gerard Debreu, *Theory of Value*, Cowles Foundation Monograph No. 17, New York 1959.

Alfred Marshall's *Principles of Economics* represents a case of its own. Marshall, deeply imbued by the English pragmatic tradition, was never really able to turn his attention away from production: he clearly felt it was practically too important to be neglected or minimised. He tried a compromise. He did accept marginal analysis, but he attempted a reconciliation with the Classical economists; to which we shall come back in chapter VII. No wonder that he has always been eliciting hostility from the purists of marginal economic theory.

maximised. No individual could become better off, without some other individuals being made worse off (a situation which has become known as one of *Pareto-optimality*). Most typically, the whole problem may be represented by a mathematical function to be maximised, subject to certain constraints to be accepted as fixed.

This is a perfectly valid theoretical scheme. Perhaps the Classical economists themselves would not have objected to it. They certainly would not have denied that there exists a rational problem of optimum allocation of the existing scarce goods. But they would never have dreamt of making of it anything more than a minor problem and an easy one to solve, so easy in fact that they felt justified in taking it for granted. The Marginalists, on the other hand, went to the other extreme. After analysing the problem of optimum allocation of given resources, they began to advance a disproportionate claim. They began to think that they had discovered a principle of universal validity, which *alone* would allow them to analyse the whole of economic reality.

From this point on, a vast theoretical movement started, the task of which has turned out to be that of *extending* the same elegant tools of marginal utility analysis to all branches of economic analysis. This tendency has become clearer and clearer especially in the twentieth century, and is in fact being continued nowadays by the great majority of economists, especially in the United States. Paul Samuelson, at the very beginning of one of the clearest versions of marginal economic theory, claims precisely this. He claims to have been able to isolate a simple principle, which, by being applied again and again, is behind every economic investigation: a mathematical function to be maximised under constraints. This is the *foundation of economic analysis*.[8] For Paul Samuelson and for all Marginalists, the whole of economics can be reduced just to that principle (and mathematical tool).[9] Under this generalising form, marginal economic analysis has even been called 'neo-classical' (a term that sounds ironical if one considers the opposition between the Classical approach and the marginalist one).

It was with reference to this vast movement and with a deep conviction on the generality of its approach, that Lionel Robbins, at the apex of the marginalist era, epitomised the new conception of economic

8 Paul A. Samuelson, *Foundations of Economic Analysis*, Cambridge, Mass. 1947; see especially Chapter I: *Introduction*. The same concepts are resumed and expanded by Tjalling C. Koopmans in *Three Essays on the State of Economic Science*, New York 1957, pp. 4–5.

9 Samuelson has restated his conviction that maximisation is 'the very foundation of our subject' in his Nobel Memorial Lecture: 'Maximum Principles in Analytical Economics', *Les Prix Nobel en 1970*. (See his *Collected Scientific Papers*, vol. 3, Cambridge, Mass. 1972, pp. 2–17).

analysis with a celebrated definition. 'Economics,' Robbins said, 'is the science which studies human behaviour as a relationship between ends and scarce means which have alternative uses.'[10]

But this is precisely the question. Is economics really all here – in a problem of optimum allocation of scarce goods – or is this not rather a narrowing down of the subject of economics itself to one aspect, perhaps not even the most important, of economic reality? Unfortunately, the Ricardian distinction between produced commodities and scarce commodities had by this time been pushed aside and forgotten;[11] and it was no longer so easy to see that the Classical economists had been talking about different things.

6. The baffling 1870s

The astonishing success of marginal utility theory in the 1870s (what has been called 'the marginal revolution') will remain for a long time a fascinating subject for the historians, and the sociologists, of economic thought to study. What strikes one about it is that it took off apparently out of nothing. Utility had been no novel subject of discussion among economists,[12] and the marginal principle was not new either.[13] But before the 1870s these concepts had been taken as rather secondary, and in any case always as complementary to the (more basic) ones coming from the sphere of production.[14] By contrast, in the 1870s, all of a

10 Lionel Robbins, *An Essay on the Nature and Significance of Economic Science*, London 1935, p. 16.
11 The process through which this has happened is itself very interesting. Economic goods have positive prices. Now, within a pure exchange model, the only goods that have positive prices are the 'scarce' goods. The Marginalists have therefore turned things upside down and *defined* the scarce goods as those goods that have positive prices. But this procedure, though justified in a pure exchange model, is illegitimate in general. All the produced commodities do have positive prices, and yet they are not 'scarce', in the Classical sense of the word. But the Marginalists did not go back to check their definitions. The consequence has been that they went on to (illegitimately) apply to produced goods the conclusions of their theories about scarce goods. For the Marginalists, all economic goods have become *scarce* – not because they are really *scarce*, but simply because they have been *called* so.
12 The numerous writings of Jeremy Bentham had very prominently introduced utility (and the measurement of utility) into economic discussions since the end of the eighteenth century. Even with reference to the specific problem of value, discussions had been widespread. See, for example, Ferdinando Galiani (*Della Moneta*, Naples 1751) and Jean-Baptiste Say (*Traité d'économie politique*, Paris 1803 and later editions).
13 Ricardo had used it for his own theory of rent.
14 Jean Baptiste Say, to take an authoritative example, always took the line that 'le prix des produits s'établissait en chaque endroit au taux où les portent leurs frais de production, pourvu que l'utilité qu'on leur donne fasse naître le désir de les acquérir'. (*Traité d'économic politique*, p. 321, 6th and last edition, Guillaumin, Paris 1841).

sudden, they were laid down as the very foundation of economic analysis. What is even more fascinating is that this happened not in one place alone, but almost simultaneously all over Europe;[15] and, moreover, precisely the same concepts, in precisely the same places, had already been tried before, but without success.[16]

A satisfactory and comprehensive explanation of such a striking turn-about may yet require a long time to emerge clearly. But it seems to me that in the end it cannot be abstracted from the combined effects of two major features of the European environment of the time: the appearance of Marx's critique of economic theory (Marx's *Das Kapital* first appeared in 1867), and the widespread social unrest which characterised those troubled years.

Objectively, Karl Marx was a Classical economist in the full sense of the word. He picked up and pursued the Classical approach to economic reality. This gave a sweeping drive to his analysis, since production – and production with capital – undoubtedly is the central feature of any modern industrial system. Subjectively, however, he used classical theory for purposes which were diametrically opposite to those of the classical economists. The Classical economists (in a line descending directly from physiocratic thinking) had accepted the society in which they lived as part of the order of Nature; Marx regarded it as a passing phase in the transition from the feudalism of the past to the socialism of the future. The Classical economists had generally been arguing in terms of harmony of interest among the various sections of society; Marx conceived economic life in terms of conflicts of interest and class struggle. The Classics had aimed at finding out how the established system works in order to help it work better; Marx aimed at uncovering its contradictions in order to hasten its end through turmoil and revolution. Even the purest of all analytical problems was turned upside down. Consider, as an example, Ricardo's labour theory of value, bogged down by the difficulty of relative prices changing when income distribution changes, even if relative quantities of embodied labour

---

15 The 'marginal revolution' is by now jointly attributed to W. Stanley Jevons (*The Theory of Political Economy*, London 1871), Carl Menger (*Grundsätze der Volkswirtschaftslehre*, Vienna 1871), and Léon Walras (*Elements d'économie politique pure*, Lausanne 1874). They all wrote their works independently of one another.

16 The list of 'precursors' is long and is continually being lengthened (Galiani, Lloyd, Longfield, Senior, Dupuit, Jennings, etc.). Some of them actually are more than precursors, as is the case of Cournot and Gossen, who were marginalists in the full sense of the word, with only the bad luck of having published their works before the 1870s (Augustin Cournot, *Recherches sur les principes mathématiques de la théorie des richesses*, Paris 1838; Hermann Heinrich Gossen, *Entwickelung der Gesetze des menschlichen Verkehrs und der daraus fliessenden Regeln für menschliches Handeln*, Braunschweig 1854).

remain the same. Marx could waste no time to untwine such Gordian knots: he just cut them. He *defined* values as being embodied quantities of labour, and then turned the argument against the capitalist system. Marx argued that if, in practice, prices turn out to be different from 'values', that is the fault of the capitalist system, which, by disguising 'surplus value' under the form of profits, distorts the 'price of production' from 'values'. Precisely those features that appeared to the Classical economists as insoluble analytical difficulties were turned by Marx into further indictments of capitalist society.

This was upsetting. To many people it sounded preposterous. Yet Marx's overall arguments were not easy to challenge. The obvious procedure to follow would have been to question the premises. But this is precisely what was so difficult. Marx's premises were exactly the same as those of Smith and Ricardo, i.e. of all established economics.

If only one could find an economic theory that made no reference to labour, no reference to means of production, possibly even to production itself. . . that would surely be the sort of thing that a frightened Establishment could not but most warmly welcome. Marginal utility theory provided precisely that.[17]

It is worth recalling that the whole of Europe had just been under the impact of shivering revolutionary waves. A concentration of events had taken place precisely in those years. The first Socialist International – formed in London in 1864 – had held its four congresses in the four successive years of the late 1860s (1866 in Geneva, 1867 in Lausanne, 1868 in Brussels and 1869 in Basle). And, at the end of the Franco-Prussian war of 1870, Europe had witnessed the first communist revolutionary attempt ever to be made (the Paris Commune, March–May 1871). The Papacy itself was openly acknowledging the challenge. And shortly afterwards, Pope Leo XIII was going to overcome all hesitations and take the unprecedented step of pronouncing on social matters (encyclical letter *Rerum Novarum*, 1891).

It cannot be surprising that when, in the 1870s, peace-loving academic economists began strongly to press with a theory which sharply drifted attention away from all the features which had so ruthlessly been put at the basis of the revolutionary trends of the time, the public to whom theoretical economic works are addressed should have a second look at what was proposed, no matter how unimportant or queer it had been

7 There is absolutely no need to think that the marginal utility theorists developed their theories with such a purpose in mind. Marginal utility theory may well have been, as Schumpeter puts it (*History of Economic Analysis*, New York 1954, p. 888), 'a purely analytic affair without reference to practical questions' (actually too much so). The point which is made here is that historical circumstances made the 1870s, in sharp contrast to earlier decades, extraordinarily receptive to such a theory.

considered before.[18] And what happened is indeed striking. Wherever, in the 1870s, marginal utility theory was proposed, it had an astounding success.

7. The theory of marginal productivity

What has happened to the theory of production, within the marginal economic framework, is worth considering in detail. Marginal utility theory had to be extended beyond its original field (the optimum allocation of scarce goods) – it would have had a rather limited impact otherwise. And an extension (or, using a word which sounds deceptively more attractive, a 'generalisation') was soon made to the more important problems of production. Thus, in the 1890s, the theory of marginal productivity emerged.

The point is worth stressing. Marginal productivity theory did not spring from an examination of the problems to which it was meant to apply: the problems of production. It came artificially from an *extension* to these problems of a set of ready-made analytical tools developed for completely different purposes.

The starting point was again provided, not by what is most important in an industrial society, but by what could most easily be fitted in, namely land (a scarce natural resource). Labour was then immediately assimilated to land, as one of the many scarce resources. All the original illustrative examples are in fact in terms of land and labour. But there was a big stumbling block, represented by the treatment of capital goods. Capital goods are not 'given'; they are themselves produced. Early attempts to deal with the problem had spontaneously considered capital goods as accumulated labour and time.[19] But this labour-time approach has put the natural resource model into such a series of

18 Cournot and Gossen provide the impressive examples. Their books (in 1838 and 1854 respectively) were complete failures. Cournot thought at first that economists might not have paid attention to his work because of lack of acquaintance with mathematics. He patiently rewrote the whole work in plain words, making it three times as long (*Principes de la théorie des richesses*, Paris 1863). But the second version was as bad a failure as the first one (and remained so). Gossen, in his turn, was deeply disappointed. His book did not arouse any interest: it remained practically unsold. He died (in 1858) without glory. But three decades later a shrewd publisher (R. L. Prager of Berlin), after realising that marginal utility had become fashionable, got hold of the old printed material, which was still lying unsold. He added a short foreword, put up a new title-page with the new date (1889) and the simple addition 'neue ausgabe'; and reissued the book. This time it was a great success.
19 See, for example, W. Stanley Jevons, *The Theory of Political Economy*, London 1871, Chapter VII. It is interesting to notice that Jevons, who in general was harsh on the Classical economists, is in no opposition to them on this point. See also: Eugen von Böhm-Bawerk, *Positive Theorie des Kapitales*, Innsbruck 1889.

inextricable difficulties that it had to be abandoned and resumed and abandoned many times. There is in fact only one logical solution compatible with that scheme: namely to assume that capital goods are in no way different from land.[20] This is the approach that has prevailed in the end. All means of production have either been merged into a homogeneous factor, called 'capital', which is put on exactly the same footing as labour and land, or have all been considered as many land-like factors, to be put on the same footing as many different types of labour and land. In the latter case there is not even the necessity of insisting any more on any distinction between capital, labour and land of various types or of the same type, as they are all treated in the same way. They are all assumed to be land-like 'factors of production'.[21]

Thus, with a series of natural-resource-like factors of production, one could go on and faithfully duplicate the marginal utility scheme. The same convex smooth differentiable 'well-behaved' function was assumed – called 'production function' instead of utility function – the same partial derivatives were considered – called 'marginal productivities' instead of marginal utilities. But there was a further difficulty. Production (unlike utility) must be measurable, which implies that marginal productivities must actually be equal (and not only be proportional) to the 'factor prices'. And since the total net product, by being always appropriated by somebody, can always be written as the sum of the various factor quantities multiplied by the corresponding factor prices, marginal productivities had to be such that they could be freely substituted for the factor prices without affecting the total (i.e. without leaving any residual, positive or negative). There is only one type of mathematical function that gives this result: a linear and homogeneous function. So production functions have been assumed to be linear and homogeneous.

20 Consider, for example, the involution that took place in Pareto's own analysis. In the *Cours* (1896), he tried to apply Walrasian analysis to capital goods, but he was not satisfied and in the *Manuel* (1909) he abandoned all processes of production of capital goods altogether. (Cf. the mathematical appendix, especially sections 77 and ff.) What he continued to call *capitaux* are quantities which are given and not produced: they are in no way different from scarce resources.
21 On the way from a labour-time approach to a scarce-resource approach, the intermediate link may be found in a late article by Knut Wicksell ('Real Capital and Interest', a comment on Dr Gustaf Åkerman's book *Real Kapital und Kapitalzins*. It appeared in the *Economisk Tidskrift*, 1923, and has been republished in English as an appendix to the first volume of Wicksell's *Lectures on Political Economy*, ed. by Lionel Robbins, in 2 vols., London 1934). In this article Wicksell keeps the labour-time approach for that part of his analysis that refers to the capital-good producing sector. Then he goes on to treat produced capital as if it were a natural resource by inserting it, for the first time, into a linear and homogeneous technical function for the production of consumption goods.

A striking feature is that any difficulty that came in the way was eliminated by introducing a further assumption. No concern was ever shown about the *substance* of such assumptions; only about the logical consistency which they obviously required. For the Marginalists it is rigour, not relevance, that counts. No concern has ever been shown, for example, about extending, by assumption, the properties of givenness and definiteness, which are characteristic of scarce natural resources, to the state of technical knowledge, namely to something which is exactly the opposite. What is interesting is that, by adding, onto that fixed framework, a rational behaviour postulate (profit maximisation, parallel to utility maximisation) the theory provided a well defined and fixed relation between final (produced) goods on the one hand and the natural resources which go into them on the other. To take the former or to take the latter is the same thing in this model: there is a one–one correspondence between the two. Demand for the final commodities is transformed into demand for the scarce resources. The two poles – utility on the one hand and natural resources on the other – had thereby been re-established, with everything in between reduced to irrelevance. For all essential purposes, the model had, so to speak, eliminated the process of production from the analysis, in the sense that all conclusions drawn at the stage of the scarce resources could be carried over, directly and without the slightest modification, to the final commodities.[22]

We may note that this is exactly the opposite of what the Classical economists did. The Classical economists eliminated from their analysis the complications raised by scarce goods in order to concentrate their investigations on produced commodities. The Marginalists have eliminated from their analysis all the relevant features of the production process in order to maintain intact the model they have built for the problem of optimum allocation of scarce goods. Out of this symmetry, however, there emerges a deep contrast, which reduces to a basically opposite criterion for the choice of the hypotheses: practical relevance (i.e. the singling out of those problems that were thought to be the most

22 This analytical procedure of, one may say, trivialisation of the aspects concerning production is not just something that has happened once. It is happening all the time In what is known nowadays as general equilibrium analysis, all problems, all theorems are first of all framed and proved within a pure exchange model, i.e. for a hypothetical world in which the process of production does not exist. Only then – when all things look fine for a pure exchange model – is a production process introduced. But at this stage, obviously, a production process can be introduced only if it does not upset the already built scheme. And what inevitably happens is that all aspects that might upset such a scheme are taken away by assumption. All important problems concerning production are either ignored altogether or stripped of their relevant features devitalised and reduced by one assumption over another, to an innocuous form that does not upset the pre-conceived scheme of the optimum allocation of scarce goods

important) in the case of the Classical economists; logical consistency with a pre-conceived pure-exchange theoretical scheme, in the case of the Marginalists.

8. New contributions to economic theory

To illustrate further the process – brought out in the previous pages – of extension by modification, that marginal economic theorists have constantly been pursuing, it may be interesting to consider briefly the contributions to economic theory that have come to light since the 'marginal revolution'.

Let us consider the following five of them:

(i) Keynes/Kalecki's short-run theory of unemployment;
(ii) the discussion on the behaviour of firms, started by Sraffa's criticism of Marshall, and continued (after a parenthesis of revival of marginal analytical tools) by the empirical studies which led to the formulation of the full-cost principle and to the studies of oligopolistic behaviour; and more recently to 'managerial economics' theories;
(iii) Leontief's input–output analysis and Sraffa's production of commodities scheme;
(iv) the whole series of theories of the business cycle;
(v) Harrod–Domar's macro-dynamic model and the post-Keynesian theories of growth and income distribution.

If we consider all these contributions carefully, their most remarkable common characteristic is that they have not come from marginal economic analysis. On the contrary, they have mainly come out in bitter polemic with, and as a challenge to, it. Moreover, they all deal with problems of production. None of them touch on problems of optimum allocation of scarce goods. None of them comes from the application of the so much cherished mathematical tool of maximisation under constraints![23]

---

23 A case apart, and a very interesting one, is represented by von Neumann's growth model (John von Neumann, 'Über ein ökonomisches Gleichungssystem und eine Verallgemeinerung des Brouwerschen Fixpunktsatzes', in *Ergebnisse eines Matematischen Kolloquiums*, vol. VIII, ed. by Karl Menger, Vienna 1937, translated into English with the misleading title of 'A Model of General Equilibrium', *The Review of Economic Studies*, 1945–46). Von Neumann's approach is typically Classical, even to the point of considering the workers as themselves commodities that can be reproduced *ad libitum* at a subsistence wage defined in physical terms. But von Neumann invents (and applies) a new analytical tool (the minimax principle) which, at a first superficial look, might be associated with the maximisation tools of marginal economics. A more careful analysis, however, reveals that von Neumann considers produced

(*continued*)

The way in which the marginal school has responded to this challenge has always been the same: namely by making every possible effort to absorb the new developments into the old theory. By adding some assumptions, by introducing some new 'more general' functions and by reducing the others, the really important ones, to an irrelevant form, marginal economics theorists have always tried to play down the new theories, to twist and force them into the strait-jacket framework of a scarcity world. It might even be polemically argued that, in the last half century, not the process of making new contributions, but this very process of 'marginalisation' of concepts invented outside marginal analysis has been the main task of marginal economic theory.[24] To the extent that this operation has succeeded it has patently rendered the new theories sterile. It is no wonder that the vitality of the new theories has always remained with their original formulations.

At this point of our discussion, it is not difficult to see that all the contributions to economic theory just mentioned stem from what has been called above the production or industry approach to economic reality, as opposed to the optimum allocation of scarce resources approach. But their authors themselves did not perceive this very clearly. Each of those theories has been presented under the compulsion of certain facts, which current theory was unable to explain. As a consequence, they have been presented independently of one another, without an explicit relation to any unifying principle. This has made things easier for the Marginalists. It seemed natural to look for a unifying theoretical framework and marginal economics had one to offer. Although the authors of the new theories have, most of the time

---

commodities – commodities that are produced in practically unlimited quantities (and not 'scarce' goods). Moreover, he applies the minimax principle to rates of growth (and not to absolute quantities), by taking *technology* as a constraint (and not the natural resources, which in fact are assumed to be entirely free). Von Neumann' analysis reveals, therefore, that the mathematical tool of maximisation under constraints has a much wider applicability than marginal economic theory.

To summarise, I would say that economics is much wider a field of investigation than that which is open to the applications of the mathematical tool of maximisation under constraints; and moreover that this specific mathematical tool is itself applicable to a much wider field of investigation than that covered by marginal economics.

24 Interestingly enough, the process of 'marginalisation' of concepts which were not, a source, marginal has gone on even through the successive works of the same author. Léon Walras is a good example. He originally conceived a theory of production (with coefficients, and not with convex functions) which, as such, might easily have been developed within a Ricardian framework. But he had to insert it into, and render symmetrical to, his pre-conceived model of pure exchange. He went on modifying it, in the successive editions of his work, until he reduced and confused it with that of the marginal productivity theorists. (See the different versions of his production theory in the successive editions of his main work, Léon Walras, *Elements*, Jaffé edition, *op cit.*).

strongly protested that their theories had nothing to do with Marginal-ism, the Marginalists have been at an advantage. They have had the advantage of synthesis. For they have always clearly presented their arguments around a unifying problem (optimum allocation of scarce resources) and a unifying principle (the rational process of maximisation under constraints).

Yet it seems to me that it is possible to build a unifying theory behind all the new contributions to economics mentioned above. The foregoing discussion has been constantly pointing towards it. It is a theory the basic elements of which can be traced back to various stages in the development of economic thought; they can be found, here and there, in Smith, in Ricardo, in Malthus, in Marx, in Keynes, in Kalecki, in Leontief, in Sraffa, and in the recent models of economic growth and income distribution. However, these basic elements have not yet been brought out and fitted together in a unifying theoretical scheme. Those economists, who understood remarkably well the requirements of production, did not go into the dynamics of it, which is indeed the aspect that gives it full relevance. The others mainly concentrated on the exploration of particular – though important – aspects, or only on the macro-economic aspects of the process of production in a modern society. There was an economist – Joseph Schumpeter – who particular-ly understood the role of technical progress and singled it out as the prime mover of modern industrial societies. Unfortunately, he failed to grasp the requirements of a theory of production. He adopted the marginal approach, and his sparkling insights died in a long description of a process which his analytical tools were unable to tackle.[25]

9. An alternative conception of the material world

The present work is an attempt to build a unifying scheme of the type hinted at above. The scheme, to be effective, will necessarily have to be simple. At the same time, however, the simplifications will have to be such as not to sacrifice those aspects of economic reality which are basic to the new approach.

It may therefore be helpful – before starting – to state explicitly the sort of schematisation that is behind the choice of the simplifications. And a useful way to do it seems to me that of carrying out this task by way of contrast with the type of schematisation of the real world which has been put behind marginal economic analysis.

We may say that the marginal economic theorists have chosen to look

25 Joseph A. Schumpeter, *The Theory of Economic Development*, Cambridge, Mass. 1934, and *Business Cycles*, in 2 vols., New York 1939.

at the real world through the lens of a scarcity model. All aspects of reality have been magnified or eliminated according to whether they did or did not fit into the pattern of a scarcity world. The conception which has thereby arisen is that of a world where the material goods, which are the object of man's desire, and technical knowledge, have been shaped by some kind of external Agent – let us simply call it 'Nature' – and given to man in scarce quantities, with a haphazard distribution, and in immutable form. Of course some changes in the state of technical knowledge may now and then suddenly come in from outside; but this is not the model's concern. In the model, these changes actually represent a nuisance, because they come to disturb the beautiful equilibrium of the system. If they do come, they must of course be accepted, but they must not be thought about. The individual members of the community must convince themselves that those changes are rare accidents on which they cannot rely. Similarly, the original distribution of the given resources is taken as given, even if it were patently inequitable. If an economist wants to talk of problems of this type, he must divest himself of any pretence of being an economist and say explicitly that he is speaking in some other capacity (as a politician, a philanthropist, etc.). All that remains to be done, or to be talked about, is a possible series of exchanges of the existing goods. In other words, the only economic problem that the members of this society are facing is a problem of rational behaviour in order to increase – when possible – the enjoyment they obtain out of what is given and immutable. By combining and exchanging the existing goods – on the basis of their given preferences and knowledge – they may reach a better allocation than the one which happened to be given to them by Nature at the beginning.

This type of schematisation will be discarded altogether in the following pages. Useful though it might have been in interpreting the problems of a society of merchants a good many centuries ago, it seems to me that it has become obsolete for the interpretation of the economic systems which have emerged from the industrial revolution. Adam Smith, two centuries ago, was already aware of this when he heavily stressed the pre-eminence of 'the skill, dexterity and judgement with which labour is applied' over the quality of 'the soil, climate and extent of territory', in determining the wealth of nations.[26] And since the time of Adam Smith the cumulative technical progress of the industrial societies has gone a long way ahead. Technical change – far from being a disturbance to the behaviour of individuals or something they must not think about – has emerged as the very focal point of any economic activity in the industrial societies.

26 See above, p. 6.

A cursory look around us is enough to perceive this most clearly. The constantly advancing technology in the more modern parts of the world has by now freed entire populations, for the first time in history, from the yoke of hunger and starvation. Technical change has made and is constantly making men less and less dependent on nature and more and more dependent upon themselves. The commodities that nowadays men produce, and the surroundings in which they live, are more and more shaped by them; the product of their own decisions. Even the raw materials and the traditional sources of energies, which at the beginning of the industrial revolution absolutely conditioned the rise of industries, are becoming less and less important, as men themselves learn how to make, in whatever place they like, a great part of the raw materials (or their synthetic substitutes), and are moreover developing entirely new sources of energy.[27] The traditional economic activity which kept man at the mercy of nature – agriculture – becomes a minor branch of the whole economy in an advanced society, and this minor branch itself becomes more and more industrialised, controlled, snatched away from the flukes of Nature and subdued to the exigencies of man. And what is most important to point out is that technical progress is continually going on, so that all these propositions are constantly acquiring a stronger and stronger content. The world of the future is going to become more and more a man-made world.

The economists seem to have failed for a long time to realise this. After the original insights of Adam Smith, they have persistently shied away from paying attention to technical progress. Ricardo and Malthus – to take two major figures among the Classical economists – utterly underestimated the effects of technical progress and ended up with a gloomy view on the future of the society which was emerging. Marx himself, the theorist of historical change, did not foresee the enormous possibilities of increasing productivity.[28] Paradoxically enough, it was the turn of the Marginalists to take at least a non-pessimistic view by developing the economic theory of a stationary state! Only in the middle of the twentieth century has technical progress begun to creep – timidly and in simplified forms – into the theoretical schemes of the economists.

27 The recent 'oil crisis' is a powerful reminder of the direction in which technical progress will have to go eventually. Less and less will we be able to rely on sources of energy that are given (and exhaustible), and more and more on sources of energy, or on the development of sources of energy, that are permanent (not exhaustible).
28 In Marx's theory, 'the material forces of society', which grow and eventually come into contradiction with the existing production relationships, are regarded as an effect of capital accumulation, but this process is not connected with improvements in technical knowledge in any essential way. On the contrary, technical progress, if considered, actually introduces complications.

But to shuffle off the anachronistic idea of a stationary state is not easy now, when it has permeated every single corner of economic thought.

It may be interesting to point out that in almost all fields of knowledge other than economics, in the meantime, the very idea of progress has been so active as sometimes to revolutionise the whole way of thinking, and to suggest the boldest hypotheses. The most outstanding example is perhaps Darwin's theory of the evolution of species. But we do not need any special hypothesis of evolution of the human species in order to explain technical and economic progress. A sufficient condition is to suppose that human beings are able to learn from past experience and to communicate among themselves the results of their learning activity. Then, if men, on the average, are born with the same degree of intelligence in time, each generation is bound to go further than the previous one; not because it is more intelligent, but because it starts from a better position, by taking advantage of longer experience. Therefore, as long as the intellectual abilities of mankind do not deteriorate, technical progress is an inherent characteristic of human history. Of course, the rate of technical progress has not always been the same in the past. The process of systematic learning itself took quite a long time to be learnt. But we must admit that since it has been discovered (let us say, with the inception of the 'age of science and experiment') the results have been impressive. The modern world has come into being!

Of course, technical progress cannot be taken as automatically leading to *social* progress. Actually, a failure to understand the nature and implications of technical progress may well lead to social unrest and destruction. But this only comes to underline even more the absolute necessity we have of developing analytical tools that are appropriate to the investigation of the basic features of our technological age. How to learn systematically in the fields of social progress is perhaps something that has yet to be learnt. But we shall not nearly begin to do this if we do not first understand correctly all the implications of technical change.

To conclude this long justification, technical progress, or more generally the learning process of human beings, is going to be put at the centre of the schematisation of the external world which is to be adopted in the following pages. A world will be considered where nothing is absolutely fixed. At any given point of time, there is a stock of means of production and of technical knowledge which is inherited from the past, but as time goes on this stock is continuously changing. Any of its components is susceptible to being increased and improved, if not directly, through substitutes; provided that enough time is allowed for the members of the community to learn (through investigation and experiment) how to do it. It is this learning activity that represents the spring moving the whole system, by its constant application to improving the production processes and to starting new productions. Thus the commodities which are exchanged and consumed are not goods that may be found in nature. They are goods produced by men, practically in whatever quantity men like, provided that they think it worth devoting to them the amount of effort they technologically require, this effort being itself changing as an effect of technical progress.

In this scheme, therefore, Man and not Nature represents the central focus.[29] Man is the mover of the whole system, in a double role: by providing with his likings and preferences the criterion for deciding on the quantities and types of commodities to produce, and by inventing and operating the process of production. Accordingly, the gravitational centre of the whole analysis that follows will reside in the learning power of the members of the community and not – as it has been in traditional economics – in the limited amount of natural resources. It will reside, in other words, not in the caprice and scarcity of Nature, but in the progress and ingenuity of Man.[30]

10. A pure production model

Going back now to the beginning of the previous section, the task ahead may be outlined more clearly. In the following pages, a theoretical model will be developed for an industrial economic system. Symmetrically to, but in contrast with, the procedure followed by marginal economic analysis, the scheme will refer to a certain type of commod-

29 When the Classical economists adhered to a labour theory of value, they evidently had this intuitive idea at the back of their minds. But they left it open to confusion, by the tripartition of the factors of productions into Labour, Land and Capital; a tripartition which somewhat leads one to associate Man only with the first factor (the other two factors appearing as inanimate factors). But Man is equally behind all of them. Labour, Land and Capital stand for three different categories of men: men as workers, men as owners of land and men as owners of capital. For it is clearly Man, in his multifarious roles and activities that is the only mover and the only beneficiary of the process of production.
30 It may be useful to add a warning at this point. To take human activity, i.e. labour, as the only ultimate factor of production must not be interpreted as meaning that 'labour is the only scarce factor' as – I have noticed – many of my (economist) friends have tended to do, when discussing the present work with me. Such an interpretation would be incorrect: scarcity of a factor presupposes a specific aim (or objective), the attainment of which is limited by the existing quantity of that factor. But no such aim is present here; the existing quantity of labour does not constrain or limit anything. As the reader will see presently, the systems of equations which will be considered yield solutions for *relative* prices and *relative* quantities, which are independent of the total quantity of labour available. To say, in such a context, that labour is 'scarce' has no sense.

ities (this time the commodities of the production type), will centre around a definite problem (the problem of production), and will be dominated by a general principle (represented by the learning process of human beings, in its twofold aspect of technical improvements and consumers' preference evolution). As against the pure exchange model of marginal economics, the scheme itself might well be called a *pure production* model. All commodities considered are produced, and can be made in practically whatever quantity may be wanted, provided that they are devoted that amount of effort they technically require.

To avoid unnecessary complications, scarce resources will not be considered. This does not imply any disregard of the problems of rationality. When problems of rational choice arise, with reference to consumers' behaviour or to producers' choice of techniques, they will be discussed explicitly. Also, the procedure does not mean that natural resources are assumed to be homogeneous and non-scarce. Not to consider a problem does not mean assuming that it does not exist. What it means is that the basic theory will be developed *independently* of the problems of optimum allocation of the scarce resources.

This again might appear as exactly symmetrical, though opposite, to what has been done by the marginalist economists, who have developed a theory of optimum allocation of scarce resources to begin with, independently of the problems concerning production. But there is an important asymmetry. The economists who have taken the production approach to economic reality have always claimed that production can in fact be investigated independently of the problems concerning scarce resources. This claim goes back to Ricardo, who 'eliminated' land from his analysis of value and distribution by referring his arguments to the 'marginal' land (that piece of land that yields no rent). But the Ricardian claim has recently been given a powerful backing by Piero Sraffa's analysis. Sraffa has shown[31] that lands, or more generally, natural resources of various types, by entering the production process though not themselves being produced, play, in reverse, a role similar to that of non-basic commodities (which are produced, but do not enter the process of production). They do not affect the rest of the analysis, and can therefore be left aside, to begin with. They may, of course, be introduced later on, and when they are introduced they bring with them the required necessary information about their rents and prices. But their effects remain limited to that part of the model that refers to them, without affecting the results of the previous analysis. This gives a powerful analytical justification to the approach which is taken here. It

31 Piero Sraffa, *Production of Commodities by means of Commodities – Prelude to a Critique of Economic Theory*, Cambridge 1960.

means effectively that the model, though not explicitly dealing with the problems concerning the scarce resources, will be kept open to their introduction.

There is, moreover, another important asymmetry with respect to traditional analysis. Marginal economic theorists have almost always considered efficient positions as the result of specific behaviour (maximising behaviour) in a specific institutional set-up (that of an ideally competitive free market economic system). It is my purpose, instead, to develop first of all a theory which remains neutral with respect to the institutional organisation of society. My preoccupation will be that of singling out, to resume Ricardo's terminology, the 'primary and natural' features of a pure production system. And these 'primary and natural' features – which will take the form of an evolving structure of the economic system defined by the conditions under which it may grow and take advantage of all its potential possibilities – will simply emerge as necessary requirements for equilibrium growth. Again this does not mean avoiding at all cost any reference to specific institutions. When the more basic features that are investigated have immediate implications for a specific institutional set-up, these implications will be pointed out explicitly; thereby showing explicitly how the investigation of problems associated with particular institutions may themselves be introduced later on. The procedure, again, may sound unusual nowadays.[32] Yet, it belongs to one of the oldest traditions of economic analysis.

This takes me to a final general remark. The hypotheses and the procedures of the inquiry which follows are very simple. They have always appeared so to all my non-economist friends with whom I have talked about them. Yet economists, who inevitably have in their education the deep mark of a century of marginal economic theory, may find them unusual. There is little I can do about this, except to remind them to keep in mind the basically different conception of the external world on which the present work is built. The difficulties here, it seems to me, are not objective, but subjective. It took a painful process and a long time for me as well to free my mind from modes of thought which I had been taught. In some places I myself might still not have been entirely successful. I should very much like, therefore, to begin by asking the reader to approach the following analysis with an open mind.

---

32 If the reader finds some difficulty in accepting it, I would suggest the following device. We have normally been used to thinking in terms of a free market economy and then extending the results to the case of centrally planned economies. In the present work, the opposite procedure may turn out to be much more helpful, namely to think first in terms of a centrally planned economy – a case for which the requirements of long-run equilibrium relationships emerge immediately – and then to extend the results to the case of market economies.

PART I

A multi-sector model of economic growth

Chapter II

Production in the short run

1. A well-diversified economic system

We may begin our analysis by considering the process of production in an economic system at a given point of time or, to be more realistic, within a *short period of time*, defined in such a way that, within it, changes in population, productive capacity, technical knowledge and consumers' preferences are negligible.

The economic system we are considering is *closed* and consists of a society of individuals whose purpose is to produce goods in order to derive enjoyment (or relief from pain) by consuming them. Two types of activities are therefore performed: a production activity and a consumption activity. At the beginning of the time period considered, the production processes are programmed in the best way that is technically known and, at the end of the production processes, the consumption goods are consumed. Technical knowledge is supposed to be quite advanced so that each process of production requires division of labour and a marked specialisation. Therefore, each individual consumes only a very small part of the commodities he (or she) produces (or contributes to the production of), and obtains all the others through exchange. Total production (and therefore consumption) is well diversified: the economic system produces many types of commodities, according to the needs and preferences of its individual members.

In order to keep the analysis in as simple terms as possible, only *final* commodities will be considered. No intermediate stage, and thus no intermediate commodity, will be explicitly represented. All production processes will be considered as vertically integrated, in the sense that all their inputs are reduced to inputs of labour and to services from stocks of capital goods.[1] It is important to stress that, for our purposes, this

1 The notion of 'vertically integrated sectors', which is here used, has been generalised in my article 'Vertical Integration in Economic Analysis', *Metroeconomica*, 1973 (reprinted in L. L. Pasinetti, ed., *Essays on the Theory of Joint Production*, London 1980).

29

entails no loss of generality. For, as will be shown in detail later on (chapter VI), it is always possible, when needed, to re-introduce intermediate stages and intermediate commodities by linear algebraic transformations.

2. Production by means of labour alone: a very simple case

It will be useful to begin by taking a very simple step. In this section and the following one, as a purely expository device, we shall develop a theoretical model where production is carried out exclusively by labour. Capital goods, as complementary to labour, will be introduced from section 4 onwards.

Even in an economic system as simple as this, there is a whole series of flows – or rather two different series of flows – which take place inside the period of time considered: flows of labour services from the individuals as labourers to the production processes, and flows of commodities from the production processes to the individuals as consumers. Suppose that the number of final commodities produced is $(n-1)$. Then, since we consider no intermediate stage, there is a production process behind each final commodity, which goes right back to what have traditionally been called the 'factors of production': labour alone in our simple case. We have, therefore, $(n-1)$ production processes or *sectors*, each of which consists of one labour input and of one product output. Finally, all the individuals may be considered as grouped into a final sector, which may be called household – sector n – which receives all outputs for consumption and provides all labour services for production.

All these flows may be framed into a usual input–output table, which in our case becomes extremely simple. As is well known, the table may be looked at from two different points of view, and accordingly represented by two systems of identities. From a *physical* point of view, the production of each commodity is identically equal to the sum of all quantities of that commodity which are delivered as inputs to the other sectors. (In our simple case this sum is reduced to one term: the amount delivered to the household sector.) Moreover, the sum of all labour services is identically equal to total labour employed. Similarly, at *current prices*, the production of each commodity must be equal to the sum of its total inputs and the sum of all productions must be equal to the total income which is distributed to the members of the community (all labourers in our case).

We therefore have:

(II.2.1)
$$
\begin{cases}
X_1 & -x_{1n} = 0, \\
\quad X_2 & -x_{2n} = 0, \\
& \cdots \\
& \cdots \\
& -x_{n-1,n} = 0, \\
-x_{n1} - x_{n2} \cdots & -x_{n,n-1} + X_n = 0;
\end{cases}
$$

and

(II.2.2)
$$
\begin{cases}
X_1 p_1 & -x_{n1} p_n = 0, \\
\quad X_2 p_2 & -x_{n2} p_n = 0, \\
& \cdots \\
& \cdots \\
-x_{1n} p_1 - x_{2n} p_2 - \cdots & +X_n p_n = 0;
\end{cases}
$$

where X_j represents the physical quantity produced of commodity j; $j = 1, 2, \ldots, (n-1)$; p_i represents the price of commodity i; $i = 1, 2, \ldots, n$; X_n represents the quantity of labour used in all production activities; x_{ij} represents the physical flow from sector i to sector j. All these magnitudes are supposed to be non-negative.

It appears now very useful, for reasons of symmetry, to put:

(II.2.3)
$$ a_{ij} = \frac{x_{ij}}{X_j}, $$

(II.2.4)
$$ a_{ij} \geqq 0, \qquad\qquad i, j = 1, 2, \ldots, n. $$

Then, systems (II.2.1)–(II.2.2) may be expressed in matrix notation:[2]

(II.2.5)
$$
\begin{bmatrix}
-1 & 0 & \cdots & 0 & a_{1n} \\
0 & -1 & \cdots & 0 & a_{2n} \\
& & \cdot & & \cdot \\
& & \cdot & & \cdot \\
& & \cdot & & \cdot \\
0 & 0 & \cdots & -1 & a_{n-1,n} \\
a_{n1} & a_{n2} & \cdots & a_{n,n-1} & -1
\end{bmatrix}
\begin{bmatrix}
X_1 \\ X_2 \\ \cdot \\ \cdot \\ \cdot \\ X_{n-1} \\ X_n
\end{bmatrix}
=
\begin{bmatrix}
0 \\ 0 \\ \cdot \\ \cdot \\ \cdot \\ 0 \\ 0
\end{bmatrix},
$$

2 Here and in all subsequent analysis, I shall be using matrices to represent the systems of linear equations (in order to evince immediately all symmetrical properties). Any compact notation will be avoided, however, and matrices will always be written in full. In this way, the whole following analysis will remain understandable also to readers who have no acquaintance with matrix algebra.

$$(\text{II.2.6}) \quad \begin{bmatrix} -1 & 0 & \ldots & 0 & a_{n1} \\ 0 & -1 & \ldots & 0 & a_{n2} \\ & & & & \cdot \\ & & & & \cdot \\ & & & & \cdot \\ 0 & 0 & & -1 & a_{n,n-1} \\ a_{1n} & a_{2n} & \ldots & a_{n-1,n} & -1 \end{bmatrix} \begin{bmatrix} p_1 \\ p_2 \\ \cdot \\ \cdot \\ \cdot \\ p_{n-1} \\ p_n \end{bmatrix} = \begin{bmatrix} 0 \\ 0 \\ \cdot \\ \cdot \\ \cdot \\ 0 \\ 0 \end{bmatrix}.$$

The $(a_{n1}, a_{n2}, \ldots, a_{n,n-1})$ represent technical coefficients of production and the $(a_{1n}, a_{2n}, \ldots, a_{n-1,n})$ represent demand coefficients of consumption. An evident property of these two systems is that they have the same, but transposed, coefficient matrix. As they have been defined, they are nothing but an algebraic representation of the flows which take place in the economic system under examination. However, they can be looked at in a different way. If we consider the a_{ij}s as parameters, then (II.2.5) and (II.2.6) form two systems of equations, and we can inquire into the nature of their solutions. These two systems are of a particular kind – they are linear and homogeneous. Therefore, in order that they may have non-trivial solutions (i.e. solutions which are not all equal to zero), the coefficient matrix must be singular, namely it must satisfy the following condition (which is the same for both systems):[3]

$$(\text{II.2.7}) \quad \begin{vmatrix} -1 & & & & a_{1n} \\ & -1 & & & a_{2n} \\ & & \cdot & & \cdot \\ & & & \cdot & \cdot \\ & & & -1 & a_{n-1,n} \\ a_{n1} & a_{n2} & \ldots & a_{n,n-1} & -1 \end{vmatrix} = 0.$$

By developing this determinant, the condition may be stated more simply as:

$$(\text{II.2.8}) \qquad a_{n1}a_{1n} + a_{n2}a_{2n} + \ldots + a_{n,n-1}a_{n-1,n} - 1 = 0.$$

If this condition is satisfied, then each of the two systems gives solutions for $(n-1)$ variables, while the nth variable can be fixed arbitrarily. In our case, there is evidently, for system (II.2.5), a magnitude which is fixed, namely $\bar{X}_n$: the total quantity of labour available. By contrast, no similar magnitude can be considered as fixed in (II.2.6). This expresses

---

3 For the sake of simplicity, the zeros will not be explicitly written from now on; so that all entries in the matrices which are left blank are to be interpreted as zeros.

the well-known property that any economic system, considered in real terms, can give solutions for *relative* prices only, but not for their absolute level. Therefore, the choice being arbitrary, let us put, for the time being, $p_n = \bar{p}_n$. Hence:

$$(II.2.9) \quad \begin{cases} X_1 & = a_{1n}\bar{X}_n, \\ X_2 & = a_{2n}\bar{X}_n, \\ \quad \cdot \\ \quad \cdot \\ \quad \cdot \\ X_{n-1} = a_{n-1,n}\bar{X}_n; \end{cases}$$

$$(II.2.10) \quad \begin{cases} p_1 & = a_{n1}\bar{p}_n, \\ p_2 & = a_{n2}\bar{p}_n, \\ \quad \cdot \\ \quad \cdot \\ \quad \cdot \\ p_{n-1} = a_{n,n-1}\bar{p}_n; \end{cases}$$

which represent, respectively, the solutions of the system for physical quantities, relative to total labour available, and the solutions of the system for prices, relative to the price of labour. The meanings of expressions (II.2.9) and (II.2.10) are fairly straightforward. Each of the coefficients $(a_{1n}, \ldots, a_{n-1,n})$ expresses average per-capita demand for each commodity, so that (II.2.9) mean that production of each commodity depends exclusively on demand. If there were no demand there would be no production. On the other hand, each of the coefficients $(a_{n1}, a_{n2}, \ldots, a_{n,n-1})$ expresses the labour input in each physical unit of output, so that (II.2.10) mean that the price of each commodity is directly proportional to the quantity of labour required to produce it. In other words, prices, in this simple case, are obviously explained by a pure labour theory of value.

3. A necessary condition for full employment

Condition (II.2.8) will recur time and again in the subsequent analysis and we may well investigate its economic meaning immediately.

From a mathematical point of view, fulfilment of (II.2.8) is a necessary condition for each of the systems (II.2.5) and (II.2.6) to have non-trivial solutions. However, non-fulfilment does not imply no meaningful solution. The coefficient matrix of (II.2.5)–(II.2.6) has a particular form (all its entries are zeros, except those in the last row, in the last column, and along the main diagonal), which means that the solutions of the systems can be derived directly, without substitution, from the first $(n-1)$ equations of (II.2.5) and from the first $(n-1)$ equations of (II.2.6) respectively. Therefore, relative prices and relative quantities are determined independently of condition (II.2.8), whose binding restrictions fall entirely on the last equation of each of the two systems. Let us see what this means. Suppose, for example, that

$$\sum_{i=1}^{n-1} a_{ni} a_{in} < 1.$$

This inequality implies two things. In the context of system (II.2.6) it implies[4] that $\sum a_{in} p_i < \bar{p}_n$, namely that average per-capita expenditure is less than the income each worker receives: a situation of under-consumption. In the context of system (II.2.5) it implies that $\sum a_{ni} \bar{X}_i < \bar{X}_n$, namely that total labour employed is less than total labour available: a situation of under-employment. Conversely, the fulfilment of (II.2.8) implies both full expenditure of national income and full employment.

Looking at condition (II.2.8) more analytically, we may notice that it is a sum of binomials $a_{ni} a_{in}$ $(i = 1, \ldots, n-1)$, where each of these binomials has the property of being composed of one technical coefficient and of one consumption coefficient, both referring to the same commodity. Therefore, each $a_{ni} a_{in}$ expresses the *proportion* of total labour which is employed in that sector, or – which is the same – the proportion of full employment national income which is spent in that sector (sector i). Evidently, the sum of these proportions, for $i = 1, 2, \ldots, n-1$, must be equal to unity in order to achieve full employment. In those cases in which average per-capita expenditure turns out to be less than the income each worker receives, prices and quantities are determined all the same, but total production turns out to be less than potential production and there will be unemployment in the economic system. This situation is expressed by condition (II.2.8) being under-satisfied, i.e. by the summation of (II.2.8) being less than unity. The gap between $\sum a_{ni} a_{in}$ and unity expresses the proportion of labour that remains unemployed.

It is important to note immediately the *macro-economic* character of condition (II.2.8): it does not depend on the number of sectors that exist in the economy. (II.2.8) is just one condition referring to the economic system as a whole, no matter how many (or how few) sectors may be considered. We may express it by simply saying that total expenditure

---

4 From now on, for the sake of simplicity, the limits of the summations will also be omitted. In other words, all summations that will appear in our analysis have to be interpreted as running from 1 to $(n-1)$, unless otherwise specified.

34

must equal potential national income if full employment is to be achieved.

When put in these terms, condition (II.2.8) sounds familiar. It expresses a conclusion which has become well known in economic theory, since Keynes brought it out explicitly.[5] The novelty here is that this macro-economic result emerges immediately from a pure production model of the type we are dealing with; and moreover that it emerges from a model which has been developed on a *multi-sector* basis, thereby revealing its truly macro-economic nature.[6]

It must be added that, with the particular hypotheses of the present simple case (where no capital goods are needed) the condition that all income must be spent also means something more specific, namely that all income must be *consumed*. By adopting a Keynesian definition of savings, i.e. by defining savings as that part of personal incomes which is not spent, macro-economic condition (II.2.8) may also be expressed by saying that there can be *no savings in this economic system*, as a necessary condition for full employment. Single individuals, of course, may save, but there must be other individuals who dissave by the same amount, so that savings and dissavings, in the aggregate, cancel each other out. The only form of savings which are possible for the economic system as a whole are in *real* terms, i.e. by carrying over durable (produced) commodities from one period to another. But, within each period, total demand must be such as to induce the full utilisation of the production potential if full employment is to be reached. This is another important property of a production system. There must be demand – and in our simple case demand for consumption goods, whether durables or non-durables – for such an amount as to generate that quantity of production that requires the full employment of the existing labour force.

4. Production by means of labour and capital goods

We may now consider a more complex economic system which has all the properties of the system analysed in the previous sections, with one difference. The production processes, in order to be carried on, also

5 J. M. Keynes, *The General Theory, op. cit.*

6 There are relations, in economic analysis, which take up a macro-economic form only when the analysis itself is carried out at a macro-economic level. These relations are macro-economic only artificially. They cease to be macro-economic as soon as the analysis is carried out at a more disaggregated level. But there are other relations which maintain a macro-economic form quite irrespective of the degree of disaggregation at which the analysis is carried out. It is these relations only that may be termed as *truly* macro-economic. Expression (II.2.8) is one of them.

require, besides labour, capital goods. Each production process is characterised, as in the previous case, by a flow-input of labour and a flow-output of final commodity, but now each also requires the existence of a stock of capital goods, on which the labour services have to be performed, in order to produce the final output.

Capital goods are themselves commodities which have been produced in the economy, so that the final outputs of the economic system are now of two types: consumption goods, which are consumed, as in the previous case; and capital goods, which are invested in the process of production. Capital goods are *durable* and, therefore, once produced, they go to increase the existing stock of capital goods. However, although durable, they are not eternal. As a result of being used by labour, they wear out and must be continually replaced, if production is to go on. This means that each production process leading to a final commodity needs a further item. Besides a flow-input of labour and a stock of capital goods, each process also needs a flow-input of capital goods to keep the initial capital stock intact. Hence total production of capital goods, which represents total gross investment of the economic system, must be distinguished into two parts. A first part of it (replacement) simply goes to replace worn-out capital: in fact it is nothing but a cost of production, since it is needed in order that the production processes may end up with the same stocks of capital goods with which they began. The rest of the total production of capital goods, namely the excess over replacement, represents a net addition to the existing stocks of capital goods (*new investments*).

Capital goods may be grouped among themselves, and measured, in many different ways. How are we going to measure them here? In our analysis, all commodities have been measured so far in two ways; in terms of physical units – whatever the physical unit may be – and in terms of current prices – physical quantities multiplied by prices. The same procedure will be used for capital goods, but a particular physical unit will be adopted here, namely the unit of *vertically integrated productive capacity*. A physical unit of vertically integrated productive capacity (for the sake of simplicity, we shall simply say 'productive capacity', except where the omission of the term 'vertically integrated' may generate ambiguities) is defined with reference to the final commodity for which it is intended. There is therefore a specific physical unit of productive capacity for each final good that is produced in the economic system. Of course a unit of productive capacity is, in an ordinary sense, a very composite physical commodity: it is made up of different types of physical goods in different proportions. The reason why such a unit of measure is here used is the same that prompted the use of the concept of a final commodity. These concepts permit useful simplifications of exposition; they will actually become necessary in the dynamic analysis of the following chapters.[7]

5. The physical stocks and flows of the economic system

Let us begin by considering the physical aspect of our economic system in a given period of time. We are faced with a series of stocks and a series of flows.

At the beginning of the time period, there exists a series of stocks of capital goods which have been inherited from previous periods. We may represent them by a vector

(II.5.1) $$[K_1, K_2, \ldots K_j, \ldots, K_{n-1}],$$

where each K_j stands for the stock of capital goods, measured in terms of physical units of productive capacity, in sector j ($j = 1, 2, \ldots, n - 1$). When our analysis begins, the K_js are obviously given. However they are not given by 'nature'. They are the result of production activity in earlier periods of time, each K_j being the sum of all net investments made in the past in sector j.

We might say that, in the economic system, there is also another stock, at the beginning of the time period we are considering, namely population. However, for economic purposes, this stock is not relevant as such, i.e. as a stock (except in a slave society, which is outside our interests). Its economic relevance is connected only with the flows it calls into being.

Let us come, therefore, to consider these flows. As in the previous case, all the members of the community are grouped into a final sector n. This final sector provides the labour services to all productive processes and owns the stocks of capital goods. Moreover, it exerts the demand for all the final goods, which are now of two types – consumption goods and capital (or investment) goods.

The flows of consumption goods, as before, come from $(n - 1)$ consumption goods sectors. In addition to these, we now have a whole series of flows of investment goods, which will be denoted with the suffix k. As a first step to the more general formulation of section 7, we shall assume that capital goods are required only for the production of consumption goods, while capital goods can be produced from labour alone. Since the physical units of measurement of capital goods (units of

---

7 The notion of a physical unit of vertically integrated productive capacity is discussed at length, for the general case, in my *Metroeconomica* article already mentioned (see footnote 1 on p. 29).

productive capacity) are specific to each consumption goods sector, the process for the production of capital goods must itself be expanded into $(n-1)$ sectors. Our system thereby acquires $(n-1)$ new variables: X_{k_1}, X_{k_2}, ..., $X_{k_{n-1}}$, each of which represents the production of capital goods for the corresponding consumption goods sector. This production of capital goods is devoted partly to new investment (expressed by demand coefficients in the final sectors: $a_{k_1 n}, a_{k_2 n}, \ldots, a_{k_{n-1} n}$) and partly to replacement of worn-out capacity (expressed by replacement coefficients: $a_{k_1 1}, a_{k_2 2}, \ldots, a_{k_{n-1} n-1}$). Hence, the whole structure of physical flows can be represented by the following system of equations, which takes the place of (II.2.5):

$$(\text{II.5.2}) \quad
\begin{bmatrix}
-1 & & & & & a_{1n} \\
 & -1 & & & & a_{2n} \\
 & & \cdot & & & \cdot \\
 & & & \cdot & & \cdot \\
 & & & & -1 & a_{n-1,n} \\
a_{k_1 1} & & & & -1 & a_{k_1 n} \\
 & & \cdot & & & \cdot \\
 & & & \cdot & & \cdot \\
 & a_{k_{n-1} n-1} & & -1 & a_{k_{n-1} n} \\
a_{n1} \cdots a_{n,n-1} & a_{nk_1} \cdots a_{nk_{n-1}} & -1
\end{bmatrix}
\begin{bmatrix}
X_1 \\ X_2 \\ \cdot \\ \cdot \\ X_{n-1} \\ X_{k_1} \\ \cdot \\ \cdot \\ X_{k_{n-1}} \\ X_n
\end{bmatrix}
=
\begin{bmatrix}
0 \\ 0 \\ \cdot \\ \cdot \\ 0 \\ 0 \\ \cdot \\ \cdot \\ 0 \\ 0
\end{bmatrix}
.$$

A few words may be added about the replacement coefficients. Each a_{k_i} $(i = 1, 2, \ldots, n-1)$ represents the amount of capital, in physical terms, which is required in each period of time in order to keep productive capacity intact. This is the general definition of the a_{k_i}s. However, as an expository device, we shall find it useful in the subsequent analysis to adopt a simplification, because of its immediately apparent meaning. We may assume that, in each period of time and in each sector, a *constant* proportion of the productive capacity vanishes owing to wear and tear, so that by writing $a_{k_i} = (1/T_i)$, T_i may be interpreted as a quantity which is very near (though, depending on the sectoral rate of growth, not exactly coincident with) the average life-time of physical capital goods in sector i $(i = 1, 2, \ldots, n-1)$.

By now following exactly the same steps as in section 2, the condition that must be satisfied in order that the system of equations may have non-trivial solutions emerges as

$$(\text{II.5.3}) \qquad \sum a_{ni} a_{in} + \sum (1/T_i) a_{nk_i} a_{in} + \sum a_{nk_i} a_{k_i n} = 1,$$

and the solutions for the physical quantities take the form

$$
(\text{II.5.4}) \quad
\begin{cases}
X_1 \quad = a_{1n}\bar{X}_n, \\
\quad \cdot \\
\quad \cdot \\
\quad \cdot \\
X_{n-1} = a_{n-1,n}\bar{X}_n, \\
X_{k_1} \quad = [a_{k_1 n} + (1/T_1)a_{1n}]\bar{X}_n, \\
\quad \cdot \\
\quad \cdot \\
\quad \cdot \\
X_{k_{n-1}} = [a_{k_{n-1}n} + (1/T_{n-1})a_{n-1,n}]\bar{X}_n.
\end{cases}
$$

As can be seen, the first $(n-1)$ solutions, referring to consumption goods, are again of the simple type of the previous case: they actually coincide with the (II.2.9). But the following $(n-1)$ solutions, referring to investment goods, now contain two addenda, expressing the fact that production of these goods is generated by two distinct types of demand: demand for new investments, and demand for replacement of worn-out capacity.

6. The structure of prices

From the physical flows which have just been considered, another (dual) system of equations may be derived for prices. At first, one might think that one should write the same matrix entering (II.5.2) (but transposed) and multiply it by prices. This procedure, however, is no longer sufficient because the production processes now require capital goods, besides labour, and therefore the total income which flows to sector n has two components: a wage component, proportional to physical labour, and a profit component, proportional to the value of capital goods. In each (vertically integrated) sector, the value of output must be equal to the amount of wages due the labourers plus the amount of profits due the owners of the capital goods used in the production processes (in terms of used productive capacity: $X_1, X_2, \ldots, X_{n-1}$). By calling w the wage rate and π the rate of profit, equation system (II.2.6) is replaced by

$$(\text{II.6.1}) \quad
\begin{bmatrix}
-1 & \cdots & a_{k_1 1} & \cdots & a_{n1} \\
 & & & & a_{n2} \\
 & & \cdot & & \cdot \\
 & & & & \cdot \\
 & -1 & & a_{k_{n-1}n-1}\,a_{n,n-1} & p_{n-1} \\
 & -1 & & a_{nk_1} \\
 & & \cdot & & \cdot \\
 & & -1 & a_{nk_{n-1}} \\
a_{1n} & \cdots\, a_{n-1,n}\,a_{k_1 n} & \cdots\, a_{k_{n-1}n} & -1
\end{bmatrix}
\begin{bmatrix}
p_1 \\ p_2 \\ \cdot \\ \cdot \\ p_{n-1} \\ p_{k_1} \\ \cdot \\ p_{k_{n-1}} \\ w
\end{bmatrix}
+
\begin{bmatrix}
\dfrac{\pi X_1 p_{k_1}}{X_1} \\ \cdot \\ \cdot \\ \cdot \\ \dfrac{\pi X_{n-1}p_{k_{n-1}}}{X_{n-1}} \\ 0 \\ \cdot \\ 0 \\ (-\pi/X_n)\sum X_i p_{k_i}
\end{bmatrix}
= \;\;[
$$

Here we are faced with a complication. Comparing (II.6.1) with (II.2.6), we can see that the unknown, p_n, has been eliminated, but only in order to be replaced by *two* new unknowns, w and π. This means that, if we want to keep determinate solutions for relative prices, we must assume either w or π to be given, or alternatively we must introduce a new explanatory relation.

This is an old dilemma in economic analysis. When the Classical economists (Ricardo in particular) faced it, they thought they could take the wage rate as given from outside the sphere of economics. Ever since, economists have been looking for other explanatory relations. The neo-classical economists, as is well known, introduced a series of new hypotheses and built up a whole theory behind the technical coefficients – the theory of marginal productivity.

In the present work, I am in a sense going back to the approach of the Classical economists, but with a reversal of their hypothesis. At this stage, I shall take as given, not the wage rate, but the rate of profit. It must be made clear, however, that this step does not have, in the present analysis, the same meaning that taking a given wage rate had for the Classical economists. The rate of profit is not an *exogenous* magnitude in our theoretical scheme (as technology and consumers' preferences are). What this taking the rate of profit as given here means is a simple assertion that the rate of profit is not determined by the elements of the model so far considered. Of course, the determinants of the rate of profit come within the scope of our economic investigation and they must be examined. This will be done in chapter VII, where the basic determinants of the rate of profit will be discussed in a dynamic context. For the time being, we only need add here the assumption that the rate of profit is given exogenously *with respect to* the theoretical scheme considered so far. And there is of course no necessity to assume that the rate of profit is the same in all sectors. There may well be a particular rate of profit for each particular sector.

This allows us to express the new vector appearing in (II.6.1) in terms of prices, and to incorporate the rates of profit and all exogenous elements into the coefficient matrix. Thus, system (II.6.1) becomes:

$$
\begin{bmatrix}
-1 & & (\pi_1 + 1/T_1) & & & a_{n1} \\
& \cdot & & \cdot & & \cdot \\
& \cdot & & & & \cdot \\
& -1 & & (\pi_{n-1} + 1/T_{n-1}) & & a_{n,n-1} \\
& & -1 & & & a_{nk_1} \\
& & & \cdot & & \cdot \\
& & & & \cdot & \cdot \\
& & & & -1 & a_{nk_{n-1}} \\
a_{1n} \cdots a_{n-1,n} & (a_{k_1 n} - \pi_1 a_{1n}) \cdots (a_{k_{n-1} n} - \pi_{n-1} a_{n-1,n}) - 1
\end{bmatrix}
\begin{bmatrix}
p_1 \\
\cdot \\
\cdot \\
p_{n-1} \\
p_{k_1} \\
\cdot \\
\cdot \\
p_{k_{n-1}} \\
w
\end{bmatrix}
=
\begin{bmatrix}
0 \\
\cdot \\
\cdot \\
\cdot \\
\cdot \\
\cdot \\
\cdot \\
\cdot \\
0
\end{bmatrix}
$$

Here again we have obtained a system which is linear and homogeneous. Note that the coefficient matrix is different from the one entering (II.5.2). However it is a remarkable property of these two matrices that their determinants are exactly the same, as can easily be demonstrated.[8] The necessary condition for (II.6.2) to yield non-trivial solutions is therefore exactly the same as that which has been found already for (II.5.2), namely (II.5.3). Then the solutions for prices (relative prices) come out as:

$$
\text{(II.6.3)}
\begin{cases}
p_1 &= [a_{n1} + (\pi_1 + 1/T_1)a_{nk_1}]w, \\
& \cdot \\
& \cdot \\
& \cdot \\
p_{n-1} &= [a_{n,n-1} + (\pi_{n-1} + 1/T_{n-1})a_{nk_{n-1}}]w, \\
p_{k_1} &= a_{nk_1}w, \\
& \cdot \\
& \cdot \\
& \cdot \\
p_{k_{n-1}} &= a_{nk_{n-1}}w.
\end{cases}
$$

8 The determinant of the matrix entering (II.5.2), after substituting the $(1/T_i)$s for the a_{k_j}s, emerges as:

$$\text{(II.6.4n)} \qquad \sum a_{ni}a_{in} + \sum a_{nk_i}a_{k_in} + \sum (1/T_i)a_{nk_i}a_{in} - 1, \qquad \textit{(continued)}$$

41

As the reader can see, the last $(n-1)$ prices are still of the simple type of the previous section. But this is only because of the simplifying assumption that capital goods require no capital goods to be produced. The formulation for the $(n-1)$ prices of consumption goods are more general and more interesting. Each price is expressed as a sum of two addenda which we may call: the prime cost a_{ni} (i.e. the quantity of labour required to produce a unit of the corresponding commodity) and the gross profit mark-up $(\pi_i + 1/T_i)a_{nk_i}$. The latter is in turn composed of the rate of profit (π_i), and of the depreciation allowance $(1/T_i)$, both of them being proportional to a_{nk_i}, which represents the quantity of labour required to produce one unit of productive capacity for sector i; $i = 1, 2, \ldots, n-1$.

At this stage already, a pure labour theory of value is no longer discernible in our formulations (or, at least at a first look, is discernible only for particular cases, such as the case in which $\pi_i = 0$, for all $i = 1, 2, \ldots, n-1$ – a zero rate of profit – or the case in which $(a_{ni}/a_{nk_i}) = (a_{nj}/a_{nk_j})$ for all $i, j = 1, 2, \ldots, n-1$ – a uniform capital intensity of the production processes). But, in general, if the rates of profit are positive and the capital intensity is different from one production process to another, relative prices will depend both on labour inputs and on the rate of profit.

It is important to notice, however, from (II.6.3), that our approach has made it possible to express *all* price components in such a way as to allow the wage rate to be factored out. This means that what appears in the square brackets, by being multiplied by the wage rate, must obviously be either a physical quantity of labour or something which is made to be equivalent to a physical quantity of labour. We shall examine in chapter VII the conditions under which the magnitude here appearing in square brackets can actually be reduced to a physical quantity of labour. For the time being, let us notice that – whatever the way in which the rates of profit are determined – the (II.6.3) imply a theory of value which is based on quantities of physical labour and on

---

and the determinant of the matrix entering (II.6.2) emerges as:

$$\Sigma a_{ni}a_{in} + \Sigma (a_{k_in} - \pi_i a_{in})a_{nk_i} + \Sigma (\pi_i + 1/T_i)a_{in}a_{nk_i} - 1.$$

This second expression can easily be reduced to the first, by expansion. We obtain:

$$\Sigma a_{ni}a_{in} + \Sigma a_{nk_i}a_{k_in} + \Sigma (1/T_i)a_{in}a_{nk_i} - \Sigma \pi_i a_{in}a_{nk_i} + \Sigma \pi_i a_{in}a_{nk_i} - 1.$$

where it can be seen that the last and the last but one summations cancel each other out. What remains coincides with (II.6.4n).

Thus, the introduction of a whole series of rates of profit does not make any difference to the formulation of the macro-economic equilibrium condition, which continues to be given by physical magnitudes alone.

quantities which are made to be equivalent to physical labour. As can be seen, the indirect physical labour is weighted more than the direct physical labour when the (exogenously given) rate of profit is positive. The prices thereby express a theory of value which is indeed no longer in terms of pure labour, but is in terms of what we may call *labour equivalents*.

7. A more complex model involving capital goods for the production of capital goods

We have assumed so far that no capital goods are needed for the production of capital goods, but the simplification has been made only in order to keep the formulations as short as possible.

Dropping this assumption does not entail any conceptual difficulty; it only requires some further algebraical manipulations. We may assume, for example, in order not to go on *ad infinitum*, that each of the capital goods sectors makes capital goods for itself and for the corresponding consumption goods sector, and we may denote by γ_i, in each sector i ($i = 1, 2, \ldots, n - 1$), the ratio of one physical unit of capital goods expressed in terms of productive capacity for the consumption goods sector to one unit of capital goods expressed in terms of productive capacity for the capital goods sector. Then a new series of $(n - 1)$ replacement coefficients for the capital goods sectors have to be introduced into the matrix of (II.5.2), in addition to those already considered for the consumption goods sectors. Similarly, a new series of $(n - 1)$ profit and depreciation mark-ups, for the prices of investment goods, has to be introduced into matrix (II.6.2), in addition to those already considered for the prices of consumption goods.

In both matrices, the new $(n - 1)$ elements fall along the second half of the main diagonal. Again the two matrices are different from each other. Yet their determinants coincide, as can easily be checked. The condition under which the two matrices are singular (a necessary condition for non-trivial solutions) is therefore again the same for both of them and emerges as

$$(\text{II.7.1}) \quad \sum a_{ni} a_{in} + \sum (1/T_i) \frac{T_{k_i}}{T_{k_i} - \gamma_i} a_{nk_i} a_{in} + \sum \frac{T_{k_i}}{T_{k_i} - \gamma_i} a_{nk_i} a_{k_i n} = 1.$$

When this condition is satisfied, the solutions for relative quantities and relative prices are again easily found and come out as follows:

$$\text{(II.7.2)} \begin{cases} X_1 & = a_{1n}\bar{X}_n, \\ \quad \vdots \\ X_{n-1} = a_{n-1,n}\bar{X}_n, \\ X_{k_1} & = \dfrac{T_{k_1}}{T_{k_1}-\gamma_1}[a_{k_1 n}+(1/T_1)a_{1n}]\bar{X}_n, \\ \quad \vdots \\ X_{k_{n-1}} = \dfrac{T_{k_{n-1}}}{T_{k_{n-1}}-\gamma_{n-1}}[a_{k_{n-1}n}+(1/T_{n-1})a_{n-1,n}]\bar{X}_n; \end{cases}$$

$$\text{(II.7.3)} \begin{cases} p_1 & = \left[(\pi_1+1/T_1)\dfrac{T_{k_1}}{T_{k_1}-\gamma_1-\pi_{k_1}\gamma_1 T_{k_1}}a_{nk_1}+a_{n1}\right]w, \\ \quad \vdots \\ p_{n-1} = \left[(\pi_{n-1}+1/T_{n-1})\dfrac{T_{k_{n-1}}}{T_{k_{n-1}}-\gamma_{n-1}-\pi_{k_{n-1}}\gamma_{n-1}T_{k_{n-1}}}a_{nk_{n-1}}+a_{n,n-1}\right] \\ p_{k_1} & = \dfrac{T_{k_1}}{T_{k_1}-\gamma_1-\pi_{k_1}\gamma_1 T_{k_1}}a_{nk_1}w, \\ \quad \vdots \\ p_{k_{n-1}} = \dfrac{T_{k_{n-1}}}{T_{k_{n-1}}-\gamma_{n-1}-\pi_{k_{n-1}}\gamma_{n-1}T_{k_{n-1}}}a_{nk_{n-1}}w. \end{cases}$$

These two new series of solutions are basically similar to (II.5.4) and (II.6.3), although they are a little more complicated. Each production of capital goods now satisfies not only the demand for replacement and new investment in the corresponding consumption good sector, but also demand for replacement and new investment in the capital goods sector itself. Similarly each of the prices now covers not only the profit and depreciation allowance for the consumption good to which it refers but also the profit and depreciation allowance for the corresponding capital goods.

Since, in this case, the production processes of capital goods are explicitly assumed to require as inputs a part of their own outputs, there is a further necessary condition that must be satisfied, to ensure positive solutions for the physical quantities, or rather, there is a series of $(n-1)$

necessary conditions – one necessary condition for each (vertically integrated) sector.[9] This series of conditions emerges clearly from expressions (II.7.2) and may be stated algebraically as:

$$(\text{II.7.4}) \qquad T_{k_i} > \gamma_i, \qquad i = 1, 2, \ldots, n-1,$$

meaning that the total output from the employment of each set of machines, in the whole course of its life, must be more than one set of machine of the same type. If it were not so (i.e. if any process of production for capital goods were to require more as inputs than it can give as output) production would be impossible. As will be realised, these are the conditions that have become known in the economic literature as *viability conditions*. Their counterparts for the price system, as again emerges immediately from (II.7.3), can be expressed as:

$$(\text{II.7.5}) \qquad \pi_i < \frac{T_{k_i} - \gamma_i}{\gamma_i T_{k_i}}, \qquad i = 1, 2, \ldots, n-1.$$

In other words, for each (vertically integrated) sector, there is a finite maximum rate of profit, that cannot be exceeded if prices are to remain positive.[10]

Yet, in spite of these algebraic complications, the reader will notice that the theory of value implied by (II.7.3) has exactly the same features as the theory of value implied by (II.6.3). More specifically, all components of prices are expressed in terms of labour, or labour equivalents, multiplied by the wage rate.

This will allow us, for most of the subsequent analysis, to continue to use formulations (II.5.3), (II.5.4), (II.6.3), instead of the corresponding

9 No condition of this type emerges from the theoretical scheme of sections 5 and 6 above (at least as long as our formulations are not re-interpreted with reference to inter-industry systems; but see chapter VI below). The explanation is that, in the scheme considered in sections 5 and 6 above, no commodity is supposed to require itself for its own production; hence the maximum eigenvalue of the coefficient matrix entering (II.5.2) and (II.6.2) is zero (implying no upper limit to the rates of profit or to the rates of growth).

10 The viability condition (II.7.5), when it is written as

$$(\text{II.7.5a}) \qquad T_{k_i} > \gamma_i + \pi_i \gamma_i T_{k_i},$$

immediately appears as more restrictive than the corresponding viability condition (II.7.4) for the physical quantity system. The reason is that we are here considering production with reference to a single period of time. We shall see later on that, when exponential economic growth is introduced into the analysis, the formulations for physical new investments will become more complete. From these more complete formulations the viability conditions for the physical quantity system will emerge as perfectly symmetrical (or rather, mathematically 'dual') to the viability conditions for the price system, the rates of growth taking the place of the rates of profit. (See footnote 2 on p. 53, and footnote 8 on pp. 93–4).

(more laborious) formulations (II.7.1), (II.7.2), (II.7.3), without any loss of generality.

8. Simplifications

A further simplification becomes possible, in the analysis of the following three chapters, besides those just mentioned and concerning the use of expressions (II.5.3), (II.5.4), (II.6.3) instead of (II.7.1), (II.7.2), (II.7.3). As a purely expository device, the same rate of wear and tear (i.e. $1/T$) will be used for the capital goods of all sectors. This will cut down the number of suffixes in our formulations, without at the same time losing the possibility of reintroducing them on any occasion in which they may become relevant.

Similarly, we shall use the same rate of profit (π) for all sectors. Here the assumption of uniformity may appear to have a more important economic content, since the equalisation of the rates of profit in all sectors is a tendency normally associated with the institutions of capitalist systems. However, whatever interpretation one normally attaches to this hypothesis, in the following analysis it will simply stand as a provisional step that allows us to deal with one problem at a time. We shall come back to non-uniformity of rates of profit in chapter VII below, where we turn to a specific examination of the determinants of the rates of profit in the different sectors.

9. The equilibrium conditions

No comment has yet been made on the new form taken by the full employment condition. Expression (II.5.3) – or for that matter (II.7.1) – represents, in mathematical terms, a condition that must be satisfied in order that the corresponding two linear and homogeneous systems may have non-trivial solutions. It clearly takes the place of (II.2.8) of the previous case and has exactly the same economic meaning: a necessary condition for achieving full employment. Unlike (II.2.8), expression (II.5.3) now makes a distinction among three different types of demand: demand for consumption goods, demand for new investments and demand for replacing worn-out capital goods. However, the importance of this distinction will only be seen in the dynamic analysis which follows; for differing compositions of demand in a given period of time evidently have different consequences on the stocks of capital goods in the ensuing period. For the time being, and as far as a short-run analysis is concerned, the composition of demand does not matter. To fulfi condition (II.5.3), that is to achieve full employment, the only requirement that is imposed is that the *sum* of all types of demand be such as to imply a total over-all expenditure equal to total potential national income.[11]

What must be added, however, is that the fulfilment of (II.5.3) is no longer enough, because it only refers to the flow aspect of the economic system, and thereby implies full employment only potentially. Some other conditions must be fulfilled with regard to the stocks. First of all, there must be enough productive capacities in the economic system to make it possible to produce what is required by potential demand, i.e.

$$(\text{II.9.1}) \qquad K_i \geqslant X_i, \qquad i = 1, 2, \ldots, (n-1).$$

Yet this could not be defined as a satisfactory situation if some strict inequality were to hold, i.e. if some productive capacity were far beyond what is required by full employment. We have to impose also the conditions of full capacity utilisation, namely:

$$(\text{II.9.2}) \qquad K_i \leqslant X_i, \qquad i = 1, 2, \ldots, (n-1).$$

It follows that, for the (II.9.1) and (II.9.2) to be both satisfied, all the K_is must be equal to the X_is.

To sum up, two types of conditions are now necessary for the systems (II.5.2) and (II.6.2) to hold, namely

$$(\text{II.9.3}) \qquad \sum a_{ni} a_{in} + \sum a_{nk_i} a_{k_i n} + \sum (1/T_i) a_{nk_i} a_{in} = 1,$$

and

$$(\text{II.9.4}) \qquad K_i = X_i, \qquad i = 1, 2, \ldots, (n-1).$$

We may notice that (II.9.3), like (II.2.8), is a macro-economic condition: there must be a total amount of demand equal to potential national income if full employment is to be reached. On the other hand, (II.9.4) represent *a series* of sectoral conditions: one condition for each sector. Each sector i must be endowed with that stock of productive capacity which is necessary to produce the amount of commodity i which is demanded ($i = 1, 2, \ldots, n-1$).

At this point, one may wonder what would happen if (II.9.3)–(II.9.4) were not satisfied. And the answer is that this clearly depends on how the non-fulfilment comes about. A few interesting cases may usefully be

---

11 It must be pointed out, however, that the introduction of an exogenously given rate of profit has now made values at current prices no longer proportional to physical quantities of labour. This means that each binomial under the summations of (II.5.3), while still keeping the meaning of proportion of total labour that is employed in the corresponding sector, loses the meaning of proportion of total final national income, at current prices, that is accounted for by the same sector. We shall see later on (chapter VII) that this second meaning may be regained, under certain conditions.

considered. Inequalities of type (II.9.1), plus the left hand side of (II.9.3) being lower than its right hand side, mean idle capacity and less than full employment: a situation which we may call one of Keynesian under-employment,[12] for it is due to lack of effective demand. On the other hand, inequalities of type (II.9.2), again plus the left hand side of (II.9.3) lower than its right hand side, correspond to a situation in which the capital structure is smaller than the one which would make full employment possible: a situation which may be called one of Marxian under-employment. The two opposite cases as to condition (II.9.3) represent situations of inflation of different types, due respectively to lack of labour and to lack of productive capacity.

But a further question that may arise at this point is the following: if any of these cases, or if any other situation takes place, in which (II.9.3)–(II.9.4) are not satisfied, how is the system going to react? The answer clearly depends on the particular institutional set-up that the economic system has adopted. But it is not my purpose, as already said, to go into any inquiry of problems of this type for the time being. At this stage, no *behavioural* theory implying any particular institutional set-up will be introduced. The purpose here is simply to find and to specify the conditions that *must* be satisfied, in any case, if full employment is to be reached.

To conclude, when both (II.9.3) and (II.9.4) are fulfilled, the two systems of equations (II.5.2) and (II.6.2) hold in their entirety. This means that the economic system they represent has achieved full employment of labour and full utilisation of existing productive capacity. From now on, for the sake of simplicity, we shall simply refer to such a situation as one of *equilibrium*. It should perhaps be stressed that no connotation of automaticity and no association with any particular adjustment mechanism is intended to be implied by such an expression. *A situation of equilibrium* will simply be taken to mean a situation in

---

12 Of course, Keynes had a *behavioural* theory about this situation, with reference to a capitalist economy. In terms of the present terminology, Keynes' theory was that, for psychological reasons,

$$\sum a_{ni} a_{in} < 1,$$

namely that total demand for consumer goods on the whole tends to be smaller than full employment national income. Of course, demand for investment goods might be such a proportion of total national income as to make up for the difference from unity in the inequality stated above. But Keynes pointed out that there is no reason necessarily to expect this, because the two types of demand depend on different factors. He thought that the most likely situation to arise in practice would be one in which there is lack of effective demand and excess of productive capacity, as is the case characterised by the inequalities referred to in the text.

which there is full employment of the labour force and full utilisation of the existing productive capacity.

10. Towards a dynamic analysis

The foregoing analysis, after the introduction of capital goods, has acquired an important characteristic: although still a short-term analysis, it is no longer a static analysis. Even if we suppose that equilibrium conditions (II.9.3) and (II.9.4) are satisfied, we cannot say that we are at the end of our analysis. These conditions refer to a certain period of time; but, just in order to be fulfilled in that time period, they may contain some elements (investments) whose mere existence means modifying in the following time period those magnitudes (stocks of capital) on which the previous equilibrium situation was based. In this theoretical framework, therefore, the attainment of equilibrium in a given period of time does not mean at all that all problems have been solved.

We are inevitably led, by our own analysis, from the investigation of equilibrium conditions in a given period of time to the investigation of equilibrium conditions through time.

Chapter III

The simplest case of economic expansion – population growth with constant returns to scale

1. A simple dynamic model

Our inquiry will now venture into what happens *after* the single period so far considered has elapsed, and into what happens in general as time goes by. From an analytical point of view, there are two notions of time which may be adopted. Time may be conceived of as a succession of finite periods, with the supposition that changes take place only between one period and another. Or time may be conceived of as bringing along changes in a continuous way, so that the finite periods of the previous procedure become so short as to be infinitesimal. For our purposes, it is immaterial whether the first or the second procedure is adopted. But since the second procedure makes things analytically simpler, from our point of view, it will normally be followed in the following dynamic analysis. However, the arguments will also be re-cast now and then in terms of the first procedure, when that appears useful and illuminating.

If we look beyond a single period of time, all magnitudes considered so far must be *dated*. The previous short-run analysis remains valid within each time period, but from one time period to another those quantities which have hitherto been taken as given may undergo important changes.

Our procedure will now be to make some hypotheses about the movements through time of those magnitudes (population, technical progress, and consumption patterns) which we accept as given from outside economic investigation, and then to inquire into the equilibrium movements of the economic variables. We shall consider in this chapter the simplest of all cases of dynamic change, by supposing that, over time, the only *exogenous* factor which is changing is population. This simple case has been extensively dealt with already, in the economic literature, and the purpose of the present chapter is not, therefore, to obtain new results. The purpose is to evince the connections with the already known growth models and, at the same time, to develop formulations which will be needed in the following analysis.

Our hypotheses may now be listed schematically as follows:

(a) first of all, the *initial conditions* are such that, when our analysis begins, at a time defined as zero, there is full employment of the labour force and full utilisation of productive capacity. In our terminology, the economic system is in a situation of equilibrium;

(b) over time, population increases at a steady percentage rate g, so that

(III.1.1) $$X_n(t) = X_n(0)e^{gt},$$

where t denotes time, and e is the basis of the natural logarithms;[1]

(c) technical conditions remain fixed over time; expansion takes place at constant returns to scale. In other words, all technical coefficients (the a_{ni}s, the a_{nk_i}s and the T_is; $i = 1, 2, \ldots, n-1$) remain unchanged in time;

(d) consumers' tastes also remain constant, which means that, if individuals continue to receive the same income, their consumption – i.e. all the coefficients a_{in}s; $i = 1, 2, \ldots, n-1$ – remain constant through time.

These are all the hypotheses that are needed in this case, besides of course the convention (discussed in section 6 of the previous chapter) of taking the rate of profit as given. The reader may have noticed that there is a series of coefficients which have not been mentioned: the a_{k_n}s, namely the demand coefficients for new investments. The reason is that these coefficients cannot be specified in advance; in a dynamic analysis, they are themselves unknown, as they must be determined in such a way as to be consistent with the growing productive potential of the economic system.

Our task is now to find, first of all, the conditions under which the initial equilibrium situation may be maintained through time; and then to investigate the time-paths of the economic variables.

2. The conditions for a dynamic equilibrium

We might begin by saying that, in order to maintain equilibrium over time, conditions (II.9.3) and (II.9.4), which are satisfied *ex hypothesi* at time zero must also and constantly be kept satisfied as time goes on. A statement of this kind, however, now becomes uninteresting and

---

1 The letter g thus denotes a *percentage* rate of growth per period of time. For brevity's sake, however, we shall simply refer to it as a 'rate of growth', except in those cases where omission of the adjective 'percentage' and of the reference to the period of time might generate misunderstanding.

superficial, because those two conditions cease to be independent of one another, as soon as time is allowed to elapse.

If population is growing, both the availability of labour services and the demand for each product increase over time. In order that the new labour force may find employment and the growing potential demand may become effective, productive capacity must also increase. Thus, in time, the equilibrium conditions for productive capacity become

$$(\text{III.2.1}) \quad \frac{d}{dt}[K_i(t)] = \frac{d}{dt}[X_i(t)], \qquad\qquad i = 1, 2, \ldots, (n-1);$$

which simply means that there must be an increase in the productive capacity of each commodity, parallel to the increase in its demand.

The formulation may be expressed in a more helpful way by making use of a few definitions. We know from (II.5.4) that each demand for capital goods $(X_{k_i}; i = 1, 2, \ldots, n-1)$ is composed of two parts: replacement of worn-out capacity $[(1/T_i)a_{in}\bar{X}_n]$; and new investment $(a_{k_in}X_n)$. Denoting these two parts respectively by X'_{k_i} and X''_{k_i}, so that

$$(\text{III.2.2}) \qquad\qquad X_{k_i}(t) = X'_{k_i}(t) + X''_{k_i}(t),$$

we have

$$(\text{III.2.3}) \qquad X''_{k_i}(t) = \frac{d}{dt}[K_i(t)], \qquad\qquad i = 1, 2, \ldots, (n-1).$$

By substituting (III.2.3) into (III.2.1), we obtain

$$(\text{III.2.4}) \qquad X''_{k_i}(t) = \frac{d}{dt}[X_i(t)], \qquad\qquad i = 1, 2, \ldots, (n-1),$$

which amounts to expressing the productive capacity equilibrium conditions in the form of equilibrium relations between the demand for new capital goods in each period of time and the *rate of change* of demand for the corresponding consumption goods. Using the (II.5.4) and (III.1.1), the (III.2.4) become

$$a_{k_in}X_n(0)e^{gt} = \frac{d}{dt}[a_{in}X_n(0)e^{gt}],$$

or

$$a_{k_in}X_n(0)e^{gt} = g\,a_{in}X_n(0)e^{gt},$$

52

and finally[2]

$$(III.2.5) \qquad a_{k_i n} = g a_{in}, \qquad\qquad i = 1, 2, \ldots, (n-1).$$

This is a remarkable formulation. It states the series of sectoral productive capacity conditions in terms of flows (and no longer in terms of stocks) by specifying a very definite relation which must hold between each demand coefficient for new investments and the corresponding demand coefficient for consumption goods. Hence, as a condition to endow the economic system with equilibrium productive capacity, each sectoral new investment, in physical terms, must be equal to the corresponding sectoral final demand multiplied by the rate of growth of population. This determines sectoral equilibrium new investments in the whole economic system:

$$(III.2.6) \qquad X''_{k_i}(t) = g a_{in} X_n(t), \qquad\qquad i = 1, 2, \ldots, (n-1).$$

We shall call these conditions *the capital accumulation conditions* for keeping full employment over time (or capital accumulation equilibrium conditions).

If we like, the (III.2.6) may also be expressed in terms of ratios between physical quantities evaluated at current prices. After multiplying both sides of (III.2.6) by p_{k_i} and dividing by $p_i X_i$, we obtain

$$(III.2.7) \qquad \frac{p_{k_i} X''_{k_i}}{p_i X_i} = g \frac{p_{k_i} X_i}{p_i X_i}, \qquad\qquad i = 1, 2, \ldots, (n-1),$$

which means that, in equilibrium, each sectoral ratio of new investment to output, evaluated at current prices, must be equal to the corresponding sectoral capital/output ratio multiplied by the rate of population growth. As the reader will realise, expressions (III.2.7) represent a multi-sector version of what has become known, in the economic

---

2 In the more complex case considered in section 7 of chapter II (capital goods for the production of capital goods), these formulations become slightly more complex. Expressions (III.2.4) become:

$$(III.2.4an) \qquad X''_{k_i}(t) = \frac{d}{dt}[X_i(t) + \gamma_i X_{k_i}(t)], \qquad i = 1, 2, \ldots, (n-1),$$

and therefore expressions (III.2.5), i.e. the capital accumulation equilibrium conditions, become:

$$(III.2.5an) \qquad a_{k_i n} = g \frac{T_{k_i}}{T_{k_i} - \gamma_i - g\gamma_i T_{k_i}} a_{in}.$$

Notice also that the replacements of worn-out capacity will have to be modified accordingly. They emerge as

$$X'_{k_i}(t) = (1/T_i) \frac{T_{k_i}}{T_{k_i} - \gamma_i - g\gamma_i T_{k_i}} a_{in} X_n(t).$$

53

literature, as the 'Harrod–Domar equation'.[3] Our 'capital accumulation equilibrium conditions' are in fact nothing but a series of 'Harrod–Domar equations'; there is a particular Harrod–Domar equation that must be satisfied in each particular sector.

When these conditions are kept satisfied through time, the economic system is being constantly endowed with exactly those stocks of productive capacity which are necessary to provide full employment for all the workers. This however does not, *per se*, ensure full employment and full utilisation of productive capacity. In order that equilibrium be reached, the other necessary condition – the macro-economic relation referring to demand in the economic system as a whole – must also be satisfied. After substituting (III.2.5) into (II.9.3), this condition becomes:

$$\text{(III.2.8)} \qquad \sum a_{ni}a_{in} + (g + 1/T) \sum a_{nk_i}a_{in} = 1.$$

The economic meaning is again that total expenditure must be equal to total potential gross national income if full employment and full capacity utilisation are to be attained. However, (III.2.8) now also requires a very definite division of total expenditure between new investments, replacements, and consumption. The effect of substituting into it the capital accumulation equilibrium conditions has been to specify the magnitude of the term $(g + 1/T) \sum a_{nk_i}a_{in}$, which is nothing but an analytical break-down of the proportion of total labour required by equilibrium gross investments. This equilibrium proportion, as can be seen, is exclusively determined by the three exogenous forces of the economic system: population growth, technology, and consumers' preferences. Therefore, if (III.2.8) is to be satisfied (i.e. if full employment is to be kept), it is the effective demand for consumption goods that must absorb the whole remaining proportion of total labour – represented by the first expression of (III.2.8). Condition (III.2.8), since it thereby determines the size of total effective demand, may be called the *effective demand condition* for keeping full employment.

To conclude, two kinds of necessary conditions must be satisfied in order to keep equilibrium over time. First of all, there is a series of capital accumulation conditions (III.2.5), ensuring that each sector be endowed all the time with precisely that amount of additional productive capacity which is required by the expanding demand. These conditions state that the ratio of new investments to the level of

---

3 See R. F. Harrod, 'An Essay in Dynamic Theory', *Economic Journal*, 1939, and *Towards a Dynamic Economics*, London 1948; Evsey D. Domar, 'Capital Expansion, Rate of Growth and Employment', in *Econometrica*, 1946.

production must be equal, in each sector, to the technologically determined capital/output ratio multiplied by the rate of population growth. Secondly, in order to ensure the full utilisation of the available productive capacity and the full employment of the available labour force, a further macro-economic effective demand condition (III.2.8) must also be satisfied. This condition states that, given (by the first series of conditions and by replacement requirements) the total amount of equilibrium gross investment, total demand for consumption goods must be such as to absorb the whole remaining part of potential gross national income.

It is important to notice that these conditions, in the case we are considering here, present no problem *through time*. Since all coefficients are constant, once conditions (III.2.5) and (III.2.8) are satisfied at time zero, they will remain satisfied for all time.

3. A more complete formulation of the effective demand condition

It may be useful to take a further step, at this point, to complete formulation (III.2.8). Population has been referred to in general terms, so far, both with respect to demand for commodities and with respect to supply of labour. This has meant assuming implicitly that population and labour force are the same thing. In practice this is not so. All people do contribute to demand for commodities, but only a fraction of them (representing active population) actually take part in the process of production. Moreover, a further complication arises in connection with the fact that our coefficients have a time dimension. The point may be made clearer by supposing a finite period, for example a year, as the unit of time. In this case, the consumption coefficients refer to yearly per-capita consumption; but, normally, the technical coefficients refer to that fraction of the unit of time which corresponds to actual working time. When this is done, the a_{in}s and the a_{ni}s come no longer to be expressed in terms of the same number of people and not even to refer to the same unit of time.

To be consistent, a correction must be made to the technical coefficients in order to make them comparable with the demand coefficients; and the simplest way to do this is to divide each technical coefficient by two parameters, the first of which – let us call it μ – represents the proportion of active to total population and the second – let us call it ν – the ratio of, let us say, working hours to the total number of hours forming the unit of time considered.

Evidently:

(III.3.1) $$1 > \mu > 0,$$

55

(III.3.2) $$1 > v > 0.$$

These corrections do not affect the expressions we found for prices which contain the technical coefficients, provided of course that the wage rate refers to a unit of actual working time (as it usually does) They do affect, on the other hand, the expression for the effective demand condition for equilibrium, where both demand coefficients and technical coefficients appear together. (This is after all intuitive: the conditions for reaching full employment are different, according to the ratio of active to total population and to the length of the working week.) Hence, after introducing μ and v, (III.2.8) becomes:

(III.3.3) $$(1/\mu v) \sum a_{ni} a_{in} + (g + 1/T)(1/\mu v) \sum a_{nk_i} a_{in} = 1,$$

which must be considered as a more complete formulation of the effective demand condition for a dynamic equilibrium.

4. The dynamic movements of relative prices, physical quantities and other economic variables

To find out how prices and physical quantities move, as time goes by, is now a relatively easy task. As to prices, it can immediately be seen from the (II.6.3) that, under the present hypotheses, all their components are constant over time, so that *all relative prices remain constant over time*.

The expressions (II.5.4) for physical quantities, on the other hand, all contain one component, namely population, which is increasing at a percentage rate g. This component, however, is the same for all of them, so that *all physical quantities increase in time at the same percentage rate of growth g*. We might also say that *relative* physical quantities remain constant over time.

As a consequence, sectoral outputs at current prices, which we shall denote by $V_i(t)$, i.e.

(III.4.1) $$V_i(t) = p_i(t)X_i(t), \quad i = 1, 2, \ldots, n-1, k_1, k_2, \ldots, k_{n-1},$$

will all grow through time at the same percentage growth rate g, as can easily be checked, after substitution from (II.5.4) and (II.6.3).

Besides prices and quantities, there are other magnitudes in the economic system which are of economic interest and which are worth considering. To begin with, the time-path of the amount of employment in each sector can be derived immediately from the movements of physical quantities. Denoting sectoral employment by $E_i(t)$, we have:

(III.4.2) $$E_i(t) = a_{ni}(t)X_i(t), \quad i = 1, 2, \ldots, n-1, k_1, k_2, \ldots, k_{n-1}.$$

56

And again, after substitution from (II.5.4) it can be seen that, under the present hypotheses, *all* E_is increase in time at the same percentage rate of growth of population (g). In other words, the *structure* of employment remains invariant.[4]

Further, we may consider the capital/output ratios and the capital/labour ratios in each sector and in the economy as a whole. Denoting the sectoral capital/output ratios by $\varkappa_i$, ($i = 1, 2, \ldots, n-1$), and the over-all capital/output ratio by Γ, and using, for simplicity, formulations (II.5.4), (II.6.3), i.e. considering an economic system where capital goods are required only for the production of consumption goods, we may write them as:[5]

$$(\text{III.4.5}) \qquad \varkappa_i(t) = \frac{a_{nk_i}(t)}{a_{ni}(t) + (\pi + 1/T)a_{nk_i}(t)}, \qquad i = 1, 2, \ldots, (n-1),$$

---

4 All the conclusions drawn above on the dynamic movements of prices, physical quantities, sectoral outputs, and sectoral employment, remain exactly the same, as can easily be checked, in the case of the more complex model considered in section 7 of chapter II (capital goods required for the production of all goods).

We are in fact in a position, at this stage, to specify in more detail the physical quantity solutions. By inserting the new expressions for replacement, and for the capital accumulation equilibrium conditions (III.2.5an) – see footnote 2 on p.53 – the physical quantity solutions (II.7.2) become

$$(\text{III.4.3n}) \quad \begin{cases} X_i(t) = a_{in}X_n(0)e^{gt}, \\ X_{k_i}(t) = (g + 1/T_i)\dfrac{T_{k_i}}{T_{k_i} - \gamma_i - g\gamma_i T_{k_i}} a_{in}X_n(0)e^{gt}, \quad i = 1, 2, \ldots, (n-1). \end{cases}$$

A novelty of these formulations is that the viability conditions for the physical quantities now emerge as

$$(\text{III.4.4n}) \qquad T_{k_i} > \gamma_i + g\gamma_i T_{k_i}, \qquad\qquad i = 1, 2, \ldots, (n-1),$$

i.e. as perfectly 'dual' to the (II.7.5a), referring to prices.

5 In each sector, the capital/output ratio is

$$\varkappa_i = \frac{p_{k_i}K_i}{p_iX_i}.$$

Remembering that, in equilibrium, K_i and X_i coincide, and using the (II.5.4) and (II.6.3), we obtain:

$$\varkappa_i = \frac{a_{nk_i}w}{[a_{ni} + (\pi + 1/T)a_{nk_i}]w} = \frac{a_{nk_i}}{a_{ni} + (\pi + 1/T)a_{nk_i}},$$

which is the expression used in the text.

When the more complex formulations (II.7.2) and (II.7.3) are used, the result is:

$$(\text{III.4.6n}) \qquad \varkappa_i = \frac{a_{nk_i}}{a_{ni}(T_{k_i} - T_{k_i}\gamma_i\pi_{k_i} - \gamma_i)(1/T_{k_i}) + (\pi_i + 1/T_i)a_{nk_i}}.$$

and:[6]

$$(\text{III.4.7}) \quad \Gamma(t) = \frac{\sum a_{in}(t) a_{nk_i}(t)}{\sum a_{in}(t) a_{ni}(t) + (g + \pi + 1/T) \sum a_{in}(t) a_{nk_i}(t)}.$$

As can be seen, the components of (III.4.5) and (III.4.7) are nothing, but coefficients. And since, under the present hypotheses, all coefficients remain constant through time, it follows that all sectoral capital/output ratios and also the over-all capital/output ratio remain absolutely constant over time.

Denoting now the sectoral capital/labour ratios by χ_i ($i = 1, 2, \ldots, n - 1$), and the over-all capital/labour ratio by Λ, and again using, for simplicity, formulations (II.5.4) and (II.6.3), we may write them as:[7]

$$(\text{III.4.9}) \qquad \chi_i(t) = \frac{a_{nk_i}(t)}{a_{ni}(t)} w(t), \qquad i = 1, 2, \ldots, n - 1,$$

and:[8]

$$(\text{III.4.11}) \qquad \Lambda(t) = \sum a_{in}(t) a_{nk_i}(t) w(t).$$

---

[6] The over-all capital/output ratio is, in our notation,

$$\Gamma = \frac{\sum p_{k_i} K_i}{\sum p_i X_i + \sum p_{k_i} X''_{k_i}}.$$

Taking the (II.5.4) and (II.6.3), and again remembering that, in equilibrium, K_i and X_i coincide, we obtain:

$$\Gamma = \frac{\sum a_{in} a_{nk_i} w X_n}{\sum a_{in}[a_{ni} + (\pi + 1/T)a_{nk_i}] w X_n + \sum g a_{in} a_{nk_i} w X_n} = \frac{\sum a_{in} a_{nk_i}}{\sum a_{in} a_{ni} + (g + \pi + 1/T) \sum a_{in} a_{nk_i}},$$

which is the expression used in the text.

When the more complex formulations (II.7.2) and (II.7.3) are used, the result is:

$$(\text{III.4.8n}) \qquad \Gamma = \frac{\sum a_{in} a_{nk_i}}{\sum a_{in} a_{ni}(T_{k_i} - T_{k_i} \gamma_i \pi_{k_i} - \gamma_i)(1/T_{k_i}) + (g + \pi_i + 1/T_i) \sum a_{in} a_{nk_i}}.$$

[7] In each sector, the capital/labour ratio is:

$$\chi_i = \frac{p_{k_i} K_i}{a_{ni} X_i}.$$

Remembering again that, in equilibrium, K_i and X_i coincide, and using the (II.5.4) and (II.6.3), we obtain:

$$\chi_i = \frac{a_{nk_i}}{a_{ni}} w,$$

which is the expression used in the text.

When the more complex formulations (II.7.2) and (II.7.3) are used, the result is:

$$(\text{III.4.10n}) \qquad \chi_i = T_{k_i}(T_{k_i} - \gamma_i - \pi_{k_i} \gamma_i T_{k_i})^{-1} \frac{a_{nk_i}}{a_{ni}} w.$$

[8] The over-all capital/labour ratio is:

$$\Lambda = \frac{\sum p_{k_i} K_i}{X_n}.$$

These ratios, besides depending on the coefficients, also depend on the wage rate. But since, under the present hypotheses, both the coefficients and the wage rate (in terms of any physical commodity) remain constant, it follows that all sectoral capital/labour ratios and also the over-all capital/labour ratio remain absolutely constant over time.

It goes without saying that, as a straightforward corollary of the above results, all aggregate quantities – such as gross and net national income, total consumption, total investments, total aggregate capital, etc. – increase in real terms at the same rate of growth (g) as population over time.

5. Elegant features of the present case of economic growth

The dynamic features of the economic system considered here, as they emerge from the foregoing sections, are of an extreme simplicity. The merits of this simplicity are entirely attributable to the assumption of a fixed technology and constant returns to scale, which confers upon this case all the elegant properties it possesses. With an invariant technology, and constant returns to scale, the growth of the economic system is entirely determined by the rate of growth of population (and thus of the labour force). This growth does not affect the position of any single individual: per capita income remains constant over time, and economic growth simply means that the economic system expands all its sections at the same percentage rate, while the structure of the economic system (its relative composition) remains constant over time.

This case of growth is well known in economic theory. A clear though rudimentary picture of it can be found already in Cassel.[9] More recently, von Neumann and Leontief,[10] although in different ways, have both based their dynamic elaborations precisely on this same case. But, most interesting of all, this is the case to which macro-economic models of growth can be correctly applied. Since the economic system expands,

---

Taking formulations (II.5.4), (II.6.3) and using equilibrium relations $X_i = K_i$ ($i = 1, 2, \ldots, n-1$), we have:

$$\Lambda = \sum a_{in} a_{nk_i} w,$$

which is the expression used in the text.

When the more complex formulations (II.7.2) and (II.7.3) are used, the result is:

(III.4.12n) $\qquad \Lambda = \sum T_{k_i}(T_{k_i} - T_{k_i}\gamma_i\pi_i - \gamma_i)^{-1} a_{in} a_{nk_i} w.$

9 Gustav Cassel, *Theoretische Sozialökonomie*, Leipzig 1918, pp. 27 and ff. (English translation: *The Theory of Social Economy*, London 1921, pp. 34 and ff.)

10 Both von Neumann's and Leontief's dynamic models will be discussed in detail in an appendix to chapter VI.

while keeping its proportions constant, there is in fact no loss of generality in framing the whole analysis in macro-economic terms. The usual convention that the variables must be considered as measured in terms of a composite commodity, made up of a fixed 'basket of goods', is in this case perfectly legitimate and logically unobjectionable. As all our results have shown, all single coefficients remain constant through time, so that the composition, or structure, of the economic system, once specified at time zero, remains the same for all times.[11]

---

11 We shall come back later on (in the appendix to chapter VI) to pointing out the strict limitations of this elegant but very special case of growth. As may easily be realised, if the whole *structure* of the economic system were really to remain constant through time, any disaggregated formulation would not provide us with particularly useful insights, besides those that are provided already by the corresponding, much simpler, macro-economic formulations.

Chapter IV

Technical change and the dynamics of demand

1. Technical progress in macro-economic models

The case of the previous chapter, despite its popularity among theoretical economists, remains a very special and unrealistic case of economic growth. In practice, as soon as we look beyond a single period of time, a whole series of changes take place, besides those of population: the changes in the technical methods of production. For any analytical investigation, these changes are clearly much more complex and problematic than those in the size of population.

Technical change, as said in the introductory chapter, has been the great neglected factor in economic analysis. It is only in the last thirty years that economists have begun to consider it, through the elaboration of models of economic growth. But all the models of economic growth with technical progress have been developed in *macro-economic* terms, i.e. with the implicit assumption that one single commodity (or a composite commodity of invariable composition) is being produced in the economic system. And technical change has been introduced in the form of an over-all 'rate of technical progress', which has been treated exactly like, and symmetrically to, the rate of population growth.[1]

Unfortunately, this approach has been accepted rather uncritically in the economic literature. My purpose is now to show that it is unacceptable. But, in order to do so, I must invite the reader to take a closer look

---

1 The pioneering work has been that, already mentioned, of Harrod. After Harrod, and the similar contribution by Domar, the models of economic growth with technical progress have followed two distinctly different theoretical paths. One has been in the direction of pursuing the Keynesian approach of Harrod and Domar. (Joan Robinson, *The Accumulation of Capital*, London 1956, and Nicholas Kaldor, 'A Model of Economic Growth' in *The Economic Journal*, 1957, are perhaps the best examples.) The other has been in the direction of trying to re-absorb Harrod–Domar ideas into traditional marginal theory (e.g., Robert M. Solow, 'A Contribution to the Theory of Economic Growth', in *The Quarterly Journal of Economics*, February 1956, and James Meade, *A Neo-Classical Theory of Economic Growth*, London 1961). All these efforts, however, have been framed in macro-economic terms, or at most in terms of a two-sector (i.e. consumption and investment) economy.

at all the implications that this approach entails. Our disaggregated analysis will turn out to be very useful for this task.

As said above, any macro-economic analysis implies that all variables considered are measured in terms of a composite commodity or 'basket of goods' of fixed and invariable composition through time. Therefore, unless the macro-economic framework is given up altogether, the introduction of an over-all rate of technical progress in such an analysis necessarily implies two further and much more specific assumptions: (i) that technical progress is going on at the same rate in all sectors of the economic system, and (ii) that demand for *each* product is expanding at the same rate.

Let us carefully consider a hypothetical case of economic growth, in which productivity movements and demand expansion conform to this uniform pattern.

2. A hypothetical economy with uniform technical progress and uniform expansion of demand

After dealing with the case of population expansion with constant returns to scale, the hypothetical case of economic growth taking place with uniform technical progress and uniform expansion of demand can be treated more summarily.

The hypotheses are now as follows:

(a) the initial conditions, as in the previous case, are such that at time zero there is full employment and full capacity utilisation;

(b) over time, population remains constant;

(c) technical progress is the same in all sectors of the economic system. This means that, over time, all the technical coefficients of production decrease at a percentage steady rate ϱ, i.e.[2]

(IV.2.1)
$$a_{nj}(t) = a_{nj}(0)e^{-\varrho t},$$

$$j = 1, 2, \ldots, (n-1), k_1, k_2, \ldots, k_{n-1};$$

(d) consumers' tastes are such that *the composition* of consumption is invariant to changes in income. In other words, when income increases, each individual expands demand for *all* the commodities consumed *in the same proportion*. This means that, if per capita

---

2 As in the case of g (see footnote 1 on p. 51), ϱ represents a *proportional* or *percentage* rate of change per period of time. But again, for the sake of simplicity, we shall simply refer to it as a 'rate of technical progress' or 'rate of growth of productivity', the adjectives 'proportional' or 'percentage', and the reference to the period of time, being omitted, except in those cases where omission might generate misunderstanding.

income increases at a percentage rate ϱ through time (as in equilibrium it must do), all coefficients of consumption will also increase at the rate ϱ, i.e.

(IV.2.2) $a_{in}(t) = a_{in}(0)e^{\varrho t}, \qquad i = 1, 2, \ldots, (n-1).$

Under these hypotheses, the two conditions for a dynamic equilibrium come out rather straightforwardly. By following exactly the same procedure as in section 2 of the previous chapter, the capital accumulation equilibrium conditions emerge as

(IV.2.3) $a_{k_i n}(t) = \varrho a_{in}(t), \qquad i = 1, 2, \ldots, (n-1),$

which are similar to the (III.2.5), the only difference being that now the rate of technical progress has replaced the rate of population growth. Of course, in the (IV.2.3), all coefficients are moving, but they are moving at the same percentage rate of change, so that all relations among them remain constant through time. The effective demand condition also emerges as very similar to (III.2.8), or rather to (III.3.3), namely:

(IV.2.4) $(1/\mu v)\sum a_{ni}(t)a_{in}(t) + (\varrho + 1/T)(1/\mu v)\sum a_{nk_i}(t)a_{in}(t) = 1,$

where again the rate of technical progress has taken the place of the rate of population growth. The (mathematically) interesting feature of this case of growth is that all coefficients of production and all coefficients of consumption, although moving in time, are moving in an opposite direction and at exactly the same rate. As a result, in (IV.2.4), *each single binary product* of coefficients under the two summations *remains constant* over time – the movements of the two components exactly cancelling each other out. This means that the contribution to total employment (and to total national income) of each single sector remains constant. As in the previous case, condition (IV.2.4) does not raise any problem through time. Once it is satisfied at time zero, it will remain satisfied for ever, because, in all sectors, productivity and demand are increasing at the same rate.

The time paths of all economic magnitudes can be found immediately by substituting (IV.2.1) and (IV.2.2) into (II.5.4), (II.6.3) and (III.4.1)–(III.4.12n). As can easily be checked, if the rate of profit remains constant, the results are as follows:

(i) physical production of each commodity increases in time at the rate ϱ; therefore all relative quantities remain constant;

(ii) all commodity prices – if w is taken as the arbitrarily fixed *numéraire* – decrease in time at the rate ϱ. Alternatively – if any commodity instead of w is taken as the *numéraire* – then all commodity prices remain constant over time, while the wage rate increases at the rate ϱ. Another way of stating this result is to say that the commodity price structure (the relative prices of all commodities) remains constant through time, while the real wage rate increases at the rate ϱ;

(iii) employment in each sector remains invariant over time;

(iv) production of each commodity, evaluated at current prices, remains constant in time (if w is taken as the arbitrarily fixed *numéraire*) or increases at the rate ϱ (if any one of the commodity prices, instead of w, is taken as given):

 (v) all sectoral capital/output ratios, as well as the over-all capital/output ratio, remain absolutely constant over time. The time paths of the (sectoral and over-all) capital/labour ratios, on the other hand, depend on the choice of the *numéraire* of the price system. They also remain absolutely constant if the wage rate is taken as the arbitrarily fixed *numéraire*, or else they increase at the rate ϱ, if any one of the commodity prices, instead of w, is taken as given.

3. Analytical properties of the two cases of economic growth considered so far

The most attractive property of the case of economic growth just examined is that it still retains the most elegant features of the previous case, namely the constancy in time of all the proportions of the economic system. By the device of uniformity, both in technical change and in demand expansion, all movements of coefficients cancel out *inside* each sector and the structure of commodity prices remains unchanged. Thus, again, the economic system expands by multiplying all its sections in the same proportion, while its relative composition is invariant with respect to growth and time.

From an analytical point of view, there is a remarkable symmetrical correspondence between the two cases of economic growth considered so far. In the case of population growth, the wage rate was constant and the economic system was growing at the same rate as population; in the case of uniform technical progress just examined, population remains constant and the wage rate is growing at the same rate as technical progress. The two cases may easily be combined, and the results of such a combination are so straightforward that it is of no use to spell them out in detail. We may, however, explicitly state the conditions of dynamic equilibrium, which emerge as follows:

$$(\text{IV}.3.1) \quad a_{k_i n}(t) = (g + \varrho)a_{in}(t), \qquad\qquad i = 1, 2, \ldots, (n-1),$$

and

$$(IV.3.2) \qquad (1/\mu v) \sum a_{ni}(t) a_{in}(t) + (1/\mu v T) \sum a_{nk_i}(t) a_{in}(t)$$
$$+ (g + \varrho)(1/\mu v) \sum a_{nk_i}(t) a_{in}(t) = 1.$$

The economic meaning is immediate. Each single sector and the economic system as a whole expand at a rate which is the sum of the rate of population growth and the rate of technical progress, a sum which has become known in the economic literature by Harrod's term of *natural rate of growth*.

At this point, however, after admiring the symmetry and the analytical beauty of the two cases of economic growth considered so far, we must also draw from the results we have obtained at least two logically inescapable conclusions.

The first one refers to the method of analysis. If the hypotheses embodied in the two cases of economic growth considered above were acceptable, then there really would not be much insight gained into the working of an economic system by using any disaggregated formulation. The merit of such a formulation would only be to show the structure of the economic system at a given point of time. But since this structure remains the same for ever, the dynamics of the economic system would always be uniform, which means that no extra information could be obtained by disaggregation. In other words, a macro-economic formulation would be quite sufficient and entirely satisfactory.

The second conclusion is of a much more practical relevance. If the hypotheses embodied in the two cases of economic growth considered above were to correspond, even roughly, to what in the long run is happening in the real world, then any preoccupation with problems of economic growth would be entirely unjustified. The model considered above amounts in fact to saying that economic growth *as such* would present no problem at all. The only thing that, in any growing economic system, would have to be done is the setting up of that particular structure which is most desired – the only constraint being that it must satisfy relations (IV.3.1) and (IV.3.2). This is a *once for all problem*. Once this structure has been set up, no problem would exist any more. Thereafter, the economic system could expand for ever, its proportions remaining constant.

Attractive though the first conclusion may be, the second one is so much in striking contrast with everyday experience, and with the economic policies of all Governments, that it should immediately lead one to infer that there must be something wrong somewhere. And it is not difficult to see that the flaw is to be found precisely in the hypothetical case of economic growth considered in the foregoing section. For the hypotheses behind the case considered in chapter III (no technical progress and constant returns to scale) are unlikely, but at least they are theoretically and logically possible. On the other hand, the hypotheses behind the case just considered (uniform technical progress accompanied by uniform expansion of demand) are not only unlikely; they are impossible. And we know that they will always be impossible, as long as the world in which we live is inhabited by human beings.

To substantiate and expand these assertions will require all the rest of the present chapter.

4. The production aspect of technical change

We must now embark on a careful examination of the economic meaning and implications of technical change. When the technical coefficients of production change over time, there are two distinctly different sets of effects which are called into being. On the one side (let us say, on the production side), technical change means a variation in the methods of production and, therefore, a change in the physical quantities and qualities of goods which may be produced out of a given amount of physical inputs. On the other side (let us say, on the demand side), it means a change in the amount of per capita real income at the disposal of consumers in general, and therefore a change in their potential demand.

Let us consider the production aspect first. Here the causes of change may be manifold. For a long time, economists have been mainly impressed by those changes which are connected with the fact that natural resources are limited. To Malthus and Ricardo, for example, it appeared as a matter of logical necessity that the continuation and expansion of the process of production, on natural resources which are given, should inevitably lead to decreasing returns, i.e. to an increasing trend in the technical coefficients of production. But the economic history of the industrial countries has by now persistently brought to the fore another, more important and widespread, process of change continuously at work in any modern society: technical progress.

Technical progress is a very complex phenomenon. In the sense in which it is relevant for economic activity, it includes not only, and not so much, the great scientific discoveries (which by their own nature come about in a discontinuous and irregular way), as their practical application on an industrial scale, which takes place through a much longer and continuous process. Furthermore, it includes all the innumerable series of expedients and devices, small if considered individually, but of great relevance if jointly gauged, which are the daily upshot of experience, experiment, research and rethinking of the organisation of production. This is indeed a very complicated process, emerging from the learning activity of human beings and the application of this learning activity to production. By its nature this process is therefore a slow, but persistent, one. It consists of long and repeated attempts not only to reorganise the old methods of production, to utilise more efficiently the new materials, and to improve the quality of products, but also to invent and apply new methods of production, produce new products, find new resources, and discover new sources of energy.

It would certainly be out of place to develop a theory of technical progress here. If such a theory should ever be developed, it would pertain to a much wider field than economics, because it could not avoid some definite conceptions about the aims and ends of human society. Therefore, as far as the present work is concerned, the usual procedure will be followed of taking technology as given from outside economic analysis. However, what will be taken as given is not a fixed technology but the *movements* of the technical coefficients, in general, through time.

The concept of technical change which is thereby adopted remains a very general one, as it includes all possible types of change, from technical improvements to increasing or decreasing returns to scale. But in order to reach practically relevant conclusions, the analysis which follows will be carried out with reference to those movements of technology which empirical evidence has shown by now to be everywhere the most typical ones in modern societies. These movements may be briefly stated in three propositions:

a) in the long run, the effects of technical progress are, on a (weighted) average, by far more important and more widespread than the effects of decreasing returns to scale.[3] This means that, over time,

---

[3] The simplest empirical confirmation of this proposition is that, in all industrial countries, per capita income is enormously higher today than it was at the beginning of their process of industrialisation. In any case, a great deal of statistical material has been collected by now on productivity growth in various countries. Suffice it to mention here the series of monograph studies carried out in the United States under the auspices of the National Bureau of Economic Research of New York. (No. 39, S. Fabricant, *The Output of Manufacturing Industries 1899–1937*, New York 1940; No. 41, S. Fabricant, *Employment in Manufacturing 1899–1939*, New York 1942; No. 42, H. Barger and H. H. Landsberg, *American Agriculture 1899–1939: A Study of Output, Employment and Productivity*, New York 1942; No. 43, H. Barger and S. H. Schurr, *The Mining Industries 1899–1939: A Study of Output Employment and Productivity*, New York 1944; No. 47, J. M. Gould, *Output and Productivity in the Electric and Gas Utilities, 1899–1942*, New York 1946; No. 51, H. Barger, *The Transportation Industries 1899–1946: A Study of Output, Employment and Productivity*, New York 1951). (*cont.*)

the coefficients of production decrease (i.e. productivity increases) in most sectors, although in a few sectors the coefficients migh increase (i.e. productivity decrease);

(b) as a net effect of decreasing returns and technical progress, produc tion coefficients are persistently moving through time. Yet, each o them may be moving at a different speed. In other words, there normally is a wide dispersion amongst the rates of change o productivity in the different branches of the economic system.[4]

(c) technical progress consists not only of increases in productivity but also of continuous additions of new sectors producing new and better goods and machines.

5. The demand aspect of technical change

Let us now consider the effects of technical change on demand. If, on the whole, technical change is in the direction of a persistently increas ing trend of productivity, it means a higher and higher amount of wage and profits, or, more generally, an increasing trend in per capit incomes at the disposal of the members of the community. It follow that, in each period of time, technical progress compels the members o the community to make new decisions; they must decide on whic commodities they are going to spend the increments to their incomes And here, clearly, their preferences as consumers come to play a crucia role.

Consumers' preferences may of course be widely manipulated, bu they ultimately depend on human nature, which represents, in the sam way as the technical conditions of production do, a fundamenta external datum for any meaningful economic investigation. No com modity, whatever ingenious technique it may require, can be successful ly produced if its (real or imagined) utility for the consumers is nc sufficient to justify its cost: it would remain unsold. The relevance itsel of technical progress depends on potential demand: an increase in

---

All these studies have shown widespread and persistent increases in productivit almost everywhere. Even in the mining industries, which theoretically should provid the typical field for diminishing returns, productivity has been increasing in most case owing to the discovery of new and better mines or to higher levels of efficiency i resource extraction from currently existing mines. Only in a few cases has productivit actually been decreasing. In these cases too, however, technical progress has normall led to the discovery of substitutes.

4 See, for example, an interesting study by F. L. Hirt, 'A New Look at Productivit Growth Rates', in *Survey of Current Business*, 1957, and, also L. Rostas, *Productivit Prices and Distribution in Selected British Industries*, London 1948, and *Comparativ Productivity in British and American Industries*, London 1948; W. E. G. Salte *Productivity and Technical Change*, Cambridge 1960, especially chapters X and XII

productivity, however large it may be, loses much or even all of its meaning, if it takes place in the productive process of a commodity for which demand can only be small or negligible. This means that any investigation into technical progress must necessarily imply some hypotheses (and if not explicitly, it necessarily does so implicitly) on the evolution of consumers' preferences as income increases. Not to make such hypotheses and to pretend to discuss technical progress without considering the evolution of demand would make it impossible to evaluate the very relevance of technical progress and would render the investigation itself meaningless. Increases in productivity and increases in income are two facets of the same phenomenon. Since the first implies the second, and the composition of the second determines the relevance of the first, the one cannot be considered if the other is ignored.

Unfortunately, the economic theory which has been developed so far is hardly able to give us any help on this problem. The consumers' demand theory that we know today is a highly sophisticated logical framework, built on entirely static premises. It relies on the existence of a perfectly known and consistent set of preferences defined at a given level of per capita income. Such a theory, however admirable it may be on formal grounds, and whether it is useful or not in showing the consequences of price changes at a given level of income, is clearly unable to offer us any guide to the investigation of changes in demand following successive and persistent *increments* to income.

The regrettable consequence of this state of affairs has been that, when, recently, the elaboration of growth models with technical progress has compelled their authors to make definite hypotheses about the expansion of demand, they have made, in the absence of any guiding principle, those assumptions that best suited the mathematical properties of their models. As pointed out already, they have invariably postulated, either explicitly or implicitly, a uniform and proportional expansion of per capita demand.[5]

Now, if there is something that we do positively know about expansion of per capita demand when income increases, this is that per capita demand for each commodity *does not expand proportionally*. All the empirical investigators who in the last hundred years have looked into this matter have invariably and without exception found and stressed this tendency.

5 The effect of all this is that all recent models of economic growth share a defect which was characteristic of classical economic analysis. They have concentrated their emphasis exclusively on the technological side of economic reality and have entirely forgotten the other side, related to demand.

As is well known, the first empirical generalisation on the evolving pattern of demand in response to increases in incomes comes from an old discovery in economics which goes back to Ernst Engel[6] in the 1850s. Engel, after studying the conditions of consumption of workers in the kingdom of Saxony, stated what has since become known as 'the Engel law'. This 'law' says that the proportion of income spent on food declines as income increases. A more general formulation of this empirical law, stating that the proportion of income spent *on any type of good* changes as per capita income increases, has been confirmed ever since, and evinced by all the econometricians who have been concerned with empirical work on demand.[7]

These results come in fact as no surprise. It should not take long to realise that what they reveal is a basic tendency inherent in the human nature of the consumers. We shall go into this matter in more detail in the next three sections. Meanwhile we can safely draw the conclusion that the hypothesis of a uniform expansion of per capita demand, which has been put so far at the basis of almost all theories of economic growth with technical progress, is incompatible with one of the most fundamental empirical 'laws' of economics. Since increases in per capita income necessarily imply non-proportional expansion of demand, and since technical progress leads to increases in per capita incomes, the introduction of technical progress in any dynamic economic investigation necessarily implies a non-proportional expansion of demand. The hypothesis of proportional growth, adopted in practically all current models of economic growth, is therefore unacceptable.

6. Modifications needed to the current theory of demand

It is no doubt very significant, as an indication of practical relevance, that all empirical works on demand, even long before the elaboration of any theory of consumer's behaviour, have always and without any exception made of 'Engel's law' one of their major themes, if not their

6 Ernst Engel, 'Die Productions- und Consumptionsverhältnisse des Konigreichs Sachsen', in *Zeitschrift der Statistischen Bureaus des Koniglich Sächsischen Ministerium des Inneren*, Nos. 8 and 9, No. 22, 1857; republished in *Bulletin de l'Institut International de Statistique*, IX (1895).

7 See, for example, R. G. D. Allen and A. L. Bowley, *Family Expenditure*, London 1935; S. J. Prais and H. S. Houthakker, *The Analysis of Family Budgets*, Cambridge 1955; H. Wold and L. Juréen, *Demand Analysis: A Study in Econometrics*, Stockholm 1952; R. Stone, *The Measurement of Consumers' Expenditure and Behaviour in the United Kingdom*, 2 vols., Cambridge 1954; M. Gilbert and I. B. Kravis, *An International Comparison of National Products and the Purchasing Power of Currencies*, Paris 1953; H. S. Houthakker, 'An International Comparison of Household Expenditure Patterns', in *Econometrica*, 1957.

only major theme.[8] And it seems to me very unfortunate that the demand theory that has been developed in the economics treatises and which is contained in our textbooks today should have concentrated almost exclusively on behaviour at given levels of per capita income. This has practically amounted to giving up all attempts to incorporate the information obtainable from Engel's law into our theory of consumer's demand. Only the econometricians,[9] so far – by being faced with facts – have gone into this field. But their attitude has generally been rather accommodating. They have normally paid formal tribute to existing theory and have gone on to make a few piece-meal theoretical adjustments that suited their empirical purposes. As a result, Engel's discovery has remained until our own day at the state of an empirical law, almost entirely isolated from the main body of the theory of consumer's demand.

It is not my purpose, of course, to engage in a comprehensive theoretical investigation of demand here. Yet it is necessary at this point to go into this matter explicitly, albeit very briefly, because the evolution of demand, in response to increases in income, is going to play a crucial role in all subsequent analysis. More specifically, I shall discuss at least two theoretical aspects of consumers' behaviour, in order to make a few essential modifications and additions to current demand theory, otherwise insufficient for our purposes.

7. Sketch of a theory of the dynamics of consumers' demand – a hierarchy of needs and wants

The first point I should like to make refers to the information we do have on the shape of consumers' preferences at different levels of real income. I shall try to expound this point by using, as far as possible, the conceptual utility-function framework of existing demand theory, in order to facilitate and shorten the exposition.

We do know that there are inescapable irreversibilities in the process of consumption. The utility of almost any commodity depends on other commodities having been consumed already. For example, the decision to buy, let us say, a colour television set presupposes that the consumer has already bought – and is permanently in the condition of buying – an

---

8 See the interesting survey by George Stigler: 'The Early History of Empirical Studies of Consumer Behaviour', in *The Journal of Political Economy*, 1954. Stigler points out that empirical studies on the effect of income on consumer's demand began seventy years before the elaboration of any theory of consumer's behaviour, while empirical studies on the effect of prices on consumer's demand did not start until forty years after.

9 See footnote 7 above.

adequate quantity of food, clothes, dwelling space, etc. The TV set itself would not have for him (or her) the same utility (it might even have no utility at all) if he (or she) were not well-fed, well-clad, etc. And this means that if we insist on representing a consumer's field of preferences by a utility function, this function may turn out to have very different shapes indeed in correspondence to each good and service, according to whether and how other goods and services have been consumed. In other words, *absolute levels* of utility do not simply depend on all consumption which has taken place already; they depend also, sometimes crucially, on the *order* in which the various goods have been consumed. This order, by the way, has nothing to do with the speed of variation of *marginal* utilities. We know, for example, that there are some basic human needs (like eating) for which the goods which are necessary have a utility (absolute utility) which is incomparably higher than, and absolutely conditional to, that of any other commodity: without them we would die! Yet, once these needs are satisfied, the marginal utility of successive increments of the same basic goods may fall dramatically and very quickly even become negative. Before this happens, obviously, other commodities become capable of producing utility, and demand will shift to them. But the property that those basic needs saturate rapidly in no way alters the fact that they must be saturated first of all if any other commodity is to bring any utility at all.[10]

Now, on orders of priority, very little empirical research has been carried out since the early rudimentary investigations of Ernst Engel. But, at least on the shape that demand *for each commodity* takes as per capita real income increases, the econometricians have provided us with a great deal of information by now. Since each level of per capita real income presupposes that a certain basket of commodities has been consumed already, when, graphically, expenditure for any particular good or service is plotted as a function of per capita real income, one normally obtains families of curves (which have precisely been called *Engel curves*) of the type indicated in figure 1. Curves of type (a) are likely to fit the cases of goods which are absolutely necessary for

10 It may be pointed out, incidentally, that current demand theory (especially after its recent most elegant refinements) has focused our attention exclusively on what happens *at the margin* – on marginal rates of substitution among commodities if a price changes, or on equalisation of marginal utilities. Such an approach may have a justification in a static world, where everything which may happen cannot but happen at the margin (which always remains the same). But in a world where per capita incomes are moving, there is very little help we can get from marginal utilities unless they are specified over the whole range of the utility functions, i.e. unless we pass from them to absolute levels of utilities. It is the absolute level of utility of each commodity that will tell us which of the various commodities comes next into the range of consumer's preferences, even if the corresponding want will then rapidly saturate.

physiological reasons (e.g. food), and curves of type (b) are likely to fit almost all other cases; while curves of type (c) represents the typical behaviour of inferior goods.[11]

It must be stressed that the relation between expenditure on each single commodity and real income, represented in figure 1, is necessarily

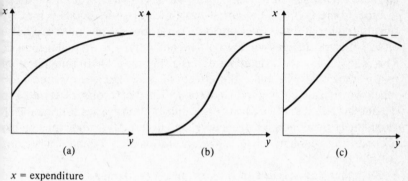

x = expenditure
y = real income

Fig. 1

limited by the two-dimensional character of the diagrams. The actual path of each single expenditure will also depend on variations of the structure of prices. The important point to make, however, is that price changes cannot but flatten out or steepen these relations; they cannot affect their basic shapes. In other words, *price changes can only postpone or anticipate a time path which, if real income increases, is going to take place anyhow.* This means that, in the long run, it is the level of real income – not the price structure – that becomes the relevant and crucial variable. To elucidate this assertion we must consider in some detail the position of each consumer.

At any given point of time, which also means at any given income and price structure, the demand of each consumer for each good and service will be at a particular level (different from one good and service to another) on the corresponding individual Engel curve. All goods and services may, therefore, from the single individual's point of view, be classified into three categories: those goods for which demand is at the bottom of the corresponding Engel curves (zero demand); those goods for which demand is somewhere in the middle of the corresponding

11 In chapter 12 of *The Lognormal Distribution* (Cambridge 1957), J. Aitchison and J. A. C. Brown suggest a general function, based on the log-normal distribution, capable of fitting almost all cases of Engel curves. The shape of such a function is of the type (b) represented in figure 1.

Engel curves; and those goods for which demand is at, or is near, the top of the corresponding Engel curves (i.e. at saturation level).

It is only for the commodities in the second category that changes in income and changes in prices can play a relevant role, the income changes normally influencing demand positively (as is intuitively clear) and price changes negatively. For, at any given level of personal income, some goods – or partial quantities of some goods – may be substituted for others if their prices increase. But the magnitude of these effects of price changes will always depend on the level of real income.[12] This is so much so that, in general, it is always possible to find a level of real income that will make the effects of price changes disappear. In other words, for each good and service in the second category, the dependence of demand on prices (i.e. substitution) varies continually all along the corresponding Engel curve; and eventually – when income has become high enough as to allow saturation – is bound to become entirely negligible.

For goods and services in the first category, demand is simply zero, quite irrespective of changes in prices and even quite irrespective of changes in income at least up to a certain threshold (i.e. up to the point necessary to shift the goods into the second category). And for goods and services in the third category, demand does not respond to changes in income and prices any more: it has simply come to depend on the nature of consumers' preferences. But which goods and services will fall into which category crucially depends on the level of real income. This means that if each individual's income is growing all the time, a certain structural dynamics will take place in the compositions of the three categories of goods and services defined above. Gradually, goods and services will be shifted from the first category to the second category, then their demands will be pushed up the corresponding Engel curve; and finally they will be shifted into the third category, where their demands have become independent of changes in prices and also in income.

Of course, the over-all movement of the aggregate demand for each single commodity will be much more complicated, because it will be the result of the aggregation of the demands of all individuals, for each of whom that commodity may fall into a different category. But as *all* individuals' real incomes increase, the shapes of figure 1 are bound to be reproduced for the aggregate as well, even though in a less sharp way than for the single individual.

To investigate further this process, at this point, would require us to

---

12 In other words, elasticities of demand with respect to prices are crucially dependent on the level of real income.

continue our analysis in terms of specific goods and services, or perhaps, more effectively, in terms of specific groups of goods and services.[13] But, for our purposes, this is not necessary. It is sufficient for us to conclude here that, although possibilities of substitution among commodities are of course relevant at any given level of real income, there exists a hierarchy of needs. More precisely, there exists a very definite *order of priority* in consumers' wants, and therefore among groups of goods and services, which manifests itself as real incomes increase. This order of priority is particularly clear-cut at low levels of income, where satisfaction of some wants is a *conditio sine qua non*, even to the appearance of all others. But the order persists at higher levels as well, where the decision process becomes more complicated only because the order itself may no longer be so obvious, and needs first to be discovered. This brings the present discussion to my second point.

8. Dynamics of demand continued – learning as a more basic process than rational behaviour

The second modification to current demand theory which I should like to make refers to the nature of the whole consumers' *activity*, which is behind the structural evolution of demand described in the previous section. Here again, traditional theory has been constrained, by its static approach, to dealing with only one component (the rational component) of the consumer's activity. But in an evolving society, there is another component that becomes relevant – a component which is actually more basic than, and preliminary to, rational behaviour, namely learning.

We know that, at low levels of real incomes – let us say at near-subsistence levels – consumers can have very little hesitation in expressing their consumption preferences. Their demand is dominated entirely by physiological urges. But, as per capita incomes grow higher and higher, choices grow wider and wider. Consumers' demand becomes dependent less and less on their instincts and more and more on their *knowledge*. This means that each consumer is increasingly bound to carry out a preliminary process of discovering his preferences before he (or she) can express them. Knowledge, as we know, can be acquired both from external information and from experience. Obviously, the amount of external information a consumer can obtain depends very much on the institutional set-up of the society in which he (or she)

13 In this connection, one might well take advantage also of the approach suggested by Kelvin Lancaster, in his *Consumer Demand – A New Approach*, New York 1971. In other words, one might consider as a group those commodities which basically satisfy the same objective need.

lives. But to the extent that information is imperfect and, even if it were perfect, to the extent that personal tastes are relevant, preferences can only be discovered through experience, i.e. through actual consumption. This is, after all, the usual way in which human beings learn when faced with situations which are new: they learn through experiment. And if real per capita incomes are continually rising, and consumers are enjoying extra amounts of incomes over time, they are indeed continually facing new situations. Even if they are reasonably aware of their preferences at the old levels of income, they cannot be so aware of them at higher levels because they have never experienced such levels before – they must learn their new preferences. This is not all. Over time, the quality of old goods may change, and the price structure may also change; while old needs may be satisfied with better (superior) goods. The consumers' learning activity is thus required over the whole range of their preferences. We may add that some consumers may try to educate themselves to better choices in consumption and others may simply be prone to imitate those consumers who are in the immediately higher income brackets, or may easily become the prey to deceptive advertising.

And this means that, at each point of time, we can never expect each consumer to make the best possible consumption decisions. Even if he (she) were to act according to perfect rationality, any of his (her) decisions could be 'rational' only relative to the amount of knowledge he (she) has been able to collect and which he (she) knows himself (herself) not to be entirely reliable. He (she) will always be in a position to improve his (her) absolute levels of utility by carrying on a more basic process than that of acting rationally: i.e. by learning. Thus, in any society where incomes are increasing, consumers' activity becomes more complexly motivated. Even if we wanted to preserve the traditional concepts of consumers' maximisation of satisfaction, we would clearly have to put behind them the much more basic and solid process of consumers' learning; a process which cannot but be preliminary to any rational choice.

9. The evolution of demand over time

The discussion carried out in the foregoing sections is sufficient for our present purposes. To synthesise those results which are relevant for the analysis that follows, we may simply state them in three propositions:

(a) at any given level of per capita income and at any given price structure, the proportion of income spent by each consumer on any specific commodity may be very different from one commodity to another;

b) as per capita real income increases, whatever the price structure may be, each *increment* of consumers' demand tends to concentrate on a particular group of goods and services. This group of goods and services gradually changes from one level of income to another. In other words, whatever the process through which consumers' preferences are reached, they are such as to set up a definite order in the consumption of the various goods, i.e. to saturate higher-priority wants before passing to considering the satisfaction of further wants. Hence, as income increases, the tendency is not to increase proportionately the consumption of already bought goods and services, but rather to buy new goods and services or to satisfy old needs with different (and hopefully better) goods;

c) there is no commodity for which any individual's consumption can be increased indefinitely. An upper saturation level exists for all types of goods and services although at different levels of real income: it may be reached sharply – in the case of goods satisfying physiological needs – or only through a slow and long process as income increases – in the case of services yielding very sophisticated kinds of satisfaction – but its attainment is eventually inevitable. Demand for some particular goods (inferior goods) may even decrease, after reaching saturation, if better (superior) goods exist and if real income persistently goes on growing.

10. The criterion for the choice of the hypotheses – variables and constants as against unknowns and data

Before going on to the general dynamic analysis to which the foregoing discussion has gradually paved the way, it may be useful to sharpen our awareness of the types of magnitudes in terms of which the following analysis is going to be developed.

To do this is important because, as pointed out already, any model does entail a simplification of reality and it is of paramount importance to be clear about the criterion according to which simplifications are made. One is bound immediately to make some simplifications in the choice of the variables and of the constants in any economic inquiry. For, in economics, there are – rigorously speaking – no constants. All magnitudes one may be dealing with are, in fact, variable. But since some magnitudes are more variable than others, it is commonly said that one should take as constants those magnitudes which vary the least. This is clearly a reasonable criterion to follow, provided that it is applied consistently. But there have been difficulties, connected with the development of economic thought.

From the middle of the nineteenth century to the middle of our own century, economists have mainly been interested in the static characteristics of an economic system, or in its short-term behaviour. And since in the short run hardly any quantity can vary substantially, they have tended to make the distinction between variables and constants coincide with the distinction between unknowns and data. Those economic magnitudes that were to be explained (unknowns) have also been taken as variables, and those magnitudes that were to be accepted as given (data) have also been taken as constants. Obviously, such an association did not matter very much as long as it was restricted to static analysis. But, when the attention of economic theorists shifted to dynamic problems, difficulties began to arise. For, some data – i.e. magnitudes to be accepted as given from outside economic analysis – are in fact much more variable over time than some of the economic magnitudes which had been taken as unknowns, and thus variables. In such circumstances, the traditional association has made the choice between variables and constants slowly undergo a very serious distortion. Some magnitudes have been kept as variables although their variability is not important, and other magnitudes, whose variability is an essential feature of the long-run growth pattern, have been left out of the analysis altogether, simply because they are data.

It is precisely in order to avoid this distortion that the theoretical framework developed in the present work has been laid down, straight from the beginning, with reference to the requirements of a long-run dynamic analysis. In the previous pages, we have specified explicitly the movements through time of the underlying exogenous forces of our theoretical scheme (our *data*); namely technology on one side and consumers' preferences on the other. In the following pages, we are now going to investigate the dynamics of the economic magnitudes of the economic system: those magnitudes which we purport to explain – our *unknowns*.

It follows that the distinction between unknowns and data does not coincide, and must not be confused with, the distinction between variables and constants. Unknowns may well be constant, in our theoretical scheme, and data may well be variables. For example, magnitudes such as population and technical knowledge have been taken as given from outside economic analysis (they belong to our data) and nevertheless are essential variables. And magnitudes such as the rates of profit are to be explained by economic investigation, and nevertheless are here taken as constant.

78

The *rationale* for this choice should be obvious at this point of our analysis. There is, in the long run, a profound difference in the order of magnitude of the various changes. There are some magnitudes which undergo changes of an irreversible character by incessantly moving on in the same direction. Although their changes may be negligible over a single short period of time, each period marks for them a step forward, in a slow but cumulative movement. The longer the time, the larger the change they undergo. These magnitudes I have taken as *variables*. On the other hand, there are other magnitudes which, in the long run, do not present any tendency (or for which there is no reason to expect any tendency) to move in any direction. They may of course change quite a lot from one period to another but they cannot go on indefinitely and are bound to return to where they started. Their changes cannot but be temporary and reversible; for they take place around a trend which – however long the period of time we may consider – cannot remain but roughly constant. These magnitudes I have taken as *constants*.[14] This means that in the present (dynamic) analysis, variability or constancy refer to variability or constancy of long-run trends in time, quite irrespective of whether the magnitudes concerned represent unknowns (i.e. they have to be explained) or whether they represent data (i.e. they have to be accepted as given).

The reader may realise that this is a radical departure from the standard procedure of traditional economic analysis. In fact, to have made the distinction between unknowns and data entirely independent of the distinction between variables and constants is the essential breakaway from tradition which will now allow us to go over from static to dynamic analysis.

---

14 To illustrate the difference between the two types of magnitudes, compare the US economy a century apart, at 1880 and at 1980. It is quite possible and easy to claim that, within this period, magnitudes like the average life span of equipment or the rate of profit have undergone considerable variations, as shown, for example, by a coefficient of dispersion. But the important point is that such a dispersion, if it has taken place, has done so around a roughly constant trend. The result is that, after a century, these magnitudes are in 1980 practically at the same level as they were in 1880. The case of population, per capita income, or composition of demand is radically different. Population has increased five times, per capita income has also quintupled, and total consumption is, for the most, composed in 1980 of goods and services which in 1880 did not even exist. In other words, the trends of these variables have been irreversibly and persistently increasing, and are going to persistently increase in the future.

Chapter V

A general multi-sector dynamic model

1. The hypotheses

We are by now in a position to expound a very general multi-sector dynamic model. After the foregoing analysis, the exposition need not be long and we may proceed in a schematic way. The hypotheses which are going to be made will be listed here under two headings, referring to initial conditions and to movements through time:

A. *Initial conditions.* At the time when our analysis begins, which we may denote as time zero, the economic system we are considering is defined by:

(a) a series of $(n - 1)$ stocks of capital goods, expressed in terms of units of productive capacity,

$$(V.1.1) \qquad K_1(0), K_2(0), \ldots, K_{n-1}(0),$$

which are the result of past productive activity. For simplicity, the assumption will be kept that capital goods require no capital goods to be produced;

(b) a population $X_n(0)$, which is taken as an exogenous magnitude. The flow of labour services which this population can provide in each unit of time is equal to $X_n(t)$ divided by the product of two coefficients – $\mu(t)\nu(t)$ – standing for the proportion of active to total population and the proportion of actual working time to the total time composing the time unit respectively. The subscript t has been added to both coefficients because they may be on a long-run trend;

(c) a series of $2(n - 1)$ technical coefficients,

$$(V.1.2) \qquad a_{n1}(0), \ldots, a_{n,n-1}(0), a_{nk_1}(0), \ldots, a_{nk_{n-1}}(0),$$

each expressing the input of labour, required in the unit of time to produce one physical unit of final commodity. There is moreover a series of $(n - 1)$ technical coefficients,

$$(V.1.3) \qquad T_1, \ldots, T_{n-1},$$

expressing the reciprocal of the coefficient of wear and tear of the capital goods[1] in each sector where capital goods are required;

(d) a series of $(n-1)$ consumption coefficients,[2]

V.1.4) $$a_{1n}(0), \ldots, a_{n-1,n}(0),$$

expressing per capita demand for each consumption good per unit of time,

(e) a series of $(n-1)$ investment coefficients,

V.1.5) $$a_{k_1n}(0), \ldots, a_{k_{n-1}n}(0),$$

expressing per capita demand for each investment good per unit of time.

All these magnitudes, at time zero, are assumed to be such as to satisfy the relations defining equilibrium in the economic system. This means that:

(i) the series of $(n-1)$ stocks of productive capacity mentioned under (a) are exactly of the size required by demand;

(ii) the series of $(n-1)$ investment coefficients mentioned under (e) are such as to satisfy, at time zero, the dynamic requirements of the economic system (which will be discussed in detail in section 4 below);

iii) the technical coefficients and the demand coefficients – i.e. (c), (d), (e) – taken all together, are such as to satisfy the macro-economic effective demand condition (II.9.3).

Conditions (i), (ii) and (iii) simply represent, in our formulations, a way of saying that, at time zero, there is, *ex-hypothesi*, full employment of the labour force and full utilisation of the existing productive capacity.

3. *Movements through time.* Over time, the following movements take place:

(a) population increases at a steady percentage rate g, so that

V.1.6) $$X_n(t) = X_n(0)e^{gt};$$

This is a simplification which, as pointed out in section 5 of chapter II, is made because of the immediately apparent meaning of the T_is. No modification to our conclusions would come from adopting the more general coefficients: $a_{k_11}, a_{k_22}, \ldots, a_{k_{n-1}n-1}$, in the place of the T_is.

It may be useful to point out explicitly that, although the technical coefficients and the per capita demand coefficients occupy a symmetrical place in the two equation systems they are not of the same nature. Technical coefficients represent *sectoral* concepts. Each of them is given by the state of technology in each particular sector. Per capita demand coefficients represent *macro-economic* concepts. Each of them is an average taken over the whole economic system.

(b) productivity changes at a particular percentage rate of change in each sector. It will be assumed that these rates of change (ϱ_j) are in general different from one sector to another, but that they are steady through time in each sector.[3] This means that

$$a_{nj}(t) = a_{nj}(0)e^{-\varrho_j t},$$

(V.1.7)

$$a_{nk_j}(t) = a_{nk_j}(0)e^{-\varrho_{k_j}t}, \qquad j = 1, 2, \ldots, (n-1).$$

Most ϱ_js and ϱ_{k_j}s are positive, but a few of them (referring to those sectors where, let us say, the exploitation of natural resources is becoming more and more difficult) might be negative;

(c) per capita demand changes at a particular percentage rate for each commodity. We shall denote these rates of change as r_i, ($i = 1, 2, \ldots$ $n - 1$). The r_is *are not constant over time*; they change as a result of a very complex process, as has been explained in the previous chapter. The r_is as such are not exogenous magnitudes in our analysis. What has been assumed as an exogenous datum is the process of formation of consumers' preferences. Thus, over time, the movements of technical coefficients postulated by (V.1.7) determine the time movements of the r_is. We may write:

(V.1.8) $\qquad r_i(t) = f_i\{a_{n1}, \ldots, a_{n,n-1}, a_{nk_1}, \ldots, a_{nk_{n-1}};$

$$\frac{d}{dt}[a_{n1}, \ldots, a_{n,n-1}, a_{nk_1}, \ldots, a_{nk_{n-1}}]\},$$

$$i = 1, 2, \ldots, (n-1);$$

where the f_is depend on consumers' preferences and on how they evolve through time – a process which is defined in such a way as to satisfy propositions (a), (b), and (c) of chapter IV, section 9. The technical coefficients that appear in (V.1.8) influence the r_is through the medium of two channels: the level and rate of change of real per capita incomes and the variations in the structure of prices.

Here, for purposes of simplicity and symmetry, the assumption will be made that the movements of per capita demand may approximately be broken down (if we represent them on a logarithmic scale) into stretches of straight lines. In other words, we assume that time can be divided into finite stretches of length z (larger than the unit of time we are adopting)

---

3 This is only a simplifying assumption, not at all necessary to our results. Non-steady rates of change in productivity can be dealt with by using the same procedure adopted below for the rates of change of per capita demand. This will actually be done, in the following pages, whenever it becomes useful.

within which, for each commodity i, the percentage rate of change of demand r_i remains constant. Then, passing from one stretch of time of length z to the next, r_i changes, remaining then constant again for another stretch of time z. And so on.

Therefore, by defining now a new variable θ as

(V.1.9) $$\theta = t - \eta z,$$

where η is the greatest integer that, multiplied by z and subtracted from t, leaves a positive remainder (θ), the movements through time of demand coefficients may be written as[4]

(V.1.10) $$a_{in}(t) = a_{in}(t - \theta)e^{r_i\theta}, \qquad i = 1, 2, \ldots, (n-1),$$

where each r_i is an f_i function of the technical coefficients and now also of $(t - \theta)$. In order not to complicate the notation excessively this functional dependence is not explicitly written in (V.1.10), nor will it be written hereafter, but it must always be taken as understood.

Of course, the same notation in terms of θ could be used also in formulations (V.1.6) and (V.1.7), and this will be done[5] in the following analysis, any time it is required by reasons of convenience or symmetry.

2. Restrictions

It is necessary to impose a few restrictions on the coefficients of our economic system, in order to limit our mathematical formulations to the range in which they have an economic meaning.

To begin with, all technical coefficients, whether referring to the production of consumption goods or of investment goods, and all consumption demand coefficients can never be negative, i.e.

(V.2.1) $$\begin{cases} a_{nj}(t) \geq 0, \\ a_{nk_j}(t) \geq 0, \qquad & j = 1, 2, \ldots, (n-1), \\ a_{in}(t) \geq 0, \\ T_i \geq 0, & i = 1, 2, \ldots, (n-1), \end{cases}$$

which have a quite straightforward meaning. A negative amount of

---

4 As explained in footnote 2, consumption coefficients represent *average* per capita consumption. No complication is here discussed in connection with a possible changing relative distribution of income among individuals or a changing composition of population as regards sex and age. The simplest way of interpreting our procedure is to suppose that both these features remain invariant over time. However, introducing complications of this type would not affect our conclusions, the only effect being that of anticipating or postponing turning points, without altering the nature of the trends through time.

5 See footnote 3 above.

labour or of consumption or of wear and tear would make no economic sense.

On the other hand, the coefficients of demand for new investment might become negative, although only to a certain extent, i.e. up to that point that still preserves gross investment as non-negative. The non-negativity restriction applies however to total gross investment. It need not necessarily apply to gross investment in each single sector, if capital is flexible enough to allow some transfers of capital goods from some sectors to others, when needed. In other words, taking first the most restrictive of all cases,

$$(V.2.2) \qquad a_{k_i n}(t) + (1/T_i)a_{in}(t) \geqslant 0, \qquad\qquad i = 1, 2, \ldots, (n-1).$$

Should a situation arise in which the equilibrium conditions (which will be discussed in a moment) required some of the inequalities (V.2.2) to be reversed, then some further information about existing capital stocks would be needed in order to tell what can happen. If, in those sectors where inequalities (V.2.2) need to be reversed, capital goods are specialised and cannot be transferred anywhere else, then idle capacity (which, in our model, means a discontinuity) will appear. If, on the other hand, capital goods are adaptable and can be transferred to other processes of production, then even negative gross investments can take place in some sectors.

In no case, however, as said above, can total gross investment become negative. Even if there were perfect mobility and adaptability of all capital goods, a fall of demand below the level at which total gross investments are zero would simply cause idle capacity. In other words, the inequality

$$(V.2.3) \qquad\qquad \sum [a_{k_i n}(t) + (1/T_i)a_{in}(t)] \geqslant 0$$

cannot but always and in any case be satisfied. The opposite inequality has no economic sense.

3. The flows of the economic system

Within each single period of time (finite or infinitesimal as it may be) there are flows of commodities from the production processes to the final sector and flows of labour services from the final sector to the production processes. These flows have been examined already in our short-run analysis of chapter II, and need not be further discussed here. Within each single period of time, the structure of the economic system is represented by systems of equations (II.5.2) and (II.6.2), and we may consider these two systems as re-written here. The only difference is

84

that a time subscript must now be added to each single coefficient and to each single variable, so as to obtain a pair of those systems of equations for each unit of time we are considering. And since a very specific set of hypotheses has been made (in section 1, heading B, above) about how the production and demand coefficients change over time, we shall now at last be able to look into the whole dynamics of the economic system. In other words, after finding the solutions of the equations in each particular period of time, we shall be in a position to look at the *movements* of these solutions through time.

For the same reasons discussed in chapter II (section 8), both the rate of wear and tear $(1/T)$ and the rate of profit (π) which appear in equation system (II.6.2) will here be taken as uniform and constant. There is no difficulty in introducing non-uniformity when necessary, or desired. In any case, a discussion on the determinants of (non-uniform) rates of profit will be carried out in detail in chapter VII.

A further point is that the hypotheses made in section 1, heading B, do not provide us with the dynamics of all coefficients that appear in systems (II.5.2) and (II.6.2). The movements through time of one series of coefficients – the demand coefficients for new investments – have not been specified. (We have only accepted them as given at time zero.) This series of structural coefficients is the only one that affects the stocks of the economic system, i.e. productive capacity in each sector; hence it cannot be taken as given from outside. These coefficients must be such as to be compatible with the process of economic growth and will therefore themselves be determined as a part of the equilibrium conditions.

4. The conditions for a dynamic equilibrium

According to our initial hypotheses, when our analysis begins (time zero), the economic system we are considering is in equilibrium – there is full employment of the labour force and full utilisation of productive capacity. We know already that, if this equilibrium situation is to be kept through time, two types of conditions must be satisfied.

First of all, since both population and technology are changing, the economic system must continually enlarge its productive capacity so as to keep up both with the increasing per capita demand and with the increasing labour force. This means that, in each sector, a very definite relation must be satisfied between new investment and the rate of change of the corresponding final demand for consumption goods. The problem has been discussed already in section 2 of chapter III. By following here the same procedure, and by inserting the dynamic movements of per capita demand and population which have been postulated in section 1, the mentioned relations emerge as

(V.4.1) $$a_{k_in}(t) = (g + r_i)a_{in}(t - \theta)e^{(g + r_i)\theta},$$

or, more compactly,

(V.4.2) $\qquad a_{k_in}(t) = (g + r_i)a_{in}(t), \qquad i = 1, 2, \ldots, (n - 1),$

which represent the *capital accumulation conditions* for keeping full employment over time (or capital accumulation equilibrium conditions).

If we refer the (V.4.2) to total new investment in each sector, instead of referring them to per capita investment, they may also be written as

(V.4.3) $\qquad X''_{k_i}(t) = (g + r_i)X_i(t), \qquad i = 1, 2, \ldots, (n - 1),$

which specify equilibrium new investment in each single sector. Their sum represents total equilibrium new investments in the economic system as a whole. As can be seen, equilibrium new investments, in physical terms, are exclusively determined by the expansion of demand.

Secondly, since the actual undertaking of all these investments only provides the required productive capacity, a further (macro-economic) condition concerning total effective demand must be satisfied, in order to ensure the attainment of full employment in the economic system as a whole.

In mathematical terms, all this is expressed by the fact that conditions (V.4.1) only come to complete the two systems of equations (II.5.2) and (II.6.2) by providing us, at any point of time, with the series of coefficients (demand coefficients for new investments) which was still missing. But the two systems of equations, thus completed, are of the linear and homogeneous type. In mathematical terms, their coefficient matrix must be singular if they are to yield non-trivial solutions. This condition of singularity, which was expressed by (II.9.3) with reference to a particular period of time, may now be written – after substitution from (V.4.1) and the completions carried out in section 3 of chapter III – as follows:

(V.4.4) $\quad 1 = (1/\mu v)\sum a_{ni}(t - \theta)a_{in}(t - \theta)e^{(r_i - \varrho_i)\theta}$

$$+ (1/\mu v)\sum (g + r_i + 1/T_i)a_{nk_i}(t - \theta)a_{in}(t - \theta)e^{(r_i - \varrho_{k_i})\theta},$$

This expression finally represents the *effective demand condition* for keeping full employment through time.

It is important to point out immediately that, owing to our present hypotheses, condition (V.4.4) poses a whole series of *new* problems, in the sense that it poses problems which did not exist in the cases previously analysed. As opposed to what happened in the two simpler cases of (proportional) economic growth considered in chapter III and in the first part of chapter IV, respectively, the fulfilment of conditions (V.4.4), at any given point of time, no longer automatically entails that it will remain fulfilled through time.

5. Impossibility of automatically maintaining full employment through time

We may begin at last to assess the relevance of the disaggregated type of analysis which has been developed in the previous pages.

The two simpler cases of economic growth discussed in chapter III and in the first part of chapter IV, respectively, have been conceived of in such a way as to exclude any process of structural dynamics. As the reader will remember, both the capital accumulation equilibrium conditions and the effective demand equilibrium condition, in those two cases, have been assumed to be such as to be independent of time and of the stage of development the economic system has reached. Once fulfilled at a certain point in time, they remain the same for all time. This means that the situation of a precisely adequate productive capacity and of full employment of the labour force, once achieved at a given point in time, is such as to be automatically maintained for all time.

Our analytical possibilities have become radically different with the present analytical scheme. Concentrating our attention on macro-economic condition (V.4.4), we may notice immediately that each one of its components is changing over time. It appears quite clear that there is no simple way in which condition (V.4.4) may be kept satisfied through time, *even if* all percentage rates of change were to remain absolutely constant. In this case, if we take all higher-order derivatives with respect to time, it appears immediately that all derivatives of the left-hand side of (V.4.4) vanish, while all even-order derivatives of its right-hand side are necessarily positive (except in a very special case to which we come back in a moment).

The conclusion is straightforward. Even if we start from an equilibrium position (i.e. even if full employment of the labour force and full productive capacity utilisation are realised at a given point of time) the structural dynamics of the economic system cause that position to change and therefore make it impossible in general to automatically maintain full employment through time.

87

6. A third special case of proportional economic growth

The two special cases of economic growth considered in chapter III and in the first part of chapter IV, respectively (proportional economic growth), may now be looked at as the two obvious, but very special cases in which all higher-order derivatives of the right-hand side of (V.4.4) are zero. Clearly, when the technical and consumption coefficients are all constant (the case considered in chapter III) and when all technical coefficients and all consumption coefficients move at precisely the same rate of change, but in opposite directions (the case considered at the beginning of chapter IV), both expressions in (V.4.4) remain constant with respect to time; hence all their derivatives vanish.

When the problem is put in these terms, it becomes evident that there also exists a third very special case, in which the same thing happens. That is the case in which:

$$(V.6.1) \qquad r_i = \varrho_i = \varrho_{k_i}, \qquad\qquad i = 1, 2, \ldots, (n-1),$$

namely the case in which the rates of change, although different from one sector to another, yet are such that, *in each single sector*, demand grows at exactly the same percentage rate of change as that of the growth of labour productivity (which incidentally must be moving at the same percentage rate both in the consumption good sector and in the sector producing capital goods for it).

This further case of proportional economic growth appears even more special than the two previously considered. For, in this case, all time movements are different from sector to sector and yet are such as to cancel out *inside* each single sector, so as to leave the proportions among all sectors exactly constant (in terms of both employment and their contributions to total national income).

It goes without saying that this further case of proportional dynamics, for the same basic reasons stated in chapter IV, can only be looked at as an analytical curiosity. However, this case too will become useful in the development of formulations which are relevant for the general case.

But let us now return to the general case.

7. Full employment as an actively pursued target of economic policy

The specific hypotheses made in the previous chapter allow us to go far beyond the general result of section 5 above. By going deeper into what happens to the components of (V.4.4), we can in fact trace out the basic tendencies at work.

If almost all technical coefficients are decreasing in time, as we have assumed, then macro-economic condition (V.4.4) is bound to become under-satisfied as time goes on, unless the demand coefficients increase in the same proportion. But we know already that no demand coefficient can increase indefinitely, because per capita demand for any commodity eventually reaches a saturation level. Therefore, we must conclude that condition (V.4.4) inevitably manifests a tendency to become *under-satisfied*, i.e. to generate unemployment, as time goes on.

Fortunately there are two factors, operating in the long run, which can counter-balance the above mentioned tendency. One of them is the same one which causes the whole trouble: technical progress. So far in this chapter, technical progress has been considered in the form of increases in productivity. But it has been pointed out earlier that technical progress also takes the form of introducing new goods. Our theoretical scheme must therefore be completed by opening it up to the possibility of the introduction of new sectors. This can be done by taking the number of sectors as running no longer from 1 to a fixed $(n-1)$, but from 1 to, let us say, $[n(t)-1]$, where $n(t)$ becomes a number which itself increases as an effect of technical progress. This means that, as time goes on, new equations keep on being added to our two systems of equations so that condition (V.4.4) becomes:[6]

$$
(V.7.1) \qquad \sum_{1}^{n(t)-1} a_{ni}(t-\theta)a_{in}(t-\theta)e^{(r_i-\varrho_i)\theta}
$$

$$
+ \sum_{1}^{n(t)-1} (g + r_i + 1/T_i)a_{nk_i}(t-\theta)a_{in}(t-\theta)e^{(r_i-\varrho_{k_i})\theta} = \mu(t)v(t).
$$

The effects of technical progress on the effective demand condition are thus two-fold. On the one hand, technical progress brings about a decrease through time of most of the $a_{ni}a_{in}$s, referring to the commodities so far produced, and on the other hand it keeps on *adding* new coefficients (referring to new commodities). The second tendency may succeed in counter-balancing the first.

However, even if this counter-balance were not to come about, there still is a second way in which condition (V.7.1) may be brought towards fulfilment. That is through a decreasing trend in its right-hand side – the

---

6 The expression $[n(t)-1]$, to be used as a subscript, is a rather awkward one and therefore, for simplicity's sake, we shall continue to write it as $(n-1)$, though intending n to be an increasing function of time. The more complete expression $[n(t)-1]$ will however be used any time that the argument depends crucially on the increasing number of commodities or that emphasis is to be drawn to such an increase.

coefficients μ and ν – i.e. a decreasing trend in working time (or, what amounts to the same, an increasing trend in leisure time), to be achieved by a decrease either in the proportion of active to total population or of the length of the working week or of both.

All these conclusions may seem, after all, to boil down to the commonsense proposition that technical progress gives society a choice between producing *more* (or *new*) goods and enjoying more leisure. Our analytical formulation, however, just because of its macro-economic implications, reveals something more than that: something which is, in fact, crucially important. It evinces the fixed framework within which the choice has to be made. It shows that there is a macro-economic constraint to the problem – represented by the requirement of keeping full employment – which restricts the choice to those combinations of goods and leisure which, in terms of time required, add up to that fixed amount determined by the existing working population and technical knowledge.

To express the same thing in a more effective way, we might say that the choice between more (or better) commodities and leisure is not merely a possibility, but a *necessity*, if full employment is to be maintained. There does not exist the alternative of not choosing! Technical progress, which characterises our societies and which brings with it that choice, does not come – so to speak – under the form of a free gift which, by being always susceptible of being refused, could only add to, and never diminish, the pre-existing wealth. It comes under the form of a flow which cannot be stopped and has to be continually channelled in new directions, which themselves have to be discovered anew because the old ones saturate. This entails an ever-standing problem of utilisation, under a fixed restriction represented by condition (V.7.1); a problem for which the failure to find solutions may cause damage to the situation carried over from the previous period. We shall return to these problems in further detail in chapter X.

For the time being, we may draw the important conclusion that the structural dynamics of the economic system inevitably tend to generate what has rightly been called *technological* unemployment. At the same time, the very same structural dynamics produce counter-balancing movements which are capable of bringing macro-economic condition (V.7.1) towards fulfilment, *but not automatically*. There is nothing in the structural evolution of technical coefficients on the one side and of per-capita demand on the other, as such, that will ensure fulfilment of macro-economic condition (V.7.1), i.e. the maintenance of full employment. Therefore, if full employment is to be kept through time, it will have to be actively pursued as an explicit aim of economic policy.

8. A central Agency entrusted with the task of keeping full employment

From the conclusion of the previous section it follows that, if full employment is to be kept through time, a central institutional organisation – let us call it, the Government, for simplicity – must be entrusted with the specific task of maintaining full employment.[7] This is by no means an easy task; for the problems to be solved will always be different from one period of time to the next.

In very general terms, the necessity emerges of both a long-run strategy and a series of short-run expedients.

In the long run, a sort of permanent surveillance is necessary on the evolution of the counter-balancing forces mentioned in the previous section so as to make it sure – when necessary, and with appropriate interventions – that, at least tendentially, those forces do move in the direction of counter-balancing one another. And even when this task is fulfilled, further surveillance is necessary on the process of the actual carrying out of the required new investments.

In the short run, given the difficulty of exercising an influence on technical coefficients, it is the rates of change in demand that afford the widest possibility of being influenced. For, although governed by basic tendencies, most r_is are indeed open, at least in the short run, to external influence. Some of them may not even reflect consumers' demands at all but actually be under the direct control of the Government.

We shall assume here that a Government is in fact actively vigilant so as to influence total effective demand, as may be necessary, to keep macro-economic condition (V.7.1) at least approximately and tendentially satisfied.

9. The dynamic movements of physical quantities and relative prices

When conditions (V.4.1) and (V.7.1) are (at least tendentially) satisfied, the two linear and homogeneous systems of equations representing the flows of the economy – the (II.5.2) and (II.6.2) – yield solutions for all their unknowns except one, which can be arbitrarily fixed. Since all

---

7 In theory, one might alternatively conceive of a hypothetical institutional mechanism that automatically leads the economic system towards the full employment dynamic path. Yet, even in such a hypothetical case – and apart from whether such an institutional mechanism is or is not possible – the Government would clearly have to be in charge of a general supervision and of intervening any time that such an institutional mechanism failed to work, or were disrupted.

coefficients and unknowns are now dated, these solutions no longer take the form of single values but of *movements through time*. It is evidently *one of these movements* which in each of the two equation systems can be arbitrarily fixed. However, in the case of (II.5.2) one of the Xs – namely X_n (population) – is a variable whose movement through time has been accepted as given from outside economic analysis. We have no choice in this case. On the other hand, in the case of equation system (II.6.2), no one of the prices is given, so that structural changes through time only determine the dynamic movements of relative prices. Here we have a choice. As a matter of convenience, we may begin by choosing the wage rate as the basis of our price system and take it as given ($\bar{w}$), both at a given point of time and through time, which means setting $w(t) = \bar{w}$. Then the dynamic movement of physical quantities and relative prices emerge as follows:

$$(V.9.1) \quad \begin{cases} X_i(t) = A e^{(g+r_i)\theta}, \\ X_{k_i}(t) = (g + r_i + 1/T)A e^{(g+r_i)\theta}, \end{cases}$$

$$(V.9.2) \quad \begin{cases} p_i(t) = B e^{-\varrho_i\theta} + (\pi + 1/T)C e^{-\varrho_{k_i}\theta}, \\ p_{k_i}(t) = C e^{-\varrho_{k_i}\theta}, \qquad i = 1, 2, \ldots, [n(t)-1]. \end{cases}$$

where A, B, C are constants which stand for the initial conditions, namely:

$$A = a_{in}(t - \theta)X_n(t - \theta),$$
$$B = a_{ni}(t - \theta)\bar{w},$$
$$C = a_{nk_i}(t - \theta)\bar{w}.$$

The economic meaning of (V.9.1) and (V.9.2), at a given point of time, has been discussed already in chapter II (sections 5 and 6), and there is no need for repetition here. But now, besides the determination of quantities and prices at a given point of time, the (V.9.1), (V.9.2) also bring out their *movements through time*.

Each physical quantity follows a time path of its own, expanding at a particular rate $(g + r_i)$, which is the sum of two rates of growth: the rate of growth of population and the rate of change of per capita demand. The first of these two rates is the same for all goods, while the second is different from one commodity to another. Therefore, in general, *the whole production structure in physical terms is changing over time*. This means that, in its process of growth, the economic system is continually changing the proportions in which it produces the various commodities.

In its turn, each relative price, as appears from (V.9.2), is also changing over time. With the convention of adopting a given $\bar{w}$, the wage rate, as the basis of the price system through time, each price is decreasing at a rate resulting from a weighted average of the pace at which productivity changes are taking place in the sector to which it refers, and in the sector which produces capital goods for it. But since the choice of *numéraire* is arbitrary, as said above, any of the commodity prices, instead of the wage rate, might alternatively be chosen as the basis for the price system through time. For example, if we set $p_i(t) = \bar{p}_i$, then each one of the other commodity prices would increase or decrease according to whether the rate of growth of productivity in the corresponding sector was lower or higher than the rate of growth of productivity in the sector producing the commodity chosen as *numéraire*. And the wage rate would increase through time at a rate of growth equal to the rate of productivity growth in the sector producing the *numéraire* commodity.

In any case, whatever the *numéraire*, since all rates of change of technical coefficients are, in general, different from one another, *the whole price structure is changing as time goes on*.

The time paths of sectoral productions, evaluated at current prices – the $V_i(t) = p_i(t)X_i(t)$ and the $V_{k_i}(t) = p_{k_i}X_{k_i}$; $i = 1, 2, \ldots, [n(t) - 1]$ – follow as a straightforward consequence. By multiplying each of the (V.9.1), when $w(t) = \bar{w}$, by the corresponding (V.9.2), we obtain:

$$(V.9.3) \quad \begin{cases} V_i(t) = De^{(g+r_i-\varrho_i)\theta} + (\pi + 1/T)Ge^{(g+r_i-\varrho_{k_i})\theta}, \\ V_{k_i}(t) = (g + r_i + 1/T)Ge^{(g+r_i-\varrho_{k_i})\theta}, \end{cases}$$

$$i = 1, 2, \ldots, [n(t) - 1],$$

where the constants D and G stand for the initial conditions, namely:

$$D = a_{ni}(t - \theta)a_{in}(t - \theta)\bar{w}X_n(t - \theta),$$

$$G = a_{nk_i}(t - \theta)a_{in}(t - \theta)\bar{w}X_n(t - \theta).$$

As can now be seen directly, each of the V_is and V_{k_i}s, in general, will move through time in its own way, for two reasons: because the physical quantity concerned is changing and because the corresponding price is changing. Each $V_i(t)$ is the sum of two elements (and each V_{k_i} of only one), each of which is moving through time, $i = 1, 2, \ldots, [n(t) - 1]$, according to an algebraic sum of rates of change: the rate of population growth plus the rate of change of per capita demand, minus the rate of growth of productivity in the corresponding sector.[8]

8 It may be interesting to point out explicitly that the conclusions about dynamic movements through time remain exactly the same if the more complex case considered in section 7 of chapter III were to be adopted. More precisely, as may easily be checked

(continued)

10. The structural dynamics of employment

Of particular interest and importance for the community as a whole, is the dynamic movement of employment in each sector. Having denoted sectoral employment by $E_i(t) = a_{ni}(t)X_i(t)$ and $E_{k_i}(t) = a_{nk_i}(t)X_{k_i}(t)$, we obtain:

(V.10.1)
$$\begin{cases} E_i(t) = Me^{(g+r_i-\varrho_i)\theta}, \\ E_{k_i}(t) = (g + r_i + 1/T)Ne^{(g+r_i-\varrho_{k_i})\theta}, \end{cases}$$

$$i = 1, 2, \ldots, [n(t) - 1],$$

from (II.7.2), (II.7.3), (III.2.5an) and from the fact that the rates of growth are now $(g + r_i)$, the expressions (V.9.1), (V.9.2), (V.9.3) of this section would remain:

(V.9.1an)
$$\begin{cases} X_i(t) = A'e^{(g+r_i)\theta}, \\ X_{k_i}(t) = (g + r_i + 1/T)A''e^{(g+r_i)\theta}, \end{cases}$$

(V.9.2an)
$$\begin{cases} p_i(t) = B'e^{-\varrho_i\theta} + (\pi + 1/T)C'e^{-\varrho_{k_i}\theta}, \\ p_{k_i}(t) = C'e^{-\varrho_{k_i}\theta}, \end{cases}$$

(V.9.3an)
$$\begin{cases} V_i(t) = D'e^{(g+r_i-\varrho_i)\theta} + (\pi + 1/T)G'e^{(g+r_i-\varrho_{k_i})\theta}, \\ V_{k_i}(t) = (g + r_i + 1/T)G''e^{(g+r_i-\varrho_{k_i})\theta}, \end{cases}$$

$$i = 1, 2, \ldots, [n(t) - 1],$$

where *only the constants* take up a more complex formulation, namely:

$$A' = A,$$

$$A'' = \frac{T_{k_i}}{T_{k_i} - \gamma_i - (g + r_i)\gamma_i T_{k_i}},$$

$$B' = B,$$

$$C' = \frac{T_{k_i}}{T_{k_i} - \gamma_i - \pi_i\gamma_i T_{k_i}} a_{nk_i}(t - \theta)\bar{w},$$

$$D' = D,$$

$$G' = \frac{T_{k_i}}{T_{k_i} - \gamma_i - \pi_i\gamma_i T_{k_i}} a_{nk_i}(t - \theta)a_{in}(t - \theta)\bar{w}X_n(t - \theta),$$

$$G'' = \frac{T_{k_i}}{T_{k_i} - \gamma_i - (g + r_i)\gamma_i T_{k_i}} G',$$

$$i = 1, 2, \ldots, [n(t) - 1].$$

An interesting feature that emerges from these formulations is that the solutions, in order to be non-negative, now require fulfilment of the viability conditions:

$$T_{k_i} > \gamma_i + (g + r_i)\gamma_i T_{k_i},$$

$$T_{k_i} > \gamma_i + \pi_i\gamma_i T_{k_i}, \qquad i = 1, 2, \ldots, [n(t) - 1].$$

which are 'dual' to each other.

where the constants M and N stand for the initial conditions, namely:[9]

$$M = a_{ni}(t - \theta)a_{in}(t - \theta)v^{-1}X_n(t - \theta),$$

$$N = a_{nk_i}(t - \theta)a_{in}(t - \theta)v^{-1}X_n(t - \theta).$$

I.e. employment in each sector i or k_i, $i = 1, 2, \ldots, n - 1$, moves through time at a rate of change equal to the rate of population growth plus the rate of increase of per capita demand for commodity i or k_i, minus the sectoral rate of increase of productivity.

Here new problems may arise, because the E_is and E_{k_i}s, although representing flow variables (services from labour in the unit of time), come from, and are inseparably linked to, a stock variable (the labour force), that may not be perfectly mobile. As appears from (V.10.1), when population is constant ($g = 0$), employment in each sector i increases through time if

(V.10.2) $$r_i > \varrho_i,$$

and decreases through time if

(V.10.3) $\quad r_i < \varrho_i, \qquad\qquad i = 1, 2, \ldots, n - 1, k_1, \ldots, k_{n-1}.$

This means that, even if macro-economic condition (V.7.1) is constantly being kept satisfied, i.e. even if full employment is maintained in the economic system *as a whole*, half of the sectors, on (a weighted) average, are generating technological unemployment, over time, while the other half of the sectors, on average, will be offering jobs and will thus re-absorb the technological unemployment generated by the former sectors. The important point to stress is that sectoral employment will *have* to change – workers will have to be shifted from sector to sector in order to keep macro-economic condition (V.7.1) satisfied, i.e. in order to maintain full employment through time. Clearly this might be a very serious state of affairs – especially in economic systems with large ϱ_is – if labour were highly specialised and not susceptible of being transferred from one sector to another except at the cost of heavy losses in productivity.

Fortunately, the natural movements of population come in to help here in the right direction, and in two ways. First of all, the natural process of people ageing through time permits a redistribution of

---

9 The $E_i(t)$ and $E_{k_i}(t)$ have been expressed here in terms of men per unit of time. For example, if the unit of time is one year, they would be expressed in terms of man-years; so that:

$$\sum [E_i(t) + E_{k_i}(t)] = \mu X_n(t).$$

employment among sectors by directing young workers towards expanding sectors and by not replacing retiring people in the contracting sectors. This may be a slow process, but it is one which is going on even when population is stationary. Secondly, when population is growing, its rate of increase is a net positive addition to the rate of change of demand (and therefore of employment) in *all* sectors.

It follows that the sectors which will actually lose employment, in absolute terms, are those in which

$$(V.10.4) \qquad (g + r_i - \varrho_i) < 0,$$

and the sectors which will be compelled to actually dismiss workers, are those in which

$$(V.10.5) \qquad (g + \delta_i + r_i - \varrho_i) < 0, \qquad i = 1, 2, \ldots, n - 1,$$

where δ_i denotes the rate at which workers retire from productive activity in sector i. I.e. those sectors will actually be compelled to dismiss workers (in spite of full employment being kept in the economic system as a whole) where the rate of growth of productivity is so high and the rate of increase of per capita demand so low that the difference between the two is not only negative, but negative to such an extent as to more than off-set the positive effects of both population growth and people's retirement from work. Agricultural sectors seem to be amongst the most typical sectors that have experienced such features. But there are signs, in some advanced countries (such as the U.K.) that some manufacturing sectors may begin to fall into this category (a phenomenon improperly called 'de-industrialisation').[10]

To sum up, we may say that, over time, the whole structure of employment changes, in the sense that the *proportions* in which total employment is distributed among the different sectors of the economic

---

10 At this point restrictions (V.2.2), discussed in section 2, may be re-written with reference both to the stocks of capital and to employment of labour in each single sector, in the following way:

$$(V.10.6n) \qquad g + r_i + 1/T_i \geq 0,$$

$$(V.10.7n) \qquad g + r_i - \varrho_i + \delta \geq 0, \qquad i = 1, 2, \ldots, [n(t) - 1].$$

We may say that, when all (V.10.6n)–(V.10.7n) are satisfied, our theoretical scheme retains all its properties. But if some of these inequalities were to be reversed, then, in order to find out what would happen, one would need more information about the degree of flexibility of capital – in the case of (V.10.6n) – and about the degree of mobility of labour – in the case of (V.10.7n). If no mobility of capital or of labour is possible between any one sector and the others, then some idle productive capacity – in the case of a reversal of (V.10.6n) – and some technological unemployment – in the case of a reversal of (V.10.7n) – becomes unavoidable.

system are all changing. A complex process of structural dynamics of employment is therefore required, behind macro-economic condition (V.7.1), in order to maintain full employment in the economic system as a whole. Half of the sectors, on average, will need to absorb an expanding proportion of total employment and the other half, on average, will need to decrease their proportion of total employment. Fortunately, the actual expulsion of workers from the (relatively) declining sectors will not be so sharp as might appear at first from the changes in the proportions. It will be mitigated by the expansionary effects of population growth, when $g > 0$, and by the counter-balancing (though slow) effect of not replacing people going into retirement. Nevertheless, especially in economic systems with particularly strong technical change, the necessity of moving some labour out of certain sectors and into others might pose very serious problems.

We shall come back to these problems in chapter X.

11. The dynamic movements of capital/output and capital/labour ratios

The movements through time of the capital/output and the capital/labour ratios, in each sector and in the economic system as a whole, also follow straightforwardly from the previous analysis. After substituting (V.9.1) and (V. 9.2) into (III.4.5) and (III.4.9), we obtain first of all the sectoral $\varkappa_i$s and χ_is:

$$(V.11.1) \qquad \varkappa_i(t) = \frac{a_{nk_i}(0)e^{-\varrho_{k_i}t}}{a_{ni}(0)e^{-\varrho_i t} + (\pi_i + 1/T_i)a_{nk_i}(0)e^{-\varrho_{k_i}t}},$$

$$(V.11.2) \qquad \chi_i(t) = \frac{a_{nk_i}(0)e^{-\varrho_{k_i}t}}{a_{ni}(0)e^{-\varrho_i t}}\, w(t), \qquad i = 1, 2, \ldots, n-1.$$

As may be seen, the dynamic movement of each capital/output ratio $\varkappa_i(t)$ depends exclusively on technical change in sector i and in sector k_i, $i = 1, 2, \ldots, n-1$. Over time, each $\varkappa_i(t)$ will increase, decrease or remain constant according to whether the rate of growth of productivity in the sector i is higher than, lower than, or equal to, the rate of growth of productivity in the corresponding capital good sector k_i. On the other hand, the dynamic movement of each capital/labour ratio $\chi_i(t)$ depends not only on technical change, in sectors i and k_i, but also on the movement through time of the wage rate, and therefore on the *numéraire* of the price system.

The necessity emerges of a specific choice of *numéraire* for the price system, otherwise any comparison through time would remain indeterminate. And the obvious point of reference appears to be the adoption of some notion of *real* wage rate, so as to make the increase of the wage rate express the increase of physical production per man. There is a simple way of doing this, which consists in allowing the wage rate to grow exponentially through time at a percentage rate ϱ^* – i.e. $w(t) = w(0)e^{\varrho^* t}$ – where ϱ^* is defined as the weighted average of all rates of growth of productivity (the precise expression for ϱ^* will be obtained in the following section 13). Then the (V.11.2) become:

$$(V.11.3) \qquad \chi_i(t) = \frac{a_{nk_i}(0)}{a_{ni}(0)} w(0)e^{(\varrho_i + \varrho^* - \varrho_{k_i})t}.$$

We are now in a position to say that the dynamic movement of each capital/labour ratio $\chi_i(t)$, besides depending on the rate of growth of productivity in sectors i and k_i, $i = 1, 2, \ldots, n - 1$, also depends on the over-all (or, as it will be called in a moment, the 'standard') rate of growth of productivity in the economic system as a whole. Expressions (V.11.1) and expressions (V.11.3) will actually be used in chapter IX (section 19) for a classification of technical change.

Going on now to substitute (V.9.1) and (V.9.2) into (III.4.7) and (III.4.11), we obtain the capital/output ratio (Γ) and the capital/labour ratio (Λ) for the economic system as a whole:

(V.11.4)

$$\Gamma(t) = \frac{\sum a_{in}(0)a_{nk_i}(0)e^{(r_i - \varrho_{k_i})t}}{\sum a_{in}(0)a_{ni}(0)e^{(r_i - \varrho_i)t} + (g + \pi + 1/T)\sum a_{in}(0)a_{nk_i}(0)e^{(r_i - \varrho_{k_i})t}},$$

$$(V.11.5) \qquad \Lambda(t) = \sum a_{in}(0)a_{nk_i}(0)w(0)e^{(r_i - \varrho_{k_i} + \varrho^*)t}.$$

The most remarkable property exhibited by the (V.11.4) and (V.11.5), as against the (V.11.1) and (V.11.3), is that they contain not only the technical coefficients, but also the coefficients of demand. The macro-economic ratios thus emerge as depending *both* on technology *and* on the composition of output; and their dynamic movements as depending both on all rates of change of productivity and on all rates of change of per capita demand.[11]

An important implication of this is that, if any classification of technical change is to be made, on the basis of the capital/output and capital/labour ratios, this classification is indeed possible at the sectoral

---

11 The reader may carry out the same substitution into expressions (III.4.6n), (III.4.8n), (III.4.10n), (III.4.12n), which refer to the more complex model considered in section 7 of chapter II. It is easily checked that the conclusions reached in the present section remain unaffected.

level, but is impossible at the macro-economic level. At the macro-economic level, any classification of technical change would clearly be illegitimate (except in the extreme case of a one-commodity world). For, the over-all ratios of capital to output and of capital to labour depend, not only on technology, but also on the composition of demand.

To these problems too we shall come back later on (chapter IX sections 19 and 20).

12. The price system through time – a degree of freedom at time zero and a degree of freedom among the rates of change

The analysis of the previous section brings to our attention the question of the choice of *numéraire* for the price system, and it may be useful, at this point, to face the problem openly.

We have seen that, in each of the equation systems (V.9.1) and (V.9.2), the whole movement through time of one of the unknowns is to be determined exogenously. As far as the physical quantities are concerned there is no problem, as has been said already. In (V.9.1) there is one physical quantity, namely population, the absolute value of which at a given point of time and its rate of change through time are indeed determined from outside economic analysis. But the problem is different for the price system. In (V.9.2) there is no price that is obviously determined exogenously. At least in principle, the choice of *numéraire* is arbitrary.

It is important to realise that this arbitrary choice concerns *a whole movement* of one of the prices through time. This means, in an analysis like the present one, where movements through time are expressed by exponential functions, that the magnitudes to be determined exogenously are in fact two: an absolute value at the initial point in time, and a rate of change over time.

More specifically, when we choose to reckon prices in terms of the wage rate and close the price system (V.9.2) by the equation

(V.12.1) $$w(t) = \bar{w},$$

or, even more specifically, when we reckon prices in terms of Classical 'labour commanded', and write

(V.12.2) $$w(t) = 1,$$

what in fact we do is to fix two things, namely the level of the wage rate at any initial point in time and its rate of change through time. In

99

general, we may well say that the wage rate $w(t)$ is an exponential function of time:

$$(V.12.3) \qquad w(t) = w(0)e^{\sigma_w t},$$

where $w(0)$, the wage rate at time zero, and σ_w, the percentage rate of change of the wage rate through time, may be given particular values. Thus, when we choose equation (V.12.2), it is as if we take equation (V.12.3) and insert into it the particular values:

$$(V.12.4) \qquad \begin{cases} w(0) = 1, \\ \sigma_w = 0. \end{cases}$$

Similarly, if we choose any particular physical commodity (or composite commodity) h as *numéraire*, and close the price system (V.9.2) by the equation

$$(V.12.5) \qquad p_h(t) = 1$$

we may say that, in general, p_h is an exponential function of time:

$$(V.12.6) \qquad p_h(t) = p_h(0)e^{\sigma_h t},$$

where $p_h(0)$, the price of commodity h at time zero, and σ_h, the (percentage) rate of change of the price through time, take the particular values:

$$(V.12.7) \qquad \begin{cases} p(0) = 1, \\ \sigma_h = 0. \end{cases}$$

Expressions (V.12.3), (V.12.4) may appear at first as a more complicated way of writing (V.12.2); and, similarly, expressions (V.12.6), (V.12.7) may appear as a more complicated way of writing (V.12.5). But the new expressions have important properties. First of all they make it clear and explicit that the price system, when considered over time, contains two, not one, degrees of freedom: a degree of freedom at the initial point in time (choice of the 'standard of value' at a given point in time) and a degree of freedom through time (choice of one of the rates of change of prices).[12]

Secondly, since *all* movements of prices through time come to be

12 Of course these two degrees of freedom are not always used independently of each other. For example, choosing to measure prices in terms of labour implies *both* $w(0) = 1$ *and* $\sigma_w = 0$; and similarly choosing to measure prices in terms of any physical commodity h implies both $p_h(0) = 1$ and $\sigma_h = 0$. But there is no inherent necessity in the price system for couplings of this type. The degrees of freedom are indeed two and can be used independently of each other. We shall come back to this problem in chapter VIII (section 6).

represented by exponential functions, we can see immediately from these functions that once the rate of change through time of one of them is fixed exogenously, then the rates of change of all other exponential functions are determined. This means that any one of these exponential functions – and not necessarily the specific exponential function representing the movement of the *numéraire* – can be used to close the price system, provided that its two parameters (initial condition and rate of change) are fixed in the appropriate relation to those of the *numéraire*.

To be more precise, we have seen above that choosing commodity h as *numéraire* of the price system through time, i.e. setting $p_h(t) = 1$, is equivalent to writing exponential function (V.12.6) with particular values (V.12.7). But an alternative way of obtaining the same result is to write the exponential function (V.12.3), concerning the movement of the wage rate, and inserting into it the particular values

$$(V.12.8) \qquad \begin{cases} w(0) = \bar{w}_h(0), \\ \quad \sigma_w = \varrho_h, \end{cases}$$

where $\bar{w}_h(0)$ is the wage rate, at time zero, in terms of commodity h, and ϱ_h is the rate of growth of productivity in sector h.

The important result that emerges, for our purposes, is that exponential function (V.12.3), concerning the wage rate, can be used *in general* as the equation that closes the price system (V.9.2). In other words, the choice of *numéraire*, whatever this *numéraire* may be, can simply be made by fixing the two appropriate particular values of $w(0)$ and σ_w, in the exponential function that expresses the movement of the wage rate through time, i.e. in (V.12.3). We shall take advantage immediately of this formulation.

13. The 'standard' rate of growth of productivity

As we have seen in the previous section, the evolution of the price system through time contains two degrees of freedom. These degrees of freedom may be closed, in general, by taking exponential function (V.12.3) and exogenously inserting into it the initial wage rate and its rate of change.

Since the choice is free, we may insert the following particular values:

$$(V.13.1) \qquad \begin{cases} w(0) = \bar{w}, \\ \quad \sigma_w = \varrho^*, \end{cases}$$

where $\bar{w}$ is the wage rate at time zero, measured in terms of whatever unit of account may be chosen, and ϱ^* is defined as the weighted average of the rates of change of productivity in the whole economic system. We shall call

(V.13.2) ϱ^*

the 'standard rate of growth of productivity'.

The first problem to face is clearly that of how to compute ϱ^*. An average of uneven magnitudes, such as the ϱ_is in our case, calls for a search for the appropriate weights. But, fortunately, these weights are implicitly contained already in our theoretical scheme. In order to make them emerge clearly it will be useful to proceed step by step, by beginning to consider the three simple cases of our previous analysis, in which the composition of the economic system remains constant through time. In these three simple cases the computation of ϱ^* is straightforward.

The simplified case considered in chapter III, in which all technical and consumption coefficients are supposed to remain absolutely constant (i.e. all rates of change are supposed to be zero) clearly yields $\varrho^* = 0$. The simplified case of section 2 of chapter IV, in which all technical coefficients are supposed to decrease at the uniform rate ϱ, and all consumption coefficients are supposed to grow at the same uniform rate ϱ, equally clearly yields $\varrho^* = \varrho$, the uniform rate of growth of productivity and of demand.

A little more complex, but more interesting, is the third simplified case, which has been considered in section 6 of the present chapter. In this case, the rates of growth of productivity are supposed all to be different from one another and yet each of them is supposed to be exactly equal to the growth rate of demand of the corresponding consumption good, so as to keep the composition (i.e. the 'weights') unchanged. The interest of this case is that it requires us to look for the weights explicitly. In order to do so, we may go back to the effective demand equilibrium condition, which – for our present purposes – may be written as

(V.13.3) $(1/\mu v) \sum a_{in}(t)[a_{ni}(t) + (g + r_i + 1/T_i)a_{nk_i}(t)] = 1.$

This is an interesting expression. We know that $a_{in}(t)$ is the coefficient of per capita demand for consumption good i, while $[a_{ni}(t) + (g + r_i + 1/T_i) a_{nk_i}(t)]$ is what may be called *the vertically hyper-integrated labour coefficient* for consumption good i, as it includes all labour inputs for good i (both in the sector directly producing it and in the sector producing capital goods for it). This means that each addendum under summation (V.13.3) represents the *proportion* of total labour required by the (vertically hyper-integrated) production of consumption good i,

$(i = 1, 2, \ldots, n - 1)$. As may easily be realised, this is precisely the 'weight' which is appropriate to the corresponding good. We can therefore now specify the 'weights' we have been looking for, denoting them by λ_i, as

$$(V.13.4) \quad \lambda_i(t) = (1/\mu v)a_{in}(t)[a_{ni}(t) + (g + r_i + 1/T_i)a_{nk_i}(t)],$$

$$i = 1, 2, \ldots, n(t) - 1.$$

Note that (V.13.4) is a perfectly general formulation, as it has been derived from the formulae of the general case. The elegant formal property of the special case we are considering here is that $a_{in}(t)$ increases through time at the rate $r_i = \varrho_i$, while the whole expression in square brackets (since $\varrho_i = \varrho_{k_i}$ *ex hypothesi*) decreases through time at exactly the same rate ϱ_i, so that each $\lambda_i(t)$ remains absolutely constant, while $n(t) = \bar{n}$, i.e. the number of goods remains constant, $i = 1, 2, \ldots,$ $(\bar{n} - 1)$. Hence, the standard rate of growth of productivity simply emerges, in this case, as

$$(V.13.5) \quad \varrho^* = \Sigma \varrho_i \lambda_i,$$

where each ϱ_i and each λ_i, though different between one commodity and the other, are absolutely constant. *A fortiori* the over-all standard rate ϱ^* will remain constant.

But let us now turn, at last, to the general case. It has been pointed out above that (V.13.4), as such, refers already to the general case, as it has been obtained from the general case formulations. Our problem, therefore, is already solved by formulation (V.13.4), which, for the general case, will retain the time subscript. The only modification we might introduce is to split up each weight $\lambda_i(t)$, by expansion of the square brackets, into two separate weights, for consumption good i and for the corresponding capital good k_i, respectively, any time that $\varrho_i \neq \varrho_{k_i}$. But in fact, for many purposes, and especially for present purposes, it turns out to be more convenient to refer the rates of growth of productivity to the corresponding vertically hyper-integrated labour coefficients. In other words, it turns out to be more convenient to call, let us say, ϱ_i' the percentage rate at which the whole magnitude contained in the square brackets of (V.13.4) decreases through time. This means that if we define

$$(V.13.6) \quad \varrho_1', \varrho_2', \ldots, \varrho_{n-1}',$$

as the rates of change (with negative signs) of the vertically hyper-integrated labour coefficients for commodities $1, 2, \ldots, n - 1$, then we can use (V.13.4), as it is, for the general case. The standard rate of growth of productivity therefore emerges, in general, as

$$(V.13.7) \qquad \varrho^*(t) = \sum \varrho_i^* \lambda_i(t).$$

Note that, when effective demand condition (V.13.3) is under-satisfied, the proportion of the total labour force that remains unemployed is, by (V.13.7), attributed a zero rate of productivity growth, which is precisely what is wanted.

Of course, formulation (V.13.7), concerning the economic system as a whole, may present various complexities. As opposed to what happens in the simplified case of section 6 above, the weights $\lambda_i(t)$ are all changing, and moreover $n(t)$ is increasing, i.e. new sectors, for new goods, are continually being added. Yet, for the economic system as a whole, many of the changes will no doubt compensate for each other. To the extent that, in spite of the ever-changing composition of its components, the standard rate of productivity growth may be considered as roughly steady through time, the usefulness of closing the price system by exponential function (V.12.3) with the particular values (V.13.1) – as is suggested at the beginning of this section – should now appear very clearly.

The computation of the 'standard' rate of productivity growth provides us with a concept of the *real* wage rate which possesses extraordinarily interesting properties, as it avoids all the ambiguities entailed by reference to any particular commodity. As will be seen in further detail in a moment, all prices and the wage rate come to be expressed in terms of a *physical* 'average commodity' for the economic system as a whole.

14. A 'dynamic' standard commodity

The implications of using the 'standard' rate of growth of productivity in expression (V.12.3) are manifold. In an economic system in which, as is normally the case today, the *numéraire* of the price system is a conventional unit of account (i.e. inconvertible paper money, as will be described later), rather than any actual physical commodity, there is no difficulty in accepting any number as expressing the wage rate $\bar{w}$ at time zero. Then, to let the wage rate $w(t)$ increase at the standard rate ϱ^* simply means letting it grow exactly in step with the average *physical* growth of production; i.e. it means letting it grow at the rate of growth of its 'average' purchasing power, in physical terms. This has straightforward effects on the price level.

Obviously, to close the price system by exponential function (V.12.3) with particular values (V.13.1) is equivalent to measuring all the prices, and the wage rate, in terms of a particular composite commodity for which productivity is growing through time at the 'average' growth of productivity of the economic system as a whole. In terms of such a commodity therefore, half of the prices, on (a weighted) average, will increase, and the other half, on (a weighted) average will decrease, so that the general level of prices neither increases nor decreases. This is a remarkable property.

Note that no other physical commodity, if chosen as *numéraire*, would keep the general price level constant. For, in an economic system with structural change, in general, no single price can remain constant, and so also no average of prices can remain constant, in terms of *any* commodity *numéraire*. Actually any average of prices would move differently over time according to the physical commodity that is chosen as *numéraire*. But we have found a particular 'composite' commodity that eliminates this ambiguity. The prices of its components move in time at rates of change the average of which is zero by definition. In terms of such a commodity, therefore, and only in terms of such a commodity, can we talk of stability of the general price level!

It may be useful to look more in detail into the features of such a commodity. Actually, it is easier to state the properties of such a commodity than to state precisely what it is physically made of. First of all, such a commodity is defined no longer in terms of its composition (in fact its composition is changing all the time), but in terms of the weighted rates of change of labour requirements of its components. We may say that it is a composite commodity for which the labour requirements decrease through time at the 'standard' rate ϱ^*, which is the weighted average of all rates of productivity change. In the present theoretical framework, in which technical progress is typically 'labour-potential augmenting', such a commodity appears to be a sort of physical *dynamic* counterpart of Ricardo's 'invariable standard of value'. I shall therefore call it the 'dynamic standard commodity'.[13]

13 As is well known, Ricardo's 'invariable standard of value' was a particular commodity which was supposed to satisfy two requisites; (i) a commodity which 'now and at all times requires precisely the same quantity of labour to produce it' (David Ricardo, *Principles*, Sraffa edition, *op. cit.*, p. 17); and (ii) a commodity the value of which is invariant to changes in income distribution.

Piero Sraffa (in his *Production of Commodities, op. cit.*) focussed on the second of these requisites. By 'freezing', so to speak, the economic system at a given technique, Sraffa has constructed a composite commodity (his 'standard commodity') whose value is invariant to changes in income distribution. In the present analysis I am following a symmetrical approach. I have focussed on the first of Ricardo's requisites, interpreted in dynamic terms. The economic system is again 'frozen', so to speak, at a given income distribution and a commodity has been constructed (the 'dynamic standard commodity') which through time always requires the same quantity of 'augmented' labour.

As a justification of this terminology, let me stress that what characterises the dynamic standard commodity is not its physical composition (which, in the general case, is ever changing), but its *dynamic properties*. In the two particular cases of chapter III and of chapter IV (section 2) *any* commodity fulfils the requirements of a dynamic standard commodity, while in the hypothetical case of section 6 above an over-all average is necessary, but the composition (at current prices) remains invariant. In the general case, the composition (both in physical terms and at current prices) is changing all the time. And yet something, lying much deeper, remains constant, in spite of all the complex structural dynamics changes. This something is precisely what has been called 'augmented' labour. As time goes on, technical progress renders labour more and more productive, but in a different way from one commodity to another. The dynamic standard commodity is that particular commodity for which the growth of labour productivity is exactly equal to the over-all average. It is a commodity, therefore, that always embodies the same amount of over-all 'augmented' labour.

15. Macro-economic variables through time

A few final remarks may be added about the dynamics of the aggregate magnitudes normally used in macro-economic investigations and comparisons (i.e. national income, total capital, consumption, investment, etc.). From the (V.9.1), (V.9.2), it follows that all these aggregate magnitudes move in time in a very composite way. Each of them results from a sum of physical quantities, whose proportions are changing, multiplied by prices, whose structure is also changing over time. Moreover, new and better goods are continually coming into being.

From these features, it is normally concluded that all macro-economic magnitudes have a well defined physical meaning at any specific point in time, in relation to the technical and demand conditions prevailing at that point in time; but, at the same time, that any comparison through time inevitably introduces some degree of arbitrariness. For, the simultaneous change of both component structures (physical quantities and relative prices) makes it impossible to reduce the macro-economic magnitudes to a strictly comparable physical basis. The same collections of physical quantities turn out to be expressed by different macro-economic figures according to the physical commodity (or composite commodity of fixed physical composition) in terms of which they are measured. But most all, given any specific physical (single or composite) commodity, to be used as standard of measurement, the same collections of physical quantities turn out to be expressed by different macro-economic figures according to whether the relative prices used are those of the initial, the final, or any intermediate, period of time. These remarks express what has been called the 'index-number problem' – very well known to all statisticians. The index-number problem does not mean that comparisons cannot be made; but it does mean that there is a margin of indeterminateness in all comparisons of macro-economic magnitudes through time, when the macro-economic magnitudes are expressed in terms of any physical (single or composite) commodity, facing a situation of changing relative prices. This is a margin of indeterminateness which, though small, or even negligible, when short periods of time are considered, becomes wider and wider the longer the period of time involved.

The foregoing analysis does not contradict (in fact, it confirms) these conclusions, but at the same time it does provide an entirely new basis for comparisons through time; it provides an alternative standard of measurement that allows us to escape from the ambiguities of index numbers. By going much deeper into the determinants of the evolution of an economic system, and by singling out the ultimate constituent of all production, namely embodied labour, the foregoing analysis has put us in a position to give a physical content to the continually increasing productivity of labour. A dynamic relation has been found between labour and its changing physical productivity, in terms of the average physical commodity which the consumers have chosen to demand. Such a dynamic relation is synthesised by the standard rate of growth of labour productivity and is governed, as was to be expected, by the joint operation of the two determinants of the evolution of the economic system: technology on the one side, and composition of demand on the other.[14]

14 In the present work, the whole analysis is carried out on the basis of per capita consumption coefficients, which are averaged over the whole economic system. Of course, the composition of individual consumption may be different from one consumer to another. This means that if a society were very markedly non-egalitarian, i.e. the personal distribution of income were rather uneven, then the over-all 'average' per capita consumption, though significant for the economic system as a whole, would become less significant for those individuals (or classes of individuals) whose per capita income, and thus composition of consumption, were very far away from the average, i.e. in practice for the very poor and the very rich. However, there is nothing in our analysis that prevents, at least in principle, the breakdown of consumers into as many groups as one may find useful. In practice, it might be reasonable to construct, besides the over-all average 'standard' rate of growth of productivity, at least 2 other auxiliary standard rates: a 'lower-third' standard rate and an 'upper-third' standard rate. Each of them would differ from the over-all 'average' one, but would be more significant for the individuals in the lower-third and upper-third income brackets, respectively. To the extent that these two auxiliary standard rates are substantially different from the over-all standard rate, they come to express a very real phenomenon, namely the different quantitative expression that technical progress takes for the different income

16. Short-run flexibilities

Before closing the chapter, it may be useful to point out explicitly that the relations between the equilibrium conditions of the economic system and equilibrium time-paths of the variables which have been considered are never to be taken as absolutely rigid. Any given structure of productive capacity and of the labour force, defining the production potential of an economic system is, in the short run, always susceptible of some flexible adjustments, which – at least temporarily – may allow increases in production out of the same existing physical capital and population. In our formulation, these possibilities of adaptation are connected with the degree of flexibility of the parameters μ, ν and T.

The magnitudes of μ, ν, T which have been used in our analysis represent the long-run normal values of these parameters, which may be constant or may be showing mild trends over time. But, in the short run, these parameters are always susceptible of being influenced, sometimes quite substantially. At least up to a certain degree, they can, so to speak, be stretched, thereby affecting the size of the *stocks* that the economic system can use. In other words, at any given point of time, productive capacities and available labour are never related to existing physical equipment and existing population by rigid one-to-one relations. Between these last physical quantities, which at any point in time are given, and the parts of them that are relevant for production, the flexibility of the mentioned parameters provide a sort of cushion. Temporary variations of μ and T mean temporary variations in the productive capacities of existing physical equipments, which may be attained by utilising them more intensively or by keeping in operation some machines which were due to be scrapped. Similarly, variations of μ and ν mean variations of working hours out of a given population, which may be obtained by lengthening (or shortening) the working week or by varying the proportion of active to total population – more (or fewer) working women; later (or earlier) retirement ages.

The degree of flexibility of parameters μ, ν, T, therefore represent very important characteristics of any specific economic system. They express the extent to which the system is capable of short-run adaptations and adjustments in the face of disturbances or emergencies of any kind.

---

classes. Labour is in fact being 'augmented' by technical progress in a different manner for each group of consumers depending on the composition of their per capita consumption.

Chapter VI

The empirical significance of vertically integrated analysis

1. Vertically integrated sectoral analysis versus input–output analysis

The analysis which has been developed in the previous pages has been built on the concept of vertically integrated sectors. The time has come to show explicitly its relations with inter-industry analysis. It will be remembered that, in chapter II, all inter-industry connections and intermediate commodities at a given point of time were deliberately left aside, because our aim was to arrive at a dynamic investigation as soon as possible. We may now go back for a moment to that stage. There is no need to develop here any model with intermediate commodities. Such models have been extensively developed already in the economic literature, especially during the past forty years. The task can here be limited to showing how they relate to the vertically integrated analysis used in the previous pages.

There are in particular two theoretical schemata, which may be considered as the logical static counterpart of the previous dynamic analysis. They are Wassily Leontief's input–output model, and Piero Sraffa's 'production of commodities' system.[1] The latter perhaps corresponds better than the former to the theoretical approach taken in the present work, but the former has had in practice wider empirical applications. Therefore, it will be convenient here to take Leontief's system as the static term of our comparisons.

First of all, let me point out the similarity of approach, from an empirical point of view, of the previous dynamic (vertically integrated) analysis and the static input–output analysis. Both of them share the characteristic of being built on coefficients which are intended to represent actual outcomes and which can therefore, at least in principle, be given an empirical content, simply by recording the actual performance of the economic system. Of course, the technical and the consumption coefficients, by which this actual performance is represented, come

---

1 Wassily W. Leontief, *The Structure of American Economy, 1919–1939*, New York, 1941 and 1951; Piero Sraffa, *op. cit.*

from a choice, made from among a larger set of possibilities. But all the alternative possibilities that might have, but have not, been chosen have become irrelevant. (We shall come back to this point in further detail in chapter IX, section 15.) The coefficients that appear both in the input–output analysis and in the present (vertically integrated) analysis must, therefore, be interpreted as representing those physical quantities which can actually be observed.

Notice, moreover, that input–output analysis and vertically integrated analysis also coincide in the way they look at the final sector of the economy – the last column of the coefficient matrix is the same in the two schemes (with the only difference that, in the present analysis, consumption goods and investment goods have been listed separately). However, they differ profoundly in the way they consider the production processes. The same production structure of the economy is looked at from two different points of view – one is very close to it and to what is immediately observable; the other is placed much further away, at the final stage of the consumption and investment goods. The input–output approach can certainly be more immediately grasped. One of the things by which one is most impressed, when looking at the real transactions which take place in an economic system, is the great number of inter-relations among productive units. One's first instinct is, therefore, to inquire into these inter-industry connections and try to reproduce them analytically. This is the idea which originally underlay Quesnay's *tableau economique* and which has been developed and given a full empirical content by Leontief.

A different approach is taken in the present work. Not 'industries', in the input–output sense, but 'sectors' have been taken as the basis of the whole investigation. And sectors have been defined in such a way as to be *vertically integrated*. All inter-relations which can be observed in the real world are looked at as parts of a process which has not yet come to an end. Any process reaches its completion only when the product which comes out is a final commodity (consumption or investment good). A vertically integrated sector is, therefore, from an inter-industry point of view, a very complex 'sector' as it repeatedly goes through the whole intricate pattern of inter-industry connections. However, from the point of view of the homogeneity of the inputs, it becomes a very simple one, as it eliminates all intermediate goods and resolves each final commodity into its ultimate constituent elements: a (flow) quantity of labour and a (stock) quantity of capital goods. It may be interesting to recall that this procedure was used by Léon Walras himself in his *Elements*, although in a more rudimentary way.[2]

2 Léon Walras, *Elements*, Jaffé edition, *op. cit.* p. 241.

At a given point in time, between the two ways of looking at the economic system there really is no *logical* difference. Both models represent the same thing, looked at in a different way. The difference, in other words, lies only in the classification, and we can pass from the one to the other simply by an algebraical re-arrangement, corresponding to a process of solving a system of linear equations: the production coefficients of a vertically integrated model turn out to be a linear combination of the production coefficients of the corresponding input–output model.

This can be shown immediately, if goods are expressed in physical terms. If we take an input–output equations system, and isolate the inter-industry transactions, by opening it with respect to the final sector, and if we further drop from the equations system the last row, representing the inputs of direct labour into each industry, i.e. the row: $a_{n1}, a_{n2}, \ldots, a_{n,n-1}$, we obtain:

$$(\text{VI.1.1}) \quad \begin{bmatrix} 1-a_{11} & \ldots & -a_{1j} & \ldots & -a_{1,n-1} \\ \cdot & & \cdot & & \cdot \\ \cdot & \cdots & \cdot & \cdots & \cdot \\ \cdot & & \cdot & & \cdot \\ -a_{i1} & \ldots & 1-a_{ij} & \ldots & -a_{i,n-1} \\ \cdot & & \cdot & & \cdot \\ \cdot & \cdots & \cdot & \cdots & \cdot \\ \cdot & & \cdot & & \cdot \\ -a_{n-1,1} & \cdots & -a_{n-1,j} & \cdots & 1-a_{n-1,n-1} \end{bmatrix} \begin{bmatrix} Z_1 \\ \cdot \\ \cdot \\ \cdot \\ Z_i \\ \cdot \\ \cdot \\ \cdot \\ Z_{n-1} \end{bmatrix} = \begin{bmatrix} U_1 \\ \cdot \\ \cdot \\ \cdot \\ U_i \\ \cdot \\ \cdot \\ \cdot \\ U_{n-1} \end{bmatrix}$$

where the a_{ij}s stand here for the inter-industry technical coefficients, the Z_is for the total outputs of the various commodities, and the U_is for the final demands for the various commodities ($i, j = 1, 2, \ldots, n-1$). By solving (VI.1.1), we arrive at

$$(\text{VI.1.2})$$

$$\begin{bmatrix} Z_1 \\ \cdot \\ \cdot \\ \cdot \\ Z_i \\ \cdot \\ \cdot \\ \cdot \\ Z_{n-1} \end{bmatrix} = \begin{bmatrix} 1-a_{11} & \ldots & -a_{1j} & \ldots & -a_{1,n-1} \\ \cdot & & \cdot & & \cdot \\ \cdot & \cdots & \cdot & \cdots & \cdot \\ \cdot & & \cdot & & \cdot \\ -a_{i1} & \ldots & 1-a_{ij} & \ldots & -a_{i,n-1} \\ \cdot & & \cdot & & \cdot \\ \cdot & \cdots & \cdot & \cdots & \cdot \\ \cdot & & \cdot & & \cdot \\ -a_{n-1,1} & \cdots & -a_{n-1,j} & \cdots & 1-a_{n-1,n-1} \end{bmatrix}^{-1} \begin{bmatrix} U_1 \\ \cdot \\ \cdot \\ \cdot \\ U_i \\ \cdot \\ \cdot \\ \cdot \\ U_{n-1} \end{bmatrix}$$

where the exponent -1 indicates the operation of matrix inversion. Now each column of the inverted matrix represents the amounts of all intermediate goods which directly and indirectly are going into one unit of the final commodity. This means that, by multiplying each column of the inverted matrix by the row vector of the input–output direct labour coefficients, which has been excluded from (VI.1.1), we arrive at the labour coefficients of vertically integrated sectoral analysis.

In algebraic terms, if we denote by v_i ($i = 1, 2, \ldots, n-1$) the vertically integrated labour coefficients, we obtain:

(VI.1.3)

$$
\begin{bmatrix} v_1 \\ \cdot \\ \cdot \\ \cdot \\ v_i \\ \cdot \\ \cdot \\ \cdot \\ v_{n-1} \end{bmatrix} = \left\{ \begin{bmatrix} 1 - a_{11} & \ldots - a_{1j} & \ldots - a_{1,n-1} \\ \cdot & \cdot & \cdot \\ \cdot & \cdots & \cdots & \cdot \\ \cdot & \cdot & \cdot \\ - a_{i1} & \ldots 1 - a_{ij} \ldots - a_{i,n-1} \\ \cdot & \cdot & \cdot \\ \cdot & \cdots & \cdots & \cdot \\ \cdot & \cdot & \cdot \\ - a_{n-1,1} & \ldots a_{n-1j} \ldots 1 - a_{n-1,n-1} \end{bmatrix}^{-1} \right\}' \begin{bmatrix} a_{n1} \\ \cdot \\ \cdot \\ \cdot \\ a_{nj} \\ \cdot \\ \cdot \\ \cdot \\ a_{n,n-1} \end{bmatrix}
$$

where the mark $'$ denotes the operation of matrix transposition. Equations (VI.1.3) now give the algebraic relation, existing in a given period of time, between the direct labour coefficients of an input–output model and the vertically integrated labour coefficients to be used in vertically integrated sectoral analysis. The ones may be obtained from the others, as the (VI.1.3) directly show, by a straightforward algebraic operation.

2. Fitting empirical data into a vertically integrated sectoral model

The algebraic relation which has just been obtained and which links the input–output technical coefficients with the vertically integrated labour coefficients is of course of crucial importance for the purpose of giving a vertically integrated sectoral model an empirical content. Of course, since each coefficient or variable appearing in both input–output analysis and sectoral (vertically integrated) analysis refers to actually observable magnitudes, the problem of fitting empirical data into these models is in principle very straightforward for both of them. But the criterion of classification is different. In the input–output model, the criterion is the industry producing a certain commodity, intermediate or

nal, as it may be, and the problem is to reckon where its inputs come
:om and where its outputs go to. In a vertically integrated model, the
riterion is the process of production of a final commodity, and the
roblem is to build *conceptually* behind each final commodity a vertical-
y integrated sector which, by passing through all the intermediate
ommodities, goes right back to the original inputs.

The procedures for collecting and ordering data for input–output
nalysis purposes are well known. On the other hand, collecting data for
he purposes of a vertically integrated model may seem a rather
aborious task. But the difficulties are only apparent. It is true that to
lassify production processes in a vertically integrated way would be
lmost an impossible task, if attempted directly. But this task need not
e attempted directly. The algebraical procedure which has been shown
bove allows us to go over to a vertically integrated type of classification,
y starting from a classification of the input–output type.

All this means that, in order to give a vertically integrated sectoral
nodel an empirical content, one must first of all collect data and fit
hem into an input–output table in the usual inter-industry way.
Moreover, data must be collected about physical capital goods (or about
apital/output ratios) in each single industry of the input–output classi-
ication. Then the resulting system of input–output linear equations can
e opened with respect to the final goods and solved by computing the
nverse of the coefficient matrix. This inverse matrix, or more precisely
he transpose of this inverse matrix, as shown in the previous section,
rovides both the logical and the *empirical* link between the input–
utput type of classification and the one which is needed in a vertically
ntegrated model. This means that to go over from one classification to
he other is simply a matter of computation. The procedure, which has
een shown by (VI.1.3) with reference to the labour coefficients,
emains exactly the same for the physical stocks of capital goods (or for
he series of capital–output ratios). In other words, after multiplying the
ransposed inverse matrix by the vector of the stocks of physical capital
oods (or of the capital/output ratios) of each input–output industry, we
btain the vector of the stocks of physical capital goods (or of the
apital–output ratios) of each vertically integrated sector. And since
ach vertically integrated sector is constructed with reference to a
pecific final commodity, each vector of the stocks of physical capital
oods thereby obtained may be regarded as a particular composite
ommodity representing a unit of (vertically integrated) production
apacity for the corresponding final commodity. The transposed inverse
natrix appears, therefore, as the linear operator which may be applied
o an inter-industry classification of labour and capital goods, in order to

reclassify them according to the new type of (vertically integrated) sectors.[3]

In this way, each vertically integrated sector is reduced to one flow-input of labour and to one stock-quantity of capital goods; or more specifically, to one vertically integrated labour coefficient and to one vertically integrated unit of productive capacity. These magnitudes do not correspond to labour or capital goods employed in any particular firm or industry, since the whole framework of intermediate relations has been consolidated; but they do represent all the labour and capital goods, in whatever remote corner of the economic system they may have been applied, which are necessary to produce the final commodity under consideration. Formally, the new coefficients are, therefore, *derived* concepts (derived from the consolidation of the inter-industry coefficients) but they have a deeper economic meaning and possess, as will be stressed in a moment, much more favourable characteristics for dynamic analysis.

3. The rationale of framing a dynamic analysis in terms of vertically integrated sectors

At this point, the reader may like a more explicit comparison of the purposes for which each of the two types of classification discussed above is suited, and a more explicit explanation of the reasons why the vertically integrated sectors have been preferred to input–output industries in the present dynamic analysis.

Let me begin by recalling that both the inter-industry and the vertically integrated ways of looking at the production processes of an economic system are by no means new in economic analysis; they can be found quite extensively used at different stages in the history of economic thought. It is very significant, however, that they have normally been used for different purposes and independently of each other: the inter-industry approach has mostly been associated with analyses at the micro-level and of a static nature, while the vertically integrated approach has mostly been associated with dynamic and macro-economic types of works. As a result, a sort of gap has gradually appeared between the two approaches; a gap which the foregoing discussion now puts us in a position to investigate.

At a given point of time, the two models which have been confronted above make the connections between the two approaches quite obvious and well-defined. Leontief has provided, for the inter-industry

---

3 These algebraic transformations have been worked out in detail in my *Metroeconomica* article referred to already in footnote 1, on p. 29.

approach, a much more aggregated framework than the one usually used. The analysis which has been discussed here gives, on the other hand, a much more disaggregated framework for the vertically integrated approach. Between the two, the inverse matrix mentioned above provides the analytical bridge. As a matter of fact, once we possess the inverse matrix, all relations between the two approaches at a given point of time take the form of one-to-one correspondences. No gap really exists in this case: the two ways of looking at the productive activities meet half-way, through the above mentioned inverse matrix, which represents the analytical tool for re-classifying the same transactions according to two different criteria and points of view.[4]

Of course, at any given point in time, the input–output model gives us more information. If we were simply interested in what happens at a specific point of time, the input–output model would be the obvious one to use because it provides a more complete picture. But, over time, the input–output coefficients change and the inter-industry system breaks down. The connections described above begin to vanish. Then it is only the vertically integrated model that allows us to follow the vicissitudes of the economic system through time.

Let us consider briefly how this happens. Technical change, at the level of the single units of production, usually manifests itself in a continuous way, as has been remarked earlier. Even when new technical methods or new products are invented, their introduction into the economic system very rarely takes the form of a sudden change. In most cases, the new methods or the new products are operated uneconomically for a period, until experience and slow improvements put them on a competitive footing and prepare the ground for further improvement and development. To an external observer, looking for the 'best-known technique', the methods of production may sometimes look like being introduced at a certain point and then remaining stable for long periods of time; but when a reckoning of the inputs and outputs of an industry is carried out, widely varying shifts are found from one moment to the next. Even at a given point of time, there are many directions from which the inputs may come, and to which the outputs may go.

These are well-known problems which have always caused difficulties to all builders of input–output tables and which sometimes cast serious doubts on the meaning to be attributed to the coefficients of very disaggregated input–output systems. Of course these doubts diminish the more the industries are aggregated, but in this direction the meaning of an input–output framework diminishes too. Hence input–output

4 Further elaborations on this point are given in my *Metroeconomica* article already mentioned (footnote 1, on p. 29).

experts have always tried to find a sort of optimum point at which to stop the process of aggregation–disaggregation, so as to take advantage of the usefulness of an input–output table without making its coefficients too unstable.

What has not been sufficiently realised is that the property of eliminating these shortcomings belongs to the completely aggregated quantities, not because they are aggregated but because – by being completely aggregated – they necessarily are vertically integrated. The property extends to all vertically integrated magnitudes as well. By resolving all varieties of products into the same constituent elements – a flow of labour and a stock of capital goods both expressed in physical terms – the vertically integrated approach leads to relations whose permanence over time is independent of specific technical possibilities. For example, two equivalent methods that, at a given point of time, entail the same cost for the same output, are represented, in an inter-industry equations system, by *two different* technical functions. But in a vertically integrated equations system they are expressed by exactly the *same* function. Their being equivalent means that they require the same amounts of inputs, and these inputs are expressed in the same terms (quantities of labour) independently of the industry in which they are used. Similarly, a sudden shift taking place at the level of a particular technical process in the origin of one of the inputs (for example, a shift in the provenance of a fibre from the textile industry to the chemical industry) means that less labour (or labour equivalents) than before is required to produce it through the new channel. A shift of this type changes an inter-industry relation by causing the disappearance of a commodity-input coefficient (and of the corresponding variable) and the appearance of another, *different*, commodity-input coefficient (and of the corresponding variable). In the vertically integrated relation, it only causes a small diminution of *the same* coefficient. If we imagine many of these shifts taking place over time and, along with them, corresponding changes in the consumption coefficients – which is after all, the normal path that technical progress takes – the input-output table is continuously upset and all relations change from one moment to the next. On the other hand, the vertically integrated relations remain unaffected. The only consequence for them is that their coefficients gradually diminish through time in a movement which, for analytical purposes, has been approximated in the present work by a smooth trend developing at a certain rate of change.

Concluding and summarising, we may say that, at any given point of time, between the static input–output model and the analysis presented in the previous pages there exists a very definite relation through a fully specifiable matrix of coefficients. Considered at a given point in time, the input–output model is more analytical – it has much more to say about the structure of an economic system. However, over time, and as the conditions of production and of consumption change (owing to technical progress, economies and diseconomies of scale, etc.) the inter-industry relations break down and become different from one moment to the next, so that a particular input–output table is needed for each stage in the evolution of the economy under consideration. These tables can be compared (comparative statics analysis), but they cannot be analytically linked to one another – no theory of any generality can be provided for passing from the one to the other. The continuity in time is kept, on the other hand, at the vertically integrated level, where the relations which can be set up possess – to use the Frisch–Haavelmo terminology[5] – a higher degree of *autonomy*. This means that the permanence of these relations in time is independent of technical change. In this context, the vertically integrated technical coefficients acquire a meaning of their own, independent of the origin of the single parts which compose them. The movements of these coefficients through time, and the various consequences thereof, can be investigated and followed as such. When more information is needed about the industrial structure at a particular point of time, the vertically integrated coefficients can be split and analysed into inter-industry coefficients particular to that point in time.

In this way, static input–output analysis and dynamic vertically integrated analysis appear as mutually complementary and completing each other. Inter-industry relations, referring to any particular point of time, represent a cross-section of the vertically integrated magnitudes, whose movements through time express the structural dynamics of the economic system.

5 Trygve Haavelmo, 'The Probability Approach in Econometrics', in *Econometrica*, supplement, July 1944, Chapter II. 'In scientific research,' Haavelmo writes on p. 38, 'our search for explanations consists of digging down to more fundamental relations than those that appear before us when we merely *stand and look*. Each of these fundamental relations we conceive of as invariant with respect to a much wider class of variations than those particular ones that are displayed before us in the natural course of events.' The process of going over from inter-industry to vertically integrated relations, for the purpose of dynamic analysis, seems to be a typical example of this 'digging down to more fundamental relations'.

A criticism of the von Neumann-type of dynamic models as applied to economic systems with technical change

1. The vertically integrated analysis developed in the present work, as the reader will certainly have realised by now, has taken so marked a departure from all the dynamic extensions of the inter-industry scheme, which have become so widespread in current economic literature, as to require at this point some justification. To this purpose, I shall append a brief critical assessment of the approach adopted in most of the dynamic models which are currently discussed among mathematical economists.

2. As is well known, the most outstanding of all these models is von Neumann's theoretical scheme of an expanding (fixed technology) economy.[6] Another model of particular interest to us is Leontief's dynamic version of his static input–output analysis.[7] All other works that have followed have introduced many slight variations in these two models but have not changed their basic features.[8]

Let me begin by considering von Neumann's celebrated model, which is built on a set of assumptions that may be listed as follows: (i) there is a wide, well specified, and invariant set of technical methods for producing separately or jointly the various commodities; (ii) there are constant returns to scale in the employments of all inputs of production (labour included, in the sense that labour is supposed to require a subsistence wage rate and is treated, like any other commodity, as an output which requires a series of inputs of subsistence consumption); (iii) the excess of the output of each commodity over the input of the same commodity in the production process is accumulated. Given these assumptions, von Neumann shows that there exists a particular set of techniques and

---

6 John von Neumann, *op. cit.*, see footnote 23, on p. 17.
7 Wassily W. Leontief, 'Dynamic Analysis', chapter 3 of *Studies in the Structure of the American Economy*, ed. by Wassily W. Leontief, New York 1953.
8 A case in point is the vast economic literature that has developed out of the so called 'turnpike theorem' (proposed by Dorfman–Samuelson–Solow, in *Linear Programming and Economic Analysis*, chs. 11 and 12, New York 1958, and expanded in a long series of articles in the economic literature). All this literature, which is based crucially on the assumption of a constant technology through time, shares of course *in toto* the restrictions which will be pointed out here with reference to von Neumann's model.

corresponding set of relative prices, and certain proportions among the various commodities, at which a uniform rate of growth of all products is a maximum. At this rate of growth, which turns out to coincide with the economically meaningful rate of profit, the economic system grows uniformly, i.e. all its sections are multiplied in the same proportion and the composition of production and the structure of prices are therefore kept constant over time.

Wassily Leontief arrives at results which are similar to these, although he does not go into the problem of choice of techniques and starts instead by immediately assuming given production coefficients for each process. He begins with his input–output flow matrix and adds to it a matrix of capital coefficients. Then he shows that there is a well-defined composition of the initial stocks of capital goods (determined exclusively by the structural coefficients), which yields a maximum uniform rate of growth for all industries. Even if the economic system does not start from this particular composition of the initial stocks, it will all the same tend to produce it eventually, although in the meantime it may run into various difficulties.

3. These have undoubtedly been important contributions to the development of dynamic economic analysis. They represent a most radical departure from traditional marginal economic theory, as they entail the abandonment of the concepts of given scarce resources and a return to classical economic theory. All goods considered are *produced* goods. This character is so basic that von Neumann, as a mathematician, always looking for symmetry, applied the scheme to an imaginary society where the workers themselves are treated as if they were produced goods.

There is in fact nothing in these schemes which is incompatible with the dynamic analysis of the previous pages. We might say that all von Neumann-type dynamic models represent a concentration of powerful analytical tools on one particular set of simple hypotheses: the case of constant returns to scale and absolutely no technical progress. From an analytical point of view, this is an elegant and exciting case.[9] However, it can have a sense only if considered *as an intermediate analytical step* to a more relevant type of dynamic analysis. Taken as such, it can have, on strictly empirical grounds, very little practical relevance.

In the foregoing discussion of the relation between input–output static analysis and the present vertically-integrated dynamic analysis, there is a point to which all the von Neumann type of models can be traced back. It has been said in section 3 that when, from an analysis of an

9 I have dealt with this case, in further detail, in the final chapter of my *Lectures on the Theory of Production*, New York and London 1977.

119

economic system at a given point of time, one goes over to considering movements through time, the inverse matrix of the technical coefficients, which provides the analytical bridge between the two types of analyses, breaks down, because of technical change. All the von Neumann-type models can be regarded as an attempt to resist – for analytical purposes – this hard fact, and to maintain that analytical bridge through time by assumption, if nothing else. But we must be aware that such an assumption, convenient though it may be mathematically, has nothing to do with the real world. It means omitting deliberately what, in the previous discussions, has been singled out as the basic force responsible for the dynamism of a modern society, namely the process of learning which goes on, both on the technical side and on the demand side. In point of fact, one might even question the type of dynamics which these models have adopted, as it has meant introducing time into a static framework while being sure not to affect the static framework itself. (Rather than dynamic models, they might more appropriately be called quasi-dynamic, or – from a different point of view – quasi-stationary.) In a sense, time has no importance in these models, since the features of the economic system are described independently of time, once and for all time. As a result, these models do not say any more about the structure of an economic system than is already said by the corresponding static model. They simply add to it a time expansion by 'blowing up' the size of operation, while taking the structure of the economic system at a given point in time and crystallising it, so to speak, for all eternity. The picture which emerges is that of a hypothetical economic system growing only in size but with no development. Each member of the community goes on, indefinitely, producing the same commodities, quantitatively and qualitatively, receiving the same per capita income and consuming the same consumption goods.

We have discussed this type of economic system already, in chapter III, explicitly considering it as a purely analytical intermediate step towards the, practically more relevant, analysis of economic systems with technical change. But it has also been pointed out there that any investigation of such types of hypothetical economic systems can only have analytical, not practical or empirical, relevance.

4. When an analytical intermediate step turns out to be mathematically more elegant than the final one, the temptation is always very strong to give up going ahead rather than abandoning the elegance of the intermediate stage. The economic literature on von Neumann-type models seems to be a good case in point. Over the past forty years, economic journals have been full of re-elaborations and re-formulations

of dynamic multi-sector models. But those assumptions (notably the exclusion of any sort of technical progress) which at the beginning might have been considered as a provisional analytical step have never been abandoned.

Unfortunately, once concepts are coined, they tend to be used without discrimination. And with all the enormous problems of economic development which have been pressing in the real world (both in advanced and in industrially underdeveloped countries), the tendency has been to try to apply in practice the same concepts which the economists have been using in theory. Von Neumann himself never extended his conclusions outside the fixed framework he adopted. But many of the mathematical economists who have followed in his footsteps have not been so strict. In this way von Neumann's concept of a maximum uniform rate of growth tends to be discussed as if it were a concept of general validity, and in particular *as if* it were applicable to a growing economic system in which there is technical progress.

This is a tendency that must be criticised most strongly, as it is entirely unjustified and distorts the very purposes of von Neumann's theoretical scheme. It may therefore be useful to show explicitly why any extension of von Neumann-type concepts to an economic system *with technical change* ought to be firmly resisted.

5. The point may be illustrated by considering the simplest of all types of technical progress, namely by supposing that improvements take the form of uniform increases of labour productivity in all sectors. In this case, it is only too natural to abandon von Neumann's assumption of a subsistence wage rate, and therefore of fixed coefficients at which workers can reproduce themselves, and to replace it with the assumption that the wage rate increases in time *pari passu* with productivity. But here is the crucial difficulty. How are we going to deal with an above-subsistence wage rate? We may consider two alternative ways. One way would obviously be to deal with it in the same way as von Neumann dealt with a subsistence wage. In other words, we might include the above-subsistence physical wage rate among the inputs. If we do so, we will of course, formally, obtain a solution. The meaning of such a solution is that a maximum rate of growth exists, relative to a technical *structure* which remains constant (since labour productivity is increasing, *ex-hypothesi*, at exactly the same rate everywhere). The only way to keep logical consistency is to suppose that the consumption coefficients increase at exactly the same rate of growth as labour productivity. This is the analytically elegant, but extremely special, case of economic growth which was discussed in the first part of chapter IV.

And it was pointed out there that this is again a case which can only have analytical, not practical or empirical, relevance, as it represents a purely imaginary society that, at least with reference to human beings, can never exist.

The other way of dealing with an above-subsistence wage rate would be to exclude wages from the input coefficients (or, which would analytically come to be the same thing, to exclude from the input coefficients that part of the wage rate which is above subsistence) and consider the (above subsistence) wages as part of net product, which itself is partly consumed and partly re-invested, according to a given proportion. In this case again there would formally be a solution to the von Neumann problem, but again its meaning would make no economic sense. It would mean that, of all possible compositions of total production which allow a uniform rate of growth, there is one at which this uniform rate of growth is a maximum. There is something here to which too little attention seems to have been paid so far. The von Neumann maximum rate of growth entails a very definite *composition* of production, a composition which comes to be determined entirely on *technological grounds*. It means, for example, that to achieve that maximum rate, total production will have to be composed of a high proportion of those commodities which are easier to produce.[10]

Therefore, unless the members of the community are indifferent to the type of goods they consume (which would simply be absurd to hypothesise) the pattern of growth defined by von Neumann's maximum can have no economically significant meaning. In no case ever will it represent an *optimum* pattern of growth.

The argument may be developed from two different (and complementary) points of view. Note first of all that von Neumann's scheme imposes a uniform rate of growth, i.e. a uniform (proportional) expansion of production of all commodities; this is a basic, inherent, non-relaxable feature of the von Neumann model. But, as has been argued in chapter IV, we know that the consumers who enjoy an increasing per capita income *do not want* a proportional increase in all the commodities they consume. As soon as their demand for each commodity approaches saturation, they are bound to spend the increasing income on different goods. This leads us to a strong conclusion. The von Neumann concept of a maximum rate of growth, if applied to a system with technical progress, not only may not, but actually *can never*

10 From this point of view, all von Neumann-type models share the basic defects of classical economic theories. By shaping all features of an economic system on technology, which represents one half of the determining forces, they miss entirely the other half, connected with consumers' demand.

correspond – not even by a fluke – to an optimum pattern of growth. It can never correspond to a pattern of growth that consumers may possibly like to have.

Secondly there is the reverse side of the coin. Von Neumann's model imposes on the system the requirement that *all* commodities should grow at the same rate. This inevitably implies that, if there is one commodity in the economic systems which is very difficult to produce, in the sense that its production can only grow very slowly through time, this commodity inevitably slows down the growth of the whole economic system.[11] This is an unacceptable restriction, at least as long as we refer our analysis to a society of human beings. If that commodity, for example, happens to be one that consumers do not want to increase, there is no reason why the growth of the whole economic system should be kept back simply in order to fulfil the arbitrary requirement of a uniform rate of growth. In practice, production of that commodity may quite well be kept constant or even decreased or eliminated altogether, if better and cheaper substitutes can be invented. All this means that, following what consumers want, both with regard to the composition of consumption and to the rate of expansion of each single production, it might well be possible to achieve an over-all 'standard' rate of productivity growth (as defined in the previous chapter), which, besides reflecting better choices on welfare grounds, is also numerically larger than von Neumann's 'maximum' uniform rate.

To conclude, there is no ground whatever for any extension of von Neumann's concept of maximum rate of uniform growth and related concepts to an economic system in which there is technical progress. In no case would a maximum rate of uniform growth produce an optimum pattern of economic growth. Moreover it may even turn out to be numerically smaller than an over-all growth rate achievable by following the sectoral rates of expansion indicated by the structural evolution of consumers' demand.

11 This criticism has already been raised by D. G. Champernowne in his 'A Note on J. von Neumann's Article on "A Model of General Economic Equilibrium"', *The Review of Economic Studies*, 1945–46. Incidentally, Champernowne's interesting article is quite indicative of economists' traditional preoccupations. The limitations of von Neumann's assumptions of constant returns to scale are indeed pointed out, but mainly with reference to the case of *decreasing* returns to scale.

PART II

Economic dynamics theory

Chapter VII

The 'natural' features of a growing economic system

1. Foreword

We are ready at last to progress, from the dynamic analysis developed in the previous pages, to considering a few basic economic concepts, drawing theoretical implications and singling out a series of organisational problems that arise, for society, from the very process of structural dynamics of a growing economy.

2. Two basic properties

There are two basic properties of the theoretical scheme developed so far which are worth being explicitly stressed. The first property is that it has been developed for the purpose of detecting the 'permanent' causes moving an economic system, irrespective of any accidental or transitory deviation which may temporarily occur. In other words, the aim has been that of representing what Ricardo called the 'primary and natural' determinants of the variables considered, and therefore, in a dynamic context, their basic movements through time.[1]

The second property is that the analysis has been developed independently of the institutional set-up of society, i.e. independently of the particular mechanisms which may in practice be put into operation in order to bring those 'primary and natural' features into being. The investigation has started directly from an evolving technology, a growing population and an evolving pattern of consumers' preferences. From these natural forces, and from nothing else, a series of structural movements have been derived which may indeed be called the *natural*

---

1 These 'natural and primary' determinants are bound to make themselves felt in the long run, whatever transitory short-run deviations there may be. This is something more than saying that the present analysis is a long-run analysis. We have been, and we are, concerned with the norm; and the norm is always there – even if it is not so much apparent – in the *short* no less than in the long run, whatever amount of temporary disturbances there may be.

127

features of a growing economic system. They are represented by:

(i) an evolving structure of commodity prices;
(ii) an evolving structure of production;
(iii) the time path of the wage rate and of the rate – or rates – of profit. (The rate of profit has not in fact been examined as yet, but will be examined in a moment.)

Moreover, as a requirement for all these structural movements to take place in 'equilibrium' – by which is simply meant full employment and full capacity utilisation – two types of necessary conditions have emerged, namely:

(iv) a series of *sectoral* new investment conditions, defining the evolving structure of capital accumulation;
(v) a *macro-economic* effective demand condition, referring to total demand in the economic system as a whole.

Structural features (i), (ii) and (iii), and conditions (iv) and (v) – duly supplemented, when more details are needed with reference to a given point in time, by the inter-industry relations discussed in chapter VI above – form a complete theoretical scheme representing what may be called the theoretical scheme of a *natural* economic system.

In the following pages, the components of this theoretical scheme will be examined one by one.

3. The 'natural' rates of profit

There is one problem which has been left open hitherto, and which must be settled before proceeding. One of the economic magnitudes of our theory, namely the rate of profit, has not been explained so far. We may therefore ask at this point: does the previous theoretical framework, besides evincing the factors determining natural prices and natural quantities, also logically imply a *natural* rate of profit? The answer is: yes. A *natural* rate of profit is already logically implied in the previous theoretical framework because the economic system considered is a growing one. It may be useful to consider separately the two basic cases of economic growth: population growth and technical progress.

Suppose first of all an economic system characterised by constant returns to scale (no technical progress) and by a population increasing at a steady proportional rate g. In this case, the productivity of labour is constant over time *ex-hypothesi*. But since population is increasing, the conditions of dynamic equilibrium require that the present population cannot consume the whole fruit of its productivity. In order to maintain a constant production per head over time, a part of the productive capacity must be devoted to producing capital goods. This means that, since technology requires the use of capital goods in the production processes, an increasing population causes the amount of goods that the present generation can afford to consume – i.e. the amount of enjoyable reward that the present generation obtains for its productive activity – to be less than it would be if population were constant. The proportion by which it is less is given by the rate of population growth multiplied by the over-all capital/output ratio. Another way of putting the problem is to say that since technology requires the use of capital goods in the production processes, an increasing population forces down in each period the productivity of labour in terms of the commodities that the community can actually consume. This means that if there are, for example, two commodities, A and B, of which the first is produced by labour alone and the second is produced by the same amount of labour, except that it is partly direct labour and partly labour first embodied into a machine, the second commodity is dearer for the community to produce when population is increasing because, in order to produce it at constant productivity through time, an extra amount of labour must be devoted to make *additions* to productive capacity. Thus an increasing population causes the productivity of labour in terms of B to be lower than the productivity of labour in terms of A. As a consequence, the price of B will have to be higher than the price of A by the same proportion as the corresponding labour productivity is lower. All this means that a rate of profit on the value of capital goods must be charged equal to the rate of growth of population. Therefore, in an economic system with increasing population and no technical progress, there is a *natural* rate of profit, which turns out to be equal to the percentage rate of growth of population.

Suppose now an economic system in which population is stationary but technical knowledge is continually improving. Average per capita incomes will increase, and therefore demand for consumption goods will have to increase, if dynamic equilibrium is to be maintained. The rates of growth of per capita demand for each consumption good, $r_1, r_2, \ldots, r_{n-1}$, will normally be different from one another, as has been argued in chapter IV.

Consider a particular commodity i and compare the two alternative cases in which $r_i > 0$ and $r_i = 0$. Clearly, we may now repeat the same arguments developed above with reference to the two alternative cases of a positive and of a zero rate of population growth. In the case in

129

which $r_i > 0$, commodity i is, for the economic system as a whole, more expensive to produce (in terms of final consumption goods) than in the case in which $r_i = 0$. For, in the former case, sector i will require, not only direct wages and replacement of used-up capital goods (indirect wages) but also an extra amount of capital goods (an extra amount of indirect wages: we may say 'hyper-indirect' wages) to expand its productive capacity. The value of these extra capital goods which are required will be precisely given by the sectoral rate of growth multiplied by the sectoral capital/output ratio. In this case again, an increasing demand for commodity i forces down in each period the productivity of labour in terms of the commodities the community can afford to consume. Or, to put the matter in another way, if there are two commodities, i and j, both of which are expanding at the same per capita rate of growth ($r_i = r_j$), both of which require exactly the same amount of labour to be produced, but such that the labour required by the first commodity is all direct, while the labour required by the second commodity is partly direct and partly first embodied into a machine, then for the community as a whole, when $r_i = r_j > 0$, the second commodity is more expensive to produce than the first. For, in order to produce it, an extra amount of labour must be devoted to make additions to productive capacity. Thus, the productivity of labour in terms of consumption good i and the productivity of labour in terms of consumption good j are exactly the same when $r_i = r_j = 0$; but the former is higher than the latter when $r_i = r_j > 0$. As a consequence, the price of j will have to be higher than the price of i by the same proportion – given by the new investment requirement (V.4.2) – as the corresponding productivity is lower. All this means that a rate of profit on the value of capital goods must be charged equal to the rate of growth of demand for commodity j. Therefore, in an economic system with technical progress and a constant population, there is a particular *natural* rate of profit for each particular sector of the economy. This natural rate of profit is equal to the sectoral rate of growth of per capita demand (and production).

By now combining this result with the previous one, we may conclude that a growing economic system logically implies a *natural* rate of profit. This natural rate of profit is uniform only in the case of population growth at constant technical coefficients. When there is both population growth and technical progress, there are as many natural rates of profit as there are rates of expansion of demand (and production) of the various consumption goods. Each natural rate of profit is given by the sum of two components: the rate of population growth, common to all of them, and the rate of increase of per capita demand for each consumption good (equal to the rate of increase of per capita product tion, as we are considering dynamic equilibrium situations). In formal terms, we may write:

$$(\text{VII.3.1}) \qquad \pi_i^* = g + r_i, \qquad\qquad i = 1, 2, \ldots, n-1,$$

where π_i^* represent the *natural rate of profit* for sector i. The (VII.3.1) define $(n-1)$ natural rates of profit which, without recourse any longer to any exogenously given economic magnitude, now come to complete and close the whole relative-price system of our theoretical scheme.

4. A labour theory of value and a labour theory of the rate of profit

The interpretation of the rate of profit outlined above follows directly and logically from the approach to economic reality which has been adopted in the present work. In contrast with the scarce resource approach of traditional marginal economic theory, which amounts to reducing labour to one of many natural resources (each of which is treated on the same footing, as if it had a kind of personality of its own), the theory developed in the present work has put the whole economic system immediately into relation with what is its only source and *raison d'être*: the activity and the wants of Man. Nothing in the present theoretical scheme has any economic relevance – i.e. value – other than in relation to the activity and wants of the members of the community. What nature offers is a datum – it is taken for granted. Any commodity, by itself, has no personality: it has no right or claim. Of course, commodities do physically produce other commodities – machines produce machines, animals reproduce animals – but this 'physical' productivity must be correctly interpreted. Commodities cannot appropriate the commodities that come out of them. Only Man can. The physical productivity of commodities simply is a part of their technical or biological properties, which for Man is a datum. What becomes relevant, for economic purposes, which means for the process of pricing, is only the amount of human activity which is required, whether directly or indirectly, to make a technological or a biological process work. The fact, for example, that machine A can produce 1 unit of commodity a per day and machine B can produce 100 units of commodity b per day is a technical characteristic. For pricing purposes, what matters is the amount of human activity which has been and has to be used. If the two machines have been made from the same inputs, and if they are operated by the same amount of labour, the value of their daily product – however different their *physical* productivity may be – will be the same. The price of b will be 1/100 the price of a. It is in this sense that what becomes economically relevant is only and exclusively the productivity of labour.

The theoretical consequences are far-reaching. As long as the rate of profit was simply taken as exogenously given, the theory of value implied in the previous analysis, as pointed out in chapter II (section 6), was a theory of value in terms of labour equivalents (the quantities of labour being weighted differently according as to whether they were applied directly or indirectly). But now that a natural rate of profit is introduced, all relations become much more straightforward. The theory of value implied by the present theoretical scheme becomes a theory in terms of simple labour – *a pure labour theory of value*.

To make this apparent, we may insert (VII.3.1) into the expression for prices discussed in chapters II, III, V. We may write:[2]

(VII.4.1) $$p_i(t) = [a_{ni}(t) + (\pi^* + 1/T_i)a_{nk_i}(t)]w(t),$$

$$i = 1, 2, \ldots, n - 1.$$

When all prices are expressed in terms of the wage rate, i.e. when we put $w(t) = 1$, and growth rates are inserted explicitly, we have:

(VII.4.2) $$p_i(t) = [a_{ni}(t) + (1/T_i)a_{nk_i}(t) + (g + r_i)a_{nk_i}(t)],$$

$$i = 1, 2, \ldots, n - 1.$$

The reader will realise that what appears in square brackets is precisely what has already been called (chapter V, section 13) the vertically hyper-integrated labour coefficient for consumption good i. It now appears clearly that the price of each consumption good i ($i = 1, 2, \ldots, n - 1$) is the sum of three *unweighted* physical quantities of *labour*: labour required directly in sector i (*direct labour $a_{ni}(t)$*), labour required to replace the worn-out productive capacity (*indirect labour $(1/T_i)a_{nk_i}(t)$*), and labour required to expand equilibrium productive capacity (what we may call *hyper-indirect labour $(g + r_i)a_{nk_i}(t)$*). In each price $p_i(t)$, the replacement component and the profit component thereby appear as perfectly symmetrical and as fulfilling the same function of computing amounts of labour indirectly required elsewhere in the economic system for the equilibrium production of consumption good i. They both represent charges made in order not to violate the basic principle of equal rewards for equal amounts of homogeneous labour.

All this may appear at first as very striking. But short reflection

---

2 The (VII.4.1) refer to the simpler model we have considered. Using the more complex model of section 7 of chapter II would simply complicate the formulae, but would not alter our arguments and conclusions.

should evince that it follows logically and inevitably from the very approach to economic reality taken in the present work. Labour emerges from the very logic of the present analysis as the only ultimate factor of production. And it is interesting that, in a growing economic system, this does imply a rate of profit. Contrary to what traditional economics has maintained for a long time, it is not the 'productivity of capital', or of any commodity, that turns out to be the *raison d'être* of a rate of profit. It is the growth, and the increasing productivity, of labour![3]

5. The two basic functions of the price system

The present theoretical scheme is now complete and it may be useful to briefly investigate meanings and properties of its components, both at any given point in time and through time.

We may begin with the variables emerging from the price system at any given point of time – a whole set of commodity prices, the wage rate and the rate (or rates) of profit.

We may say that, in the economic system, the price system basically performs two quite distinct and separate functions: a 'decentralised-decision-process' function and an 'income-distribution' function.

The 'decentralised-decision-process' function is performed at the intermediate stages of production. With reference to this function, the wage rate and the rates of profit are often referred to, in the economic literature, as 'factor prices'. But this terminology is misleading, though for reasons quite different from those that might be inferred from traditional economics. At the intermediate stages of the production process, *all* prices of the commodities used as inputs, and not only the wage rate and rate(s) of profit, are 'factor prices', in the sense that they

---

3 To illustrate further the contrast between this interpretation and the traditional one, consider the much exploited example, taken from the biological field, of rabbits reproducing themselves, so often used to evince Böhm-Bawerk's third ground – namely the physical productivity of goods through time – for the existence of a rate of profit. This physical productivity is a biological property which, along with all other technical properties, will set constraints. In the present case, the activity of producing rabbits (or any other commodity) is obviously incompatible with a rate of profit higher than the physical own-rate of reproduction of rabbits. But this has nothing to do with any process of determination of the rate of profit. To set a constraint to is something quite different from determining an economic magnitude. In a modern society, rabbits reproduce themselves because Man provides the favourable conditions (suitable place, fodder, organisation) for them to do so. The number of rabbits which can be taken for consumption in each unit of time is, for the economic purposes of pricing, the product of the direct, indirect and hyper-indirect labour put into this activity. It is the hyper-indirect labour (which depends on the growth of production) that determines the natural rate of profit, quite independently of rabbits' own biological productivity.

133

fulfil the same basic function of providing an appropriate evaluation of the corresponding inputs in the process of production.

In order to visualise this important 'factor price' function of the whole price system, it is useful to revert to the inter-industry relations discussed in chapter VI. In any advanced economic system, characterised by a very complex network of inter-industry relations, each producer is called upon, every day, to make decisions about inputs which, before coming to him (her), have passed through a huge number of previous intermediate stages, sometimes in the most remote corners of the economic system. If, in order to take any single decision, one were required to know everything which has gone on in all those remote corners of the inter-industry network, the working of any economy would become practically impossible. But, if, with each input, whatever the stage at which it has arrived, an index can be associated summarising all operations which have been performed on it, and therefore expressing the relative importance of that input as against any other, then decisions can be taken very quickly and efficiently, in a decentralised way.

It is precisely this remarkable decentralised-decision process that the price system as a whole makes possible at the intermediate stages of production. From this point of view, there is no difference whatever between the prices of commodities, the wages to be paid to workers and the profits to be computed on the values of capital goods: for the single producer, faced with a production decision, they are all costs, or, if we like, they are all intermediate 'factor prices'. So that, for the economic system as a whole, the problem that arises is that of ensuring that the set of indexes that are used for production decisions (commodity prices, wage rate and rate(s) of profit) are not distorted. And it is not difficult to realise that the non-distorted set of indexes is precisely represented by the 'natural' price system. For, this particular price system has the property of ultimately reducing all inputs to physical quantities of labour, no matter where and when they have been applied in the production process. And this is precisely what is required.

We may conclude, therefore, that, as far as the 'decentralised decision process' function, or 'factor price' function, of the price system is concerned, commodity prices, wage rate and rate(s) of profit all play exactly the same role of providing appropriate indexes for efficient decentralised decisions.

But if we were to restrict our attention to how things appear at the level of any single intermediate stage of production, we would remain at the surface of economic problems. The price system also fulfils another, most important, function, which we may call the 'income distribution' function of the price system. Separately from, and in a reverse direction to, the process of production, any economic system inherently and inevitably carries out a process of distribution of claims to share in the final national product. And as far as this function is concerned, commodity prices on the one side and the wage rate and rate(s) of profit on the other do set themselves in opposition to each other. While the former maintain their role of intermediate devices, the latter acquire the character of final 'distributive variables'. More specifically, wages and profits, which represent the starting stage of the process of production, appear, in reverse, as the final stage of the process of income distribution. We have seen that, at the final stage of the process of production, the final national product of an economic system is represented by a series of physical quantities with which our equations have associated a series of corresponding commodity prices. When the physical quantities are multiplied by the corresponding commodity prices, these prices fulfil the remarkable function of distributing all through the economic system an amount of purchasing power, which is equal in the end to the sum of wages and profits. In this way, all commodity prices disappear eventually, and the whole purchasing power corresponding to the final national product finds itself distributed to the members of the community either in the form of wages or in the form of profits.

It is with reference to this 'income distribution function' that commodity prices on the one hand and the wage rate and rate of profit on the other hand evince their profoundly different nature. To be more specific, the intermediate role played by commodity prices remain 'intermediate' in either direction – in one direction they carry with them the precise indication (they represent indexes) of the costs that have occurred in the previous stages of production; in the opposite direction they channel a corresponding amount of purchasing power towards those earlier stages of production. By contrast, the wage rate and the rate of profit (irrespective of what they may look like to the single producer) precisely do not let the corresponding purchasing power go back to any previous stage. They refer to something (inputs of labour) that takes place *at that* production stage, and thus directly channel purchasing power to final beneficiaries of the production process. Their basic nature therefore is that of claims to shares in final national income.

Looking at the same contrast in another way, we may say that, in the process of income distribution, any time we find a commodity price, we know we are at an intermediate stage of the distribution process: a certain amount of purchasing power is channelled back to the previous stages of production. Any time we find profits and wages, we know that the income distribution process has come to an end.

135

We may also look at these concepts in the context of the national income accounts, where we see them appearing on the two opposite sides of the balance sheet. The physical quantities of all final commodities which are produced, evaluated at their prices, appear on one side. The sum of total wages and total profits appears on the opposite side. And the sums of the two sides are identically equal to each other. They provide two different ways of looking at the same thing: the final national income – as it is produced on the one side, and as it is distributed on the other.

6. The real wage rate as a macro-economic concept

The basically different nature of the distributive variables – the wage rate and rate of profit – as opposed to the commodity prices may be stressed further by contrasting the interpretation of them that emerges from the foregoing analysis with the interpretation which is given by traditional economic theory.

As will be realised, marginal economic theory, by looking at the wage rate and rate of profit through the filter of a scarce-resource economic world, has inevitably concentrated on their decentralised-decision-process function, while almost entirely neglecting their income-distribution function. Within such a theoretical framework, it becomes inevitable to look at the wage rate and rate of profit as micro-economic concepts, along with any other commodity price. More specifically, marginal economic theory has related the wage rate and the rate of profit to corresponding 'marginal productivities', which are physical concepts referring to marginal variations of production in the specific firm where labour and 'capital' are applied. From the point of view of the present analysis, such an approach appears very primitive. To concentrate attention on physical productivities within a single sector or firm might in fact have had a lot of heuristic merit in an economic system of the pre-industrial type, where each labourer normally produces directly the major part of the goods which his family consumes. But in a modern economic system, such an approach becomes patently irrelevant – not only owing to, and quite apart from, the difficulties and ambiguities inherent in the concepts of 'marginal productivities' (to which we shall come back later on, in chapter IX), but more fundamentally because of the fact that, in a highly specialised society, the physical productivity of any single worker (whether marginal or average) can only have a negligible influence on claims that refer to the economic system as a whole. Fundamentally, in a modern economic system, the distributive variables are *macro-economic concepts*.

136

In section 3 and 4 above, it was pointed out how irrelevant the physical productivity of any single commodity is to the determination of the natural rates of profit. A similar point can now be stressed, with reference to the wage rate. On this problem, in fact, the limits of a static approach appear even more strikingly. In a hypothetical world, such as the one considered by traditional economic theory, where technology is supposed to be absolutely constant, one is led too easily to neglect what happens anywhere else in the economic system, by concentrating one's attention on what happens in the sector under consideration. But in a dynamic context, in which technology is changing in all sectors, it becomes evident that it is precisely *what happens in the other sectors* that is of paramount importance in determining the real content of the wage rate, and not the changes in productivity in the sector under consideration, whether at the margin or on the average.

The reader will notice that we are concerned here with the *real* wage rate, i.e. with the wage rate in terms of physical commodities. When this concept first emerged in our analysis in chapter V, we were compelled to define it through the construction of the 'standard' rate of growth of productivity – a typically macro-economic concept. It is important to realise how strikingly in contrast this concept is with that which is used by traditional economic theory. The 'real wage rate' of traditional economic theory is related to the 'marginal productivity' of labour. It is a single number – a number of physical units of the commodity which is produced in the sector where the worker is actually working. But this is not the concept of the real wage rate which is relevant in a modern economic system. When the degree of specialisation in production is very marked, the concept of the 'real wage rate' that becomes relevant is represented, not by a single number, but by a whole series of numbers (a vector), indicating the physical basket of goods on which the wage rate is actually spent, and, as such, depending on the physical productivity of *the economic system as a whole*.

A short example may be useful to illustrate this important point. A worker who tightens screws on the assembly line of a car factory produces tightened screws, but he is not paid in terms of the number of screws tightened. He is paid with an amount of abstract purchasing power over *all* commodities. And when, as it is usually the case, an entirely negligible proportion of this purchasing power is spent on tightened screws, to concentrate all economic analysis of wages on the worker's physical productivity in terms of tightened screws means magnifying out of proportion one tiny and negligible side of the whole problem. The real meaning of that worker's wage rate cannot but be sought in the basket of goods and services which the screws he has tightened can buy in the whole economic system. And the size of such a basket of goods and services depends on the absolute levels, and on the rates of change, of productivity in *all* the sectors that produce them. It depends, in practice, on the degree of productivity of the whole economic system. The reader has no doubt understood how important it is to realise the macro-economic nature of the concept of real wage rate.

To conclude, traditional economic theory has concentrated on one aspect of the real wage rate, which has become more and more negligible, and more and more remote from its physical content. It has concentrated on the physical productivity of each single individual, at a time when, between the physical productivity of any single worker and his (her) *real* wage rate, there has grown the entire and complex technological structure of the whole economic system.

7. The determination of relative prices and physical quantities in a dynamic context

We may now go on to investigate more specifically the movements through time. And we shall begin with the evolution of the commodity prices together with the evolution of the corresponding physical quantities. Our dynamic analysis has put us in the enviable position of being able to take a fresh look at an old economic problem – the problem of singling out the basic determinants, through time, of the relative prices and physical quantities of the commodities produced in an economic system.

Some readers may look surprised at this statement and think that this is something which no longer needs any discussion, since the answer can be found in any elementary economics textbook, under the chapter (or chapters) devoted to the theory of value. But it is precisely this conviction that I should like to dispute, because the theory of value only refers to one half of the whole problem. So far it has been impossible even to realise that there exists another half, because the static limitations imposed on economic theory have left it (this other half) in the shade. Since the issue has kept a central place in economic analysis, it is almost impossible to deal with it without opening a parenthesis and retracing the story from the beginning, by going back, albeit very briefly, to the standard works of the Classical, the Marginalist, and the Neo-classical economists.

The position of the Classical economists is masterly expressed by Ricardo in the first two pages of his *Principles*. He makes first of all the distinction – which has been singled out and stressed already in chapter I above – between *produced commodities* and *scarce commodities*. Then, on grounds of economic irrelevance, he leaves the commodities of the *scarce type* out of consideration and exclusively concentrates on those commodities which are the outcome of a process of production. 'Utility,' says Ricardo, 'is not the measure of [their] exchangeable value, although it is absolutely essential to it.'[4] Their value – he claims – is determined by their cost of production, which he mainly conceives of in terms of labour.

Fifty years later, as is well-known, the Marginalists reacted violently against this statement. They objected that the Classical economists had neglected demand. They were right. Unfortunately, however, instead of correcting the Classical economists, they went in a completely different direction. They turned their attention to the other type of goods – the goods of the scarce type – that the Classical economists did not consider at all, and, by taking them as representative of *all* goods, they claimed that *utility*, and not the cost of production, is the fundamental determinant of value. 'Repeated reflection and inquiry have led me to the somewhat novel opinion that *value depends entirely upon utility*.'[5] This was the starting point, and the central tenet, of all works of Jevons, one of the first leading and most vigorous proponents of the utility theory. It was really unfortunate that the Ricardian distinction between commodities which are scarce and commodities which are produced had not been kept in mind: it would have shown so clearly how the Classical economists and the Marginalists were talking about different things.

When, at the turn of the century, Marshall tackled the problem, he was taken up by the Marginalist arguments, but he was concerned with explaining what happens in 'industry', and he was confronted with the puzzle of whether cost of production or utility determines the value of commodities. To solve it, he proposed a famous compromise, which is still nowadays considered to be the standard answer to the problem, though it has been slightly modified by the monopolistic and imperfect competition theories.

Marshall's argument is very ingenious and it is worth recalling in detail. Both the cost of production and utility – Marshall claims – contribute to determining prices, in the same way as both blades of a pair of scissors contribute to cutting a piece of paper. He carries on his analogy very effectively by explaining that 'when one blade is held still, and the cutting is effected by moving the other, we may say with careless brevity that the cutting is done by the second'.[6] Similarly in the market,

---

4 David Ricardo, *Principles*, Sraffa edition, *op. cit.*, p. 11.
5 W. Stanley Jevons, *The Theory of Political Economy*, *op. cit.*, p. 1 (italics in the original).
6 Alfred Marshall, *Principles of Economics*, 8th ed., London 1920, p. 348.

when the structure of production is given and held still – which happens in the short run – we may say that demand is the main factor responsible for the determination of prices. On the other hand, in the long run, when there is time for the structure of production to be adapted, it is the cost of production which will determine prices. Therefore, in the long run, 'if a person chooses to neglect market fluctuations . . . he may be excused for ignoring the influence of demand and speaking of (normal) price as governed by cost of production'.[7]

This is all right but, if we consider it carefully, it only reconciles the Marginalists' difficulties in understanding the Classical economists. It *does not* solve the problem that Ricardo (and the Classical economists) left unsolved. Marshall has the merit of grasping two important features of the Ricardian analysis, which the utility theorists had missed. The first is that the commodities under discussion are those ones which are important in an industrial type of society, namely the commodities of the reproducible type; and Marshall refers his analysis to them. The second feature is that the Ricardian theory is concerned with the long run (or rather, with fundamental determinants, which make themselves felt in the long run).

Now, what Marshall's arguments amount to is simply saying that in a market economy the commodities of the reproducible type are, in the short run, assimilated to the goods of the scarce type, because the adaptation of production to unforeseen circumstances requires time. Therefore, in the short run, the market demand will influence their prices. On the other hand, in the long run, when 'adjustment of the flow of appliances' can take place, the cost of production will eventually come out as the determinant of price.

This is a statement that perhaps Ricardo would even have accepted. Only he would have pointed out that he was not terribly interested in the first part of it, because his purpose was to bring out the fundamental determinants of the economic variables, independently of any temporary and short-lived deviations due to any market fluctuation.[8]

But, in this way, we are back to where Ricardo was. Marshall – apart from beginning to explore the effects of short-run and temporary difficulties within a certain institutional system (the market economy) – does not bring that analysis ahead a single jot. In particular, Marshall's

---

7 *Ibid.*, p. 349.
8 Incidentally, we can clearly see here that Marshall's analysis, in spite of its apparent symmetry, is in fact a very hybrid one. For, it puts on exactly the same footing elements belonging to the 'natural' economic system, which are objectively given for all types of economic systems, and elements which are temporary and specific to a particular institution (the market economy).

ormulation leads one to conclude – in the same way as Ricardo's did – that demand has no role to play in the long run. This is incorrect.

With the help of a dynamic scheme representing the evolution of both technology and demand we can see the whole problem much more clearly. We may return, for a check, to the solutions of our systems of equations in chapter V. By the (V.9.2) we are told that natural prices at a certain point in time and through time depend exclusively on technical factors: labour and capital goods required in the production of each unit of output. In other words, we are told that, in the long run, the cost of production determines prices, as both Ricardo and Marshall stated. But this is only half of the story. There is another (dual) series of solutions which have been forgotten – the (V.9.1). This other series of solutions say that the quantities to be produced depend on demand factors, namely on the per capita evolution in time of consumers' preferences and on population. In other words, in the long run, demand determines the *quantity* of each commodity which has to be produced. This is the half of the problem which Ricardo did not see,[9] and which Marshall then himself failed to bring out.

The conclusions that follow are very simple and at the same time rather stringent. It is not true – as both Ricardo and Marshall implied – that demand has no role to play in the long run. Both technology and demand are indeed relevant; both of them have their own role to play. But they determine two different things. Costs of production, i.e. technology, determine *relative prices*; consumers' decisions, i.e. their demand, determine *relative quantities*. In dynamic terms, the process emerges at its clearest – the pattern of productivity increases determines the evolution over time of the structure of prices and the pattern of consumers' decisions determines the evolution over time of the structure of production.

This conclusion needs perhaps a few words of elaboration because the determining process, while conceptually straightforward in the case of relative prices, is more complex in the case of physical quantities, where the consumption coefficients that appear in our analysis change as a result both of the variation of the price structure and of the increase in

9 Now that we have discovered it, we may go back for a moment to Ricardo's original statement. Indeed he was right in saying that cost of production, and not utility, determines the *natural* price of (produced) commodities but he added: 'although utility is absolutely essential to it'. This is misleading. That 'it' must be referred to the production of the commodity and not – as in Ricardo's context – to the prices. Those (reproducible) commodities that have no utility will simply not be produced (zero quantity), although they may have positive costs and, therefore, positive 'natural' prices. The only thing we can say is that the natural price, although positive, will never have a chance of coming into being because production is zero.

141

per capita incomes. The whole process may be viewed as a succession of asymmetrical relations, which evince a definite causation chain. The first exogenous factor of our scheme, technology, which is at the origin of the whole process, directly determines the structure of natural (relative) prices, independently of anything else. But technology also determines the height of potential per capita income. At this point, when the price structure has been (conceptually) determined already, the consumers' decisions and the population size (the other two exogenous factors in our scheme) come in to determine the physical quantities to be produced.

This process is so fundamental that one can follow it even if one looks at it from a strictly traditional (marginal utility) point of view. By using traditional terminology, one may say that, at any given level of technology – i.e. at any given price structure and level of real income – each consumer acting rationally will push demand for each commodity to that point at which his (her) marginal utility equals the given price. This is indeed a typically traditional conclusion, but the reader will notice that the chain of causation emerges as exactly reversed. It is the relative prices that determine what the individual marginal utilities are going to be and not vice versa! Yet this static outlook still conceals the process which has been and is going on. It is only by considering the movements of per capita incomes and of the price structure through time that the way in which demand shapes the structure of physical production emerges in its entirety. As per capita incomes increase, consumers' preferences will determine the order of succession in which the various commodities are wanted, while the rate at which the 'marginal utility' of each commodity falls, as more and more of it is consumed, will determine the speed of variation of the structure of per capita consumption, as has been explained in chapter IV. The rate of population growth is then the final additive element for the determination for each commodity of the rate of expansion of its total production through time.

8. The dynamic paths of the wage rate and the rate(s) of profit

It also becomes important to stress, at this point, the fundamentally different movements through time of the wage rate, on the one side, and of the rates of profit, on the other.

We have seen in the foregoing sections that the very same basic principle underlying income distribution implies two different distribution criteria: profits related to rates of change, and wages related to absolute levels of production. As a consequence, precisely the same principle also implies two basically different types of dynamic movement. If rates of profits are related to rates of change, while the real wage rate is related to the absolute level of over-all productivity, then clearly the two cannot follow the same type of dynamic path. Changes in rates of change and changes in absolute levels belong to two entirely different orders of magnitude.

The real wage rate, by reflecting the absolute level of average per capita productivity, is bound to exhibit a continually and persistently rising trend over time. The longer the time, the bigger the real wage rate is bound to be. On the other hand, the rates of profit, and *a fortiori* their average, by reflecting rates of change of per capita demand and population are bound to show no monotonic trend in either direction. There may well be periods in which the rates of growth of per capita demand and population slowly increase and periods in which they slowly decrease. But the effects will remain different in a fundamental way: to increases (or decreases) in the rate(s) of profit, there will correspond accelerations (or decelerations) in the growth of the real wage rate. In the long run, therefore, while the real wage rate will *persistently* grow, the rate(s) of profit cannot but roughly remain at the same level. For, all the changes in the rates of change cannot but be of a temporary and reversible character: the rate of growth of population cannot go beyond certain strict limits, owing to simple biological reasons; and similarly the over-all rate of growth of productivity, which is the basis of the over-all rate of growth of per capita demand, is bound to remain within strict physical limits, owing to the limited amount of knowledge that human beings can acquire within each period of time.

The consequences are important. The very same hypothesis on population growth and on technological change, whatever this hypothesis may be, entails two basically different dynamic paths for the rate(s) of profit and the wage rate. In our case, the simplest of all hypotheses – namely the hypothesis that population grows exponentially and that, on average, people are born over time with roughly the same degree of intelligence, and thus ability to learn – entails a roughly constant trend for the over-all average rate of profit and a monotonically increasing trend for the real wage rate.

9. Total profits and total wages – an asymmetrical relation

A straightforward macro-economic implication follows immediately. Within any given period of time, the division of the final national product between profits and wages emerges through a chain of typically asymmetrical relations. The total amount of natural profits at (natural)

143

prices is determined first of all and independently of anything else. If w call it Π^* we have:

(VII.9.1) $$\Pi^* = \sum \pi_i^* p_{k_i} K_i.$$

Then total wages follow, absorbing all that is left over, after payin profits.

What happens to relative shares, over time, i.e. to the share of tota profits, and as a consequence to the share of total wages in the fina national income, will obviously depend on the movements of all th rates of profits and of all the capital/output ratios. If it were to happen for example, that the (weighted) average of all rates of profit and th (weighted) average of all capital/output ratios remained roughly con stant over time then, as can be seen by dividing both sides of (VII.9.1 by the final national income, the share of total profits (and thus th share of total wages) would also remain constant, over time. In general of course, relative shares will change, but there is no reason to expec any persistent trend in either direction.

In any case, within the 'natural' economic system, whether we look a profits and wages at the macro-economic level, in terms of absolut amounts, or in terms of shares, the asymmetrical nature of the deter mining process emerges very clearly. Total profits emerge as a kind o prior claim to share in the final national income, while total wages – b being (conceptually) determined after profits have been determine already – emerge as a kind of residual, or, looking at it from a differen point of view, as a 'surplus' that remains over and above what has bee charged for profits. Of course, wages represent a very big and essentia 'residual' – a very important 'surplus'. To produce, and to continuall increase this 'surplus', through technical progress, is precisely th purpose of the whole production process.

At the end of all these elaborations on profits and wages, the result may appear to be quite simple and commonsense; and of course the are. The reader will realise, however, that they are in sharp contras with the interpretation of wages and profits, and of their movements ir time, that the whole of economic theory (both Classical and Neo classical) has given so far.

10. New investments

The same role which is played by the rate(s) of profit and the wage rate in the price equations system is played by the rates of growth o productive capacity and by consumption, respectively, in the physical-quantity equations system. But here, the dynamic movement of population is taken as exogenously given and the various relations emerge in the form of necessary conditions imposed by the requirement of full employment of the labour force.

There is first of all a series of new investment equilibrium conditions, defined by the (V.4.3), which specify the amounts of additional productive capacity that must be built in each single sector if full employment is to be maintained over time.

Of course, more than one technical possibility may be available, and hence it might seem that to determine investments in terms of productive capacity, as done by the (V.4.3), is not yet to determine them in terms of actual machines and therefore in terms of current values. The problem of choice of techniques will be examined in detail later on (chapter IX, sections 10–16). But the conclusion which is relevant to our present purposes can be anticipated already. Since, in each sector, the rate of profit is determined exogenously by the same factors that enter the (V.4.3), the whole problem of choice of technique can be solved independently of the (V.4.3), and has a unique solution, except in the very particular case in which, with a discrete technology, the rate of profit happens to settle precisely at a switch point between two techniques. We shall assume, for simplicity, that this is not the case. This means that the capital accumulation equilibrium conditions (V.4.3) will normally determine investments in each particular sector, not only in terms of productive capacity, but also in terms of actual machines.

As a straightforward consequence, the total amount of new investment in the economic system as a whole, which we may call I, can be derived by a simple sum:

(VII.10.1) $$I = \sum (g + r_i) p_{k_i} X_i.$$

The importance of this expression is that, by determining total equilibrium investment, it also *ipso facto* determines the equilibrium amount of total new savings for the economic system as a whole. By dividing both sides of (VII.10.1) by aggregate final national income, we also obtain the equilibrium proportion of final national income that must be saved and devoted to new investment, if full employment is to be maintained. It is important to realise that this equilibrium ratio (the over-all savings ratio) emerges as being determined directly by the exogenous factors of our analysis. As may be seen immediately by expanding its components, it is determined by consumers' consumption coefficients, population, technology, and their movements through time.

11. Total consumption

The set of capital accumulation equilibrium conditions just examined are sectoral conditions and have a macro-economic consequence only as a result of their sum. But we know that they must be inserted into the other equilibrium condition, expressed by (V.4.4) and concerning total effective demand. As pointed out in chapters II and V, this is a genuinely macro-economic condition: it is just one condition embracing the economic system as a whole. And since a part of total demand – the sum of all demands for new investments – has been determined already by (VII.10.1), what condition (V.4.4) comes down to imposing is that the whole remaining part of equilibrium total demand must be devoted entirely to absorbing consumption goods.

We therefore find here another asymmetrical chain of relations, parallel and similar to, but distinct from, the one determining the division of the final national income between profits and wages. This new asymmetrical chain of relations governs the equilibrium division of final national income between new investment (and thus savings) and consumption.

To conclude, the exogenous magnitudes of our theoretical scheme determine equilibrium new investment (and thus the equilibrium amount of total savings), first of all and independently of anything else. Then condition (V.4.4) determines how big total demand for consumption goods can, or rather must, be. Total consumption is, therefore, another macro-economic magnitude that (conceptually) emerges as a kind of residual, or 'surplus'. It must absorb all that is left over after providing for the necessary additions to productive capacity, as a requirement for full employment growth. Again we may say, of course, that total consumption represents a very big and essential 'residual' or 'surplus', and that to produce this surplus, and to continually increase it through technical progress, is the whole purpose of the production process.

12. Profits and wages, savings and consumption in the 'natural' economic system

It will be noticed that the two systems of equations (for prices and physical quantities, respectively) representing our theoretical scheme have become at this stage perfectly symmetrical and 'dual' to each other. Out of all possibilities of completing these two systems of equations, that one which is associated with the particular features of the 'natural' economic system has remarkable properties of symmetry and simplicity.

146

Each equations system is closed by a set of sectoral conditions. The price equations system is closed by sectoral expression (VII.3.1), synthesised by their sum (VII.9.1), which defines total 'natural' profits (and, as a residual, total wages); and the physical quantity system is closed by sectoral expressions (V.4.3), synthesised by their sum (VII.10.1), which determines equilibrium savings (and, as a residual, total equilibrium consumption).

These two sets of sectoral expressions have been obtained independently of each other, as two different requirements of logical consistency (equal weight for equal quantities of labour in the first case, full employment and full capacity utilisation in the second case). They express in fact two different economic phenomena altogether. But the remarkable result is that they exactly coincide. In the 'natural' economic system, total profits turn out to be equal to total savings, and total wages turn out to be equal to total consumption.

It is important to realise that this is not a mere over-all averaging-out result, but the consequence of a whole series of equalities realised at each single sectoral stage. The best way of making this clear is again to go back to the macro-economic effective demand equilibrium condition (V.4.4) and analyse its components. We have seen that when this condition is written in the form (V.13.3) each expression i under the summation represents the *proportions* of total available labour that is employed in the vertically hyper-integrated sector i, $(i = 1, 2, \ldots, n-1)$. Earlier in our analysis, we had seen that, in a pure labour economy, the same expression also represents the proportion of final national income, at current prices, accounted for by the same sector i.[10] But then we have also seen that, in general, this coincidence ceases to hold when capital goods are introduced.[11] Now, however, a new result emerges. When the rates of profit are at their 'natural' level, a further really remarkable property of their's is that they re-establish that coincidence. In each single (vertically hyper-integrated) sector, current values become proportional to physical quantities of labour and the two proportions again come to coincide. The only variance, with respect to the case of a pure labour economy, is that here the economic system, by having to produce a whole series of (intermediate) capital goods, also has to re-absorb them, so to speak, within each (vertically hyper-integrated) sector, so that the identical proportions refer to labour on the one side and to final production of consumption goods on the other.

To conclude, in the 'natural' economic system, profits turn out to be equal to new investments; and wages turn out to be equal to

10 See chapter II, section 3.
11 See chapter II, section 9 (footnote 11).

consumption; hence values of consumption goods turn out to be proportional to quantities of labour – not only in the economic system as a whole but also (and most importantly) in each single (vertically integrated) sector.

13. The consumption goods basis of a pure labour theory of value

The remarkable property of the 'natural' economic system, which has just emerged, deserves a little further attention. When 'natural' prices are expressed in terms of the wage rate, the value of the production of each consumption good i turns out to be equal to the sum of the physical quantities of labour employed in the vertically hyper-integrated sector which is producing it: i.e. in the consumption goods sector i and in the investment goods sector k_i (the sector which produces capital goods for sector i); $i = 1, 2, \ldots, n - 1$. To put it in a different way, the physical quantity of labour which consumption good i can 'command' turns out to be equal to the physical quantity of labour embodied in consumption good i plus the physical quantity of labour embodied in the new investment goods necessary to the expansion of production of consumption good i.

The 'natural' features thus make the economic system regain all the properties of a pure labour economy, provided that all relations are referred to commodities as consumption goods. The basic equality that emerges is between labour and consumption, both in each single sector – where value at natural prices becomes equal to the physical quantity of labour – and in the economic system as a whole – where the total value of all consumption goods becomes equal to the total labour force.

As the reader will realise, this is a complete generalisation of the pure labour theory of value.

14. The 'natural' economic system and the two levels of economic efficiency

We have obtained by now a complete set of economic theories – concerning prices, production, the wage rate and the rates of profit, both at a given point in time and in their evolution through time. Moreover we have obtained a whole set of equilibrium conditions for new investments and a macro-economic equilibrium condition for total effective demand. All these theories and equilibrium requirements refer to the 'natural' economic system. But one may wonder: why should all analysis be carried out only with reference to the 'natural' economic system?

148

The answer, which is implicit in the foregoing analysis, may now be made explicit. The present theoretical construction is aimed, as said at the beginning of the chapter, at detecting the 'primary and natural' determinants of the variables characterising an economic system, in the sense of those objective forces that are so basic as to be given prior to, and independently of, any institutional set-up. All our elaborations have been the consequence of this approach.

We may compare these propositions with the relations entailed by another criterion which is widely used in economic theory: the criterion of economic efficiency. As is well known, the notion of efficiency arises whenever, at any given point of time, a choice has to be made from among many possible alternatives. A particular choice is said to be efficient if it is such as to minimise the means employed to achieve a given aim. In traditional economics, the treatment of efficiency has always started from the rational behaviour of single individuals, especially with reference to consumption. Then, all other problems have been made to crucially depend on that. But the present inquiry has turned such an approach upside down. The whole framework has been developed in its entirety without any assumption about individuals' rational behaviour. This has amounted in fact to drawing a sharp distinction between two levels at which problems of economic efficiency may arise: the level of the decisions of single individuals (or group of individuals), and the level of the economic system as a whole. Neither of these two levels necessarily implies the other. The whole previous analysis has been in fact a demonstration of this. It has been carried out on purpose without any particular hypothesis as to the individual process of decision making.

However, one can now realise that, in principle, there is no difficulty in re-introducing hypotheses about individual behaviour at this stage. Clearly there are individual decisions behind each coefficient of production and each coefficient of consumption, and even behind each of the coefficients of the inter-industry system. At the level of these decisions, the problem of efficiency is generally assumed to take the form of rational behaviour. When an investment is to be undertaken, and more than one technical method is available, it is rational to choose that technical method which minimises costs. Similarly, when a consumer is faced with a range of different goods to buy, he (she) is said to act rationally, if he (she) chooses that combination that maximises satisfaction.

We know that these arguments are subject to serious limitations in a dynamic context, as was stressed in chapter IV. However, there is no incompatibility between them and the analysis of the previous pages.

149

The important point is that – unlike traditional theory – the previous analysis *does not* depend on any one of these arguments. In other words, if the single individuals (or group of individuals) do behave rationally, then the coefficients of our analysis can be interpreted as being the outcome of rational individual choices. We shall see in fact later on (chapter IX, section 13) that the 'natural' prices, rates of profit and wage rate possess remarkable efficiency properties concerning the decision process for the choice of the technical methods of production. But the validity of the present theoretical scheme remains unaltered, even if the consumption or production choices are not strictly rational, or are rational, for example, in the field of production and not rational, as may happen more often, in the field of consumption, or are in any case more complexly motivated. In these cases, the coefficients simply represent the choices that have actually been made, whatever the process through which they have been made.

Going now to the level of the economic system as a whole, it does not take long to realise that the two equilibrium conditions that have emerged from our analysis obviously do possess efficiency properties. The effective demand condition defines an amount of effective demand – full employment demand – that is obviously better than any other possible alternative amount, as the latter would necessarily entail either unemployment or inflation. It is better because it generates, respectively, a higher production from the same available labour and capital goods or the same physical production without the distortions of inflationary demand. Similarly, the set of sectoral investments entailed by the capital accumulation conditions is obviously better than any other alternative set of investments, which would necessarily entail either over-expansion or under-expansion of productive capacity. It is better because it leads respectively to the same increase in production from fewer capital goods or to a higher increase in production from the same amount of labour. As a consequence, it also determines, for the economic system as a whole, an efficient amount of savings.[12]

To conclude, after distinguishing two levels at which problems of efficiency may arise, we may say that, at the level of the economic system as a whole, the 'natural' features of an economic system also have the property of being efficient features. At the level of the decision of the single individuals, efficient decisions are not excluded (actually, the 'natural' price system also possesses remarkable efficiency properties concerning the decision processes), but they are considered as a particular case of a more general attitude towards individual behaviour.

12 There is, by the way, another interesting corollary to these results. By making a sharp distinction between the two levels at which the problems of economic efficiency may

15. Profits and savings in a capitalist economy

The discussion of the previous section brings us back to the problem of the institutions that a society may adopt. For, after developing our analysis independently of institutions, it may well emerge that some of the 'natural' features of an economic system may be impossible to achieve within a particular institutional set-up. In fact, the foregoing analysis precisely points at the 'natural rates of profit' as a most clear example of this type of impossibility.

In a socialist economic system, 'natural' rates of profit may or may not be adopted – at least in principle, they raise no incompatibility. But in a capitalist economic system, a structure of 'natural' rates of profit would inevitably clash with a few basic institutional mechanisms.[13]

To begin with, it is a fundamental principle of a capitalist economy that capital funds are to be left free to move from one sector to another. This means that competition will drive them out of low-profit sectors and direct them towards the sectors with the highest rates of profit. A most characteristic tendency is thereby induced towards the equalisation of the rates of profit all over the economy. Of course, a perfect equalisation (even when account is taken of the different riskiness of various sectors) can never be achieved in practice. Yet the 'profit motive' is the engine of the whole system and makes that tendency an inevitable one.

Moreover, the very fact that consumption by the owners of the means of production must necessarily be positive implies that there cannot be any tendency towards 'natural' profits (not even in the aggregate) if full

---

arise, the foregoing analysis has also shown how the process of economic growth of an economic system is something different and independent of the process of taking rational decisions. An economic system might be growing very fast (because of rapid change in technical knowledge and population) and nevertheless not be making the best choices about consumption or not be adopting the most efficient production methods available at each particular point in time. Conversely, an economic system might be making the best decisions about consumption and be exploiting the best techniques which are available at each particular point of time, and nevertheless be growing slowly or not be growing at all. Growth depends on how fast a society learns, while the optimum choice of the available possibilities depends on how well a society is organised to carry out rational decisions. No doubt there are connections between the two problems but they are two separate and different problems altogether. One of the most important consequences is, for example, that there is no reason to expect that the institutional arrangements which are the best for promotion of the former should also be the best for promotion of the latter and vice versa.

13 This is the reason why, in the whole analysis of the previous chapters, I have preferred to take the rate of profit as exogenously given and to come back to it only at the stage of the present chapter. This approach has permitted avoiding any specific reference to capitalist or socialist economic systems.

employment is to be kept in the economic system as a whole. In other words, as a mere condition for keeping full employment through time, a (tendentially uniform) rate of profit can never be equal to, and in fact will have to be higher than, the weighted average of the sectoral 'natural' rates of profit. If s_c is the proportion of income that tends to be saved by the people who own the means of production, then only in the extreme, but impossible, case in which $s_c = 1$ could total profits be equal to total equilibrium investments. If, as is inevitable, $s_c < 1$, then, even at the level of the economic system as a whole (let alone at the sectoral level), to insist on actual profits being equal to 'natural' profits would become incompatible with the fulfilment of the equilibrium conditions, i.e. with both the sectoral investment conditions (V.4.3) – and thus (VII.10.1) – and the macro-economic effective demand condition (V.4.4). The only way to keep these conditions satisfied, i.e. the only way to keep the economic system on the dynamic path of full employment and full productive capacity utilisation, is to give up any aiming at 'natural' profits, and allow the over-all rate of profit to diverge from, and, more precisely, to rise above, the over-all rate of growth for the economy as a whole. Calling π_e this new rate of profit, we may write:

$$(VII.15.1) \qquad\qquad \pi_e = \frac{1}{s_c}(g + r^*),$$

where r^* is the over-all (weighted) average rate of growth of per capita demand.

The over-all, and uniform, rate of profit (VII.15.1) must therefore be taken, with reference to a capitalist economy, as the equilibrium rate of profit. It represents the rate of profit that must be realised in order to maintain full employment and full productive capacity utilisation in the economic system, over time. Expression (VII.15.1) is in fact very general. As I have shown elsewhere,[14] π_e is entirely independent, in the long run, of the savings behaviour of the workers, provided only that the workers' total savings are not as high as to provide all the over-all savings required by the equilibrium level of investment (VII.10.1).[15]

All this means that, when referring the present analysis to a capitalist economy, equilibrium relation (VII.15.1) must replace the set of the sectoral relations (VII.3.1). The (VII.15.1), when the rate of profit is uniform, becomes the extra equation which is needed in order to close

14 'Rate of Profit and Income Distribution in relation to the Rate of Economic Growth' in *The Review of Economic Studies*, 1962; reprinted in *Growth and Income Distribution – Essays in Economic Theory*, Cambridge 1974.

15 In this extreme case, the working class would come to own the entire stock of capital goods and all capitalists would disappear from the (no longer capitalist) system. See essay VI of my *Growth and Income Distribution, op. cit.*

he price equations system. An important consequence is of course that, with relation (VII.15.1) in the place of (VII.3.1), the model loses its remarkable properties concerning value, associated with the 'natural' prices, and reverts back to a theory of value in terms of labour equivalents. The jump is more than just a formal one. For, this analysis amounts to a demonstration that a theory of value in terms of pure labour can never reflect the price structure that emerges from the operation of the market in a capitalist economy, simply because the market is an institutional mechanism that makes proportionality to physical quantities of labour impossible to realise.

To conclude this discussion on the special problems arising within particular institutions, we may say that, in a capitalist economic system, an incompatibility arises between the attainment of the structure of natural' rates of profit and the maintenance of a full employment dynamic equilibrium. Full employment can, however, be maintained by giving up any pretence of aiming at the 'natural' rates of profit (and hence at the properties thereof) and allowing the over-all (tendentially uniform) rate of profit to settle at the equilibrium level expressed by (VII.15.1).

16. The role of institutions

A few final and quite general remarks may be added with reference to the institutions of any particular society, as they appear when looked at from the standpoint of the analysis concerning the 'natural' economic system.

What has just been discussed makes it transparent how important it is not to confuse the type of problems that concern the natural economic system and the type of problems that relate to the institutional mechanisms which characterise any society. The former deal with logical relations, or end results, valid in themselves, independently of anything else. The latter are (conceptually) subsidiary to the former and may actually be solved in many different alternative ways. The whole previous analysis has in fact amounted to a demonstration that it is possible to separate the two; that it is possible to build up the conceptual scheme of a 'natural' economic system quite independently of the institutional mechanisms that might bring it into existence. It is with such a conceptual scheme that the present analysis has mainly been concerned. All quantities have been defined on the basis of movements of magnitudes which are given from outside economic analysis; and all relations among economic variables have been investigated, so to speak, in their pure economic form, and in the logical succession in which they determine one another within the logical scheme which has been called the natural economic system, quite independently of the order (which may be different) in which they may be aimed at in practice, within any particular institutional set-up.

But when this is granted, i.e. when it is granted that it is possible, on purely logical grounds, to (conceptually) build up the framework of a natural economic system, it becomes inevitable to think that it must be one of the aims of any society to bring the actual economic structure as near as possible to the one defined by the natural economic system; i.e., to organise itself, to devise institutional mechanisms, such as to make the actual economic quantities permanently tend towards their 'natural' levels or dynamic paths.

This task, however, should not be taken as an all-or-nothing undertaking. Some of the 'natural' features of an economic system may not be attainable, or may be attainable only approximately, within any specific institutional set-up. We have seen in the previous section, for example, that in a capitalist economy it is impossible to actually attain the natural structure of the rates of profit, and therefore to achieve a price structure proportional to physical quantities of labour. This does not prevent the operation of institutional mechanisms leading to prices and to choices of technique that are the most profitable in terms of labour equivalents, nor does it exclude the setting up of institutional bodies in charge of full employment policies. Similarly, as we have seen since chapter II (section 3), the sectoral variables of our systems of equations – prices and quantities – have been determined independently of the equilibrium conditions. This means that society may set up institutional mechanisms to achieve efficient structures of prices and outputs even if it is still failing in other respects, e.g. even if it is still far away, for lack of capital accumulation in the past, from the possibility of achieving full employment. And so on, and so forth.

Therefore, while the evaluation of analyses and of problems concerning the natural economic system should not, at least in principle, give rise to discussions that go beyond the application of the logical method in economic analysis, an appropriate evaluation of the institutions of society necessarily encompasses much wider fields of analyses, which may go far beyond economic theory. It may actually be impossible, in the end, to arrive at definite conclusions valid for all times and all places on the suitability of one type of institution or another. Different institutional arrangements may turn out to involve different types of failures, and thus to have different advantages and disadvantages, or to work reasonably well at some stages and not so well at other stages of economic development and technological change.

All these considerations only come to confirm how important it is to keep the logical problems concerning the 'natural' economic system quite separate from those concerning the institutions, and to consider the institutions for what they really are – means, and not ends in themselves. Once their instrumental role is properly understood and recognised, it becomes much easier also to operate on them in as detached a way as is possible; to treat them as instruments susceptible to being continually improved and changed, in relation to their suitability (or unsuitability) to ensure tendencies, or near-tendencies, towards agreed ends.

Chapter VIII

The 'natural' rate of interest

1. Personal savings as distinct from over-all savings

Savings and consumption, in the whole of the previous analysis, have
been considered from the standpoint of the economic system as a whole.
Total savings have emerged from the equilibrium investment conditions
(V.4.3) – summarised by (VII.10.1) – and total equilibrium consumption has emerged, by subtraction, from the macro-economic effective
demand condition (V.4.4).

But savings for the economic system as a whole, physically determined by the amount of total investments, must not be confused with
the vast possibilities of *personal* savings which are open to the single
individuals. The best way to make this distinction clear is to begin by
analysing the case of a hypothetical economy in which no investment is
required and in which therefore there is absolutely no over-all saving.
This is the case of the hypothetical economic system considered in
chapter II above, sections 1–3, in which goods are supposed to be made
by labour alone – a 'pure labour' economy. It is absolutely clear, in this
case, that no savings whatever are possible for the economic system as a
whole.[1] Yet, for the single individuals, the possibilities of personal
savings are entirely open. In the following pages we shall concentrate
precisely on these possibilities of personal savings. Once the inter-
personal savings relations have been clarified for this simple case, it will
become easy to show how they remain basically the same in the more
general case of production with capital goods.

2. The emergence of financial assets and liabilities

In a pure labour economy, there can be no savings for the economic
system as a whole, as has just been pointed out. This is a straightforward
macro-economic consequence of the effective demand equilibrium

---

1 With the exception, of course, of physical hoarding of consumption goods. See footnote
2, below.

condition (II.2.8). The whole productive capacity of the economic system must be devoted to the production of consumption goods. If total demand for consumption goods were to fall short of total potential national income, the difference would simply represent lost consumption, i.e. consumption goods that have been lost through idle productive capacity. This also means that, for the economic system as a whole, foregone consumption in any period of time cannot be transferred to any other period of time. It is lost for ever.[2]

Yet all this does not entail any impossibility for single *individuals* of postponing or bringing forward consumption, i.e. it does not entail any impossibility of *personal* savings and dissavings. Any single individual may indeed abstain from consuming part of his (her) current income, and postpone its consumption, in time, provided that he (she) can find some other individual, or individuals, who are willing to do the opposite.

Operations of this type may be carried out to a very large extent indeed. Individuals have natural lives that are longer than their active lives; moreover they normally have families whose components vary in age, requirements and number, in each particular time period. This means that the time profile of each family's consumption needs will normally differ from the time profile of the family's incoming income, even when their total sums coincide. Hence there may be periods in which a particular family needs to save (income exceeding consumption) and periods in which the same family needs to dissave (consumption exceeding income). Normally these needs for savings and dissavings will arise at different times for different families, so that – within each period of time – those people whose incomes are in excess of their consumption needs may lend their excess purchasing power to those people whose incomes fall short of their consumption needs, and then have it back when the personal situations have reversed.[3]

It is quite evident that, in an economic system with millions of

---

2 The possibility is always open, of course, of physically storing up some non-perishable consumption goods and carrying them over in time. This physical hoarding is indeed possible, though it is subject to strict physical limits. But in order to make our relations emerge clearly and without complications, we shall assume, in the whole of the present chapter, that all consumption goods are perishable, and therefore that there is no physical hoarding of consumption goods. The introduction of physical hoarding of non-perishable consumption goods can always be done at a second analytical stage.

3 This is, of course, the phenomenon that has been at the basis of the 'life-cycle hypothesis' theories of savings, of the type proposed, for example, by Modigliani–Brumberg (Franco Modigliani and Richard Brumberg, 'Utility Analysis and the Consumption Function: An Interpretation of Cross-Section Data', in *Post-Keynesian Economics*, edited by Kenneth K. Kurihara, London, 1955, pp. 388–436) and then extensively developed in the economic literature.

individuals, inter-personal lending and borrowing may take place with very little complication. In theory, in each single period of time, any individual may lend to others an amount of purchasing power up to the whole amount of his (her) current income; and, at other times, may even borrow multiples of the amount of purchasing power corresponding to his (her) current income. There is no practical limit to this lending and borrowing.[4] The only constraint is of a different type – it is a macroeconomic constraint and is imposed by the over-all effective demand equilibrium condition. In any closed economic system, all personal lending and borrowing must cancel each other out. There can be no net savings or dissavings for the economic system as a whole, however large personal savings and dissavings may be.

Now we come to a consequence of crucial importance. The coming into being of inter-personal lending and borrowing relations, in any economic system, entails the emergence of financial assets and liabilities. This means that even when no physical stocks of goods are carried through time (as in the case we are considering here) the economic system will normally carry *financial* stocks through time, representing claims to future consumption by some individuals as against others. Over-all, positive and negative claims – i.e. financial assets and liabilities – necessarily cancel each other out. Yet they may grow to very large amounts indeed and, through them, single individuals have the possibility of making their annual consumption go well beyond or restrict it much below the (physically determined) amounts of their annual incomes.

3. The emergence of a rate of interest

The immediate consequence of the introduction of financial stocks into our analysis is that it becomes no longer indifferent which commodity is chosen as the *numéraire* of the price system (as opposed to the case in which financial stocks do not exist). For, the choice of *numéraire* ties down all debts and credits to being constant through time in terms of the particular commodity chosen as *numéraire*; while, at the same time, all 'natural' prices are changing in terms of that *numéraire*.

If the percentage rates of growth of productivity in the $n-1$ (vertically integrated) sectors are $\varrho_1, \varrho_2, \ldots, \varrho_h, \ldots, \varrho_{n-1}$, ranked in a decreasing order, and if commodity h is the one that is used as *numéraire*, which means that all debts and credits are stipulated in terms of commodity h, then all debts and credits will clearly remain constant

---

4 Note the contrast with physical hoarding, which meets strict physical limits.

only in terms of commodity h. In terms of any other commodity, the purchasing power of all debts and credits will change. More precisely, over time, all debts and credits will revalue at rate $(\varrho_1 - \varrho_h)$ in terms of commodity 1, at rate $(\varrho_2 - \varrho_h)$ in terms of commodity 2, . . ., at rate $(\varrho_{h-1} - \varrho_h)$ in terms of commodity $(h-1)$. And they will devalue at rate $(\varrho_h - \varrho_{h+1})$ in terms of commodity $(h+1)$, . . ., at rate $(\varrho_h - \varrho_{n-1})$ in terms of commodity $(n-1)$.

This also means that if, for instance, we wanted to change the *numéraire* of the price system, we could not do so without altering the relations among debtors and creditors. If we want to change the *numéraire* and at the same time keep inter-personal relations unaltered, we must introduce a correction in the form of a *rate of interest*,[5] even if no rate of interest had originally been stipulated on the debts and credits in terms of commodity h. For example, if a change of *numéraire* were to be made from commodity h to commodity 1, in order that all debt and credit relations remain unaltered, a rate of interest equal to $(\varrho_1 - \varrho_h)$ would have to be introduced on all debts reckoned in terms of the new *numéraire* (on the top of whatever rate of interest had been stipulated already when debts were reckoned in terms of the old *numéraire*).

A discussion becomes necessary, at this point, on the meaning and foundations of a rate of interest.

4. A whole series of own-rates of interest implied by the same (actual) rate of interest

We may notice that the existence of financial assets and liabilities, when coupled with a structural dynamics of natural prices, implies the existence, not of one rate of interest, but of a whole series of rates of interest. More precisely, it implies the existence of a particular own-rate of interest for each commodity.

To illustrate the point, suppose that the wage rate is chosen as the *numéraire* for all time, i.e. $w(t) = 1$, and suppose that loans, in terms of the wage rate, are stipulated at a rate of interest equal to zero. Thus, when a loan expires, the lender simply receives back from the borrower an amount of purchasing power (in terms of labour) equal to the amount that was lent at the beginning, without having received any interest in the meantime. However, the natural price of each commodity j, in terms of labour, has been decreasing in the meantime at the percentage rate ϱ_j; $j = 1, 2, \ldots, n-1$. Hence the amount of the loan repaid at time t, although unchanged in terms of labour, could purchase a quantity of

---

5 For simplicity's sake, as before, we shall talk of a 'rate of interest' to mean a *percentage* rate of interest per period of time.

each commodity j equal to $q_j(0)e^{\varrho_j t}$, *where* $q_j(0)$ is the quantity of commodity j which the amount that is repaid could purchase at time zero. This means that the amount of the loan, though unchanged in terms of labour, has grown in terms of each specific commodity j at a compound rate of interest equal to ϱ_j; $j = 1, 2, \ldots, n-1$. Percentage rate ϱ_j therefore represents, in this case, what may be called *the own-rate of interest for commodity j*. There are $(n-1)$ such own-rates of interest, namely:

(VIII.4.1)
$$\varrho_1, \varrho_2, \ldots, \varrho_{n-1},$$

for commodities $1, 2, \ldots, n-1$, respectively; all implied by an actual rate of interest equal to zero in terms of the wage rate. If the actual rate of interest, stipulated on loans in terms of the wage rate, were $i_w > 0$, instead of being zero, then the series of own-rates of interest implied by i_w would be:

(VIII.4.2)
$$(i_w + \varrho_1), (i_w + \varrho_2), \ldots, (i_w + \varrho_{n-1}),$$

for commodities $1, 2, \ldots, n-1$ respectively.

The same concepts may alternatively be illustrated with reference to the case in which a particular commodity (instead of the wage rate) – let us say commodity h – is chosen as *numéraire* in terms of which loans are reckoned through time, i.e. the case in which $p_h(t) = 1$. In this case, if an actual rate of interest i_h is stipulated, to be paid on loans reckoned in terms of commodity h, then this actual rate of interest i_h clearly implies a series of own-rates of interest:

(VIII.4.3)
$$(i_h + \varrho_1 - \varrho_h), (i_h + \varrho_2 - \varrho_h), \ldots, (i_h + \varrho_{h-1} - \varrho_h),$$
$$i_h + \varrho_h - \varrho_h = i_h, (i_h + \varrho_{h+1} - \varrho_h), \ldots, (i_h + \varrho_{n-1} - \varrho_h),$$

for commodities $1, 2, \ldots, h-1, h, h+1, \ldots, n-1$, respectively; and also an own-rate of interest,

(VIII.4.4)
$$i_h + 0 - \varrho_h = i_h - \varrho_h,$$

for labour.

5. The 'nominal' or 'money' rate of interest

The rates of interest considered in the previous section (though one of them is explicit, and the other $n-1$ own-rates are implicit) are all 'real' rates of interest, in the sense that each of them refers to purchasing power in terms of a specific physical commodity.

But situations usually arise in which the *numéraire* that is chosen is neither the wage rate nor any physical commodity, but that particular unit of account which is at the basis of money.

In the past, money has actually been a particular commodity, notably gold. And even when gold disappeared from actual circulation, all monetary authorities tried, for some time, to keep a link between the monetary unit and a certain physical quantity of gold (the so called 'gold exchange standard' monetary system). But this system has by now ceased to operate.

In our own day, money is nothing but a particular type of credit. It is normally represented by paper credit certificates, issued by a Central Bank, that are accepted in settlement of debts. Such credit certificates – paper money – are issued in terms of a purely conventional unit of account (the pound-sterling, the dollar, the rouble, the franc, the lira, etc.). This means that when loans are stipulated in terms of such a conventional unit of account, the rate of interest which is paid on them is itself reckoned in terms of the same monetary unit. And since the monetary unit of account is a purely conventional one, the rate of interest, in terms of money, or *money rate of interest*, which we shall call i_M, cannot but be a *nominal* rate of interest.

The problem arises, at this point, of finding the relation between the 'nominal' (or 'money') rate of interest and the n 'real' own-rates of interest.

6. Price changes and the 'rate of inflation'

We know that all the (relative) 'natural' prices and the wage rate are linked to one another according to relations (II.6.3), and we know that their relative movements through time are linked to one another by relations (V.9.2). These relative movements through time, in the particular case considered here of a pure labour economy, can even more simply be written in terms of the (percentage) rates of change of commodity prices, which will be denoted by $\sigma_1, \sigma_2, \ldots, \sigma_{n-1}$, and of the (percentage) rate of change of the wage rate, σ_w. We may simply write:

(VIII.6.1) $\qquad \sigma_j = \sigma_w - \varrho_j, \qquad\qquad\qquad j = 1, 2, \ldots, n-1.$

If the economic system keeps to its 'natural' structure, as we are supposing here, it is the *relative* prices that are linked to one another, both at any initial point of time and through time. The absolute level of prices – i.e. one of the prices in (II.6.3) – and the speed of the over-all movement of prices through time – i.e. one of the rates of change in

(V.9.2), or alternatively, in (VIII.6.1) – are to be fixed from outside the price system. These are the two degrees of freedom that need to be closed from outside the price system. We have seen in chapter V (section 12) that this can be done, in general, by simply fixing the initial wage rate and its rate of change through time in exponential function (V.12.3), in terms of any arbitrarily chosen *numéraire*.

When the *numéraire* of the price system is a conventional monetary unit of account (paper money), we may fix:

$$(VIII.6.2) \qquad w(0) = \bar{w}^{(M)}(0),$$

at time zero, where $\bar{w}^{(M)}$ is the wage rate in terms of the conventional monetary unit of account. Then, through the (II.6.3), all prices are determined in terms of money at time zero. And moreover we may fix:

$$(VIII.6.3) \qquad \sigma_w = \bar{\sigma}_w.$$

Then the rates of change of all prices, in terms of money, are determined by the (VIII.6.1).

But what are now the relations of the monetary with the 'real' magnitudes? It is here that a profound difference comes to light between a price system in which a physical commodity is used as *numéraire* and one in which prices are measured in terms of a conventional unit of account (paper money). In the former case, the unit of reference is a well defined physical magnitude (e.g. an ounce of gold). Its price is equal to unity, by definition, and remains unity through time (its rate of change cannot but be zero). More specifically, in this case, the two degrees of freedom contained in the price system are inherently coupled to each other and in fact reduce to one. On the other hand, in the case of prices expressed in terms of a conventional monetary unit of account (paper money), even after fixing one of the prices, in terms of money, at time zero (or alternatively after fixing the wage rate, in terms of money) complete freedom still remains as to its movement through time. The degrees of freedom of the price system, as was pointed out in chapter V, remain two in this case. A further equation is needed besides the initial one, and this is precisely what is provided by equation (VIII.6.3).

Note that, in (VIII.6.3), $\bar{\sigma}_w$ can be given *any* value. In other words, the wage rate, in terms of money, can grow at *any* rate. But of course an arbitrary growth of the wage rate would be a purely nominal growth. What becomes important is to find its relation to the movements of the 'real' magnitudes. It is precisely for this purpose, as we may now realise, that the 'dynamic standard commodity' defined in chapter V (section 14) becomes of particular relevance.

The dynamic standard commodity is an ideal commodity for which productivity changes through time at the 'standard' rate ϱ^*, i.e. at the weighted average of the rates of change of productivity in the whole economic system. It may therefore be taken as the 'real' standard of reference. We know that if the wage rate, in terms of any conventional unit, were to move through time precisely at the 'standard' rate of growth ϱ^*, i.e. if it were to happen that

(VIII.6.4)
$$\bar{\sigma}_w = \varrho^*,$$

then all prices would *ipso facto* turn out to be measured in terms of the dynamic standard commodity. Each price $p_j(t)$ would change through time at the very specific rate:

(VIII.6.5)
$$\varrho^* - \varrho_j, \qquad j = 1, 2, \ldots, n-1.$$

This means that half of the prices, on average, would decrease (those referring to commodities with above-average increases in productivity) and the other half of the prices, on average, would increase (those referring to commodities with below-average growths of productivity), while the weighted average of all the rates of change would be exactly zero.

We may indeed refer to a situation of this type as a situation of (average) price stability. This ideal situation represents our basic point of reference.

Clearly any time that:

(VIII.6.6)
$$\bar{\sigma}_w > \varrho^*,$$

i.e. any time that the money wage rate increases at a rate of growth higher than ϱ^*, the over-all level of prices is increasing, even though some prices might still be decreasing. This is the situation which in common parlance is generally referred to as one of *price inflation*. Conversely, any time that:

(VIII.6.7)
$$\bar{\sigma}_w < \varrho^*,$$

the over-all level of prices is decreasing, though some of the prices might still be increasing – a situation of price deflation.

Therefore, the difference $(\sigma_w - \varrho^*)$, which we may denote by σ_A, i.e.

(VIII.6.8)
$$\sigma_A = \bar{\sigma}_w - \varrho^*,$$

becomes of crucial importance in any monetary economy. By expressing the rate of change through time of the price of the 'dynamic standard commodity' in terms of the monetary unit, it comes to represent the rate of change of the over-all level of prices. It comes to represent what may indeed be called 'the general rate of price inflation'.[6]

We may look at the same concepts in another way. When $(\sigma_w - \varrho^*)$ is different from zero, *all* prices are undergoing the same change through time, over and above whatever change each of them may be undergoing owing to the relative changes of productivity, as expressed by (VIII.6.5). As opposed to changes (VIII.6.5), which are specific to each price, change (VIII.6.8) affects all prices in the same way. Each one of the rates of change (VIII.6.1) may in fact now be rewritten in the following way:

(VIII.6.9) $\qquad \sigma_j = (\bar{\sigma}_w - \varrho^*) + (\varrho^* - \varrho_j), \qquad j = 1, 2, \ldots, n - 1.$

This is a general formulation of considerable interest. It evinces explicitly the two components that make up the total rate of change of each price. There is a particular component $(\varrho^* - \varrho_j)$, which is specific to each price, and there is a general component $(\sigma_w - \varrho^*)$, which is common to all prices.

The general component $\sigma_A = (\sigma_w - \varrho^*)$ is precisely the 'general rate of price inflation'; or, as we may say more simply, the 'rate of inflation'.

There is also a reciprocal way of looking at these movements. Rate of change σ_j, with a negative sign, also represents the rate of fall of the purchasing power of the monetary unit in terms of each specific commodity j, $(j = 1, 2, \ldots, n - 1)$. And the rate of change σ_A, with a negative sign (i.e. the opposite of the rate of increase of the money price of the dynamic standard commodity), represents the weighted average rate of fall of the purchasing power of the monetary unit – what may simply be called the rate of fall (through inflation) of the purchasing power of money.

7. The relation between the nominal rates of interest and the 'real' rates of interest – the 'standard' real rate of interest

We are now in a position to specify all the 'real' rates of interest in an

6 Note that no other physical commodity, when chosen as *numéraire*, would enable us to use unambiguously the concept of price inflation. The choice of *numéraire* must therefore be made with care, if the movement of the price level is of any concern. This was hinted at in chapter V (section 14). Even when the *numéraire* is a physical commodity, the movement through time of the average price level does indeed depend on the *numéraire*. For example, choosing as *numéraire* the physical commodity with the fastest growing productivity would yield an over-all level of prices which is constantly increasing; and conversely, choosing as *numéraire* the physical commodity with the slowest growing productivity would yield an over-all level of prices which is constantly decreasing. Only measurement in terms of the dynamic standard commodity can keep the over-all level of prices constant, thus providing the basic point of reference for using the concept of price inflation.

economy with prices based on a conventional monetary unit of account. All debt/credit relations being in terms of money, the rate of interest i_M will also be in terms of money – i.e. it will be a nominal rate of interest.

We can immediately say that, if $\bar{\sigma}_w$ is the rate of growth of the wage rate, in terms of money, the own-rate of interest for labour will be

$$(\text{VIII.7.1}) \qquad i_M - \bar{\sigma}_w = i_M - \sigma_A - \varrho^*,$$

and consequently the own-rate of interest for each commodity j – as obtained from (VIII.6.1), (VIII.6.8), (VIII.6.9) – will be:

$$(\text{VIII.7.2}) \qquad i_M - \sigma_j = i_M - (\bar{\sigma}_w - \varrho_j) = i_M - \sigma_A - (\varrho^* - \varrho_j),$$
$$j = 1, 2, \ldots, n-1.$$

These are the n 'real' rates of interest (own-rates of interest) corresponding to the nominal rate of interest i_M and to the rate of increase $\bar{\sigma}_w$ of the wage rate, in terms of money.

But we now also possess a more synthetic expression for the whole set of real rates of interest taken together. By considering the nominal rate of interest i_M with reference to that particular composite commodity which we have called the 'dynamic standard commodity', we obtain from (VIII.7.2), as a particular case:

$$(\text{VIII.7.3}) \qquad i_M - (\bar{\sigma}_w - \varrho^*) = i_M - \sigma_A,$$

which, as we may see, is simply the difference between the money rate of interest and the rate of inflation. This is the own-rate of interest for the dynamic standard commodity. It represents a sort of average 'real' rate of interest for the economic system as a whole. We may call it the 'standard' real rate of interest.

It may be interesting to bring attention again to the difference between the case of any physical commodity (or the wage rate) used as *numéraire*, and the case of a conventional monetary unit of account (paper money). In the former case the own-rates of interest, as appear from (VIII.4.2) or (VIII.4.3), (VIII.4.4) depend on the actual rate of interest, in terms of the chosen *numéraire*, and on the rates of growth of productivity. In the case of paper money, the own-rates of interest, as appear from (VIII.7.1), (VIII.7.2), (VIII.7.3), depend not only on the actual money rate of interest and on the rates of growth of productivity, but also on the changing purchasing power of money, as expressed by the rate of price inflation. In other words, a nominal rate of interest (the money rate of interest) does not acquire any 'real' meaning until it is put into relation with the rate of price inflation.

8. The correct problem concerning the rate of interest

It should be evident, from the foregoing analysis, that it would make no sense at this point to posit the question of whether there should be or whether there should not be a rate of interest. A *whole structure* of rates of interest exists in any case, whatever the actual 'nominal' rate of interest (even if it were fixed at zero) and whatever the *numéraire* chosen as the basis of the price system. In other words, a whole structure of own-rates of interest – all of them 'real' rates of interest – is unavoidably inherent in the structural dynamics of relative prices.

If a problem is to be posited at all, therefore, this problem is that of finding which is the appropriate level at which to peg the whole structure of the own-rates of interest. Given the *numéraire* that has been chosen – let us say a conventional monetary unit – and given the rate of change of the wage rate in terms of money (or alternatively the rate of change of any one of the commodity prices), we have seen that there are well defined relations between the evolution of the money prices and the evolution of the purchasing power of the monetary unit, in terms of each physical commodity. The problem that arises is therefore that of singling out which money rate of interest is the correct one to apply to all debt/credit relations, stipulated in terms of the monetary unit.

More specifically, the problem to be solved – within the present theoretical framework – may be stated in the following manner. From the infinite number of possible levels of the actual rate of interest (and by implication of the structure of the own-rates of interest), is there a particular one that may be called the 'natural' level of the rate of interest? (And, by implication is there a 'natural' level of the whole structure of the own-rates of interest?)

9. The 'natural' rate of interest

Any answer to the question stated at the end of the previous section requires the adoption of a certain criterion. And in the present context, the logical criterion to adopt is quite straightforward, as it follows from the basic approach to economic reality which has been taken. We may begin by stating it straight away in the following manner. In an economic system in which all contributions to, and benefits from, the production process are regulated on the basis of quantities of labour, the 'natural' rate of interest cannot but be a zero rate of interest in terms of labour.

We have seen already, in section 4, that a zero rate of interest in terms of labour implies a rate of interest equal to ϱ_1 in terms of commodity 1, a rate of interest equal to ϱ_2 in terms of commodity 2, . . ., a rate of interest equal to ϱ_{n-1} in terms of commodity $n-1$, and, we may now add, a rate of interest equal to ϱ^* in terms of the 'dynamic standard commodity'. We may therefore call this the 'natural' structure of the own-rates of interest. Clearly, given this structure of own-rates of interest, what the actual rate of interest will have to be in order to bring that structure into being depends on the *numéraire*. Hence, the (actual) natural rate of interest does depend on the *numéraire*. If we denote the natural rate of interest by an asterisk, i.e. if we represent it by i^*, we shall normally have to add a subscript to this symbol in order to specify the *numéraire* in terms of which all debt/credit relations are reckoned.

When the *numéraire* chosen is the wage rate (i.e. when $w(t) = 1$) and all debt/credit relations are reckoned in terms of labour, then the natural rate of interest, to be denoted by i_w^*, turns out to be:

(VIII.9.1) $$i_w^* = 0.$$

When the *numéraire* chosen is any commodity j (i.e. when $p_j(t) = 1$) and all debt/credit relations are stipulated in terms of commodity j, then the natural rate of interest i_j^* turns out to be:

(VIII.9.2) $$i_j^* = \varrho_j, \qquad\qquad j = 1, 2, \ldots, n-1.$$

And when, as a particular case, the *numéraire* chosen is that singularly interesting composite commodity which we have called the 'dynamic standard commodity', the natural rate of interest (which we may denote in this case by i_A^*) turns out to be equal to the 'standard' rate of productivity growth:

(VIII.9.3) $$i_A^* = \varrho^*.$$

The usual case, however, will be the one in which the *numéraire* chosen is a conventional monetary unit of account and all debt/credit relations are stipulated in terms of such a monetary unit. In this case the natural rate of interest (in terms of money) may be expressed with reference to the average movement through time of all prices. We know that such movement coincides with the movement of the price of the 'dynamic standard commodity'. Hence we only need to take (VIII.9.3) and add to it the rate of change σ_A. We obtain:

(VIII.9.4) $$i_M^* = \varrho^* + \sigma_A.$$

This is the natural, *money*, rate of interest. It is simply equal to the standard rate of productivity growth plus the rate of inflation.

We may note that all these expressions are equivalent, in real terms. They simply represent different ways, in relation to the particular choice of *numéraire*, of making the price system produce the same 'real' effects, i.e. of making it produce the same structure of (natural) own-rates of interest and thus of preserving intact through time the original purchasing power of all loans in terms of labour.

But there is a particularly remarkable expression that emerges from all these elaborations. Since $\varrho^* + \sigma_A = \varrho^* + \sigma_w - \varrho^* = \sigma_w$, (VIII.9.4) may also be written:

(VIII.9.4a) $\qquad\qquad\qquad i_M^* = \sigma_w.$

But the same can also be said of (VIII.9.3), of (VIII.9.2), of (VIII.9.1)! In other words, these expressions may also be written, respectively, as:

(VIII.9.3a) $\qquad\qquad\qquad i_A^* = \sigma_w,$

(VIII.9.2a) $\qquad\qquad\qquad i_j^* = \sigma_w,$

(VIII.9.1a) $\qquad\qquad\qquad i_w^* = \sigma_w,$

where the wage rate is measured, in each expression, in terms of the corresponding *numéraire*. Thus, in general, whatever the *numéraire* may be, the natural rate of interest possesses the remarkable property of always being equal to the rate of change of the wage rate.

We may therefore write, without the need of any subscript,

(VIII.9.5) $\qquad\qquad\qquad i^* = \sigma_w,$

where σ_w is the percentage rate of change of the wage rate, expressed in whatever *numéraire* is chosen as the basis of all debt/credit relations.

This is the simplest of all expressions of the 'natural rate of interest' – a rate of interest which preserves intact through time the purchasing power of all loans in terms of labour.

10. Natural rate of interest and income distribution

A practical implication of the definition which has just been given is that, since productivity growth is normally positive, the (actual) natural rate of interest will normally be positive (the only exception occurring when the *numéraire* chosen is the wage rate, which implies by definition $\sigma_w = 0$). This means that, at the end of each time period, interest will normally have to be paid on loans. And it may not be immediately clear what implications this may have for income distribution in an economic system in which income is to be distributed in proportion to labour contributed to the production process.

168

To investigate this question, we may begin by considering first the case in which the *numéraire* chosen is the wage rate and all debt/credit relations are reckoned in terms of labour. One can see clearly, in this case, that in each time period the whole national income is distributed to people in proportion to labour contributed. Then, side by side with the income distribution process carried out by natural prices, a whole series of debt/credit relations may come into being owing to the needs of single individuals to transfer personal consumption through time. Some people may save and other people may dissave by exchanging positive and negative purchasing power among themselves, while all financial transactions cancel out for the economic system as a whole. Since all debts and credits are in terms of the wage rate, and the natural rate of interest is therefore equal to zero, each creditor will receive, at maturity, an amount of purchasing power, in terms of labour, which is exactly equal to the amount originally lent. It appears absolutely clear, in this case, that an income distribution process is in operation which distributes income, through time as well as at any given point in time, on the basis of quantities of labour. All national income, whether at any given point of time or through time, is distributed to the people in proportion to the labour they have contributed to the production process. We may well say that income is distributed according to a 'labour principle of income distribution'.

But we can also easily see that the situation remains exactly the same, in real terms, with any other *numéraire*, provided that a *natural rate of interest is charged*. Suppose for example that a particular (single or composite) commodity h is taken as the *numéraire* of the price system and that all debt/credit relations are reckoned in terms of commodity h. Then the natural rate of interest on loans is $i_h^* = \varrho_h$. At the end of each time period, the national income, measured in terms of commodity h, is distributed in proportion to labour contributed to the production process. But now loans are stipulated in terms of commodity h, and since labour productivity in sector h is increasing at rate ϱ_h, the wage rate, in terms of commodity h, will increase through time at rate ϱ_h. This means that, *in terms of the wage rate*, all financial assets are devaluing through time at rate ϱ_h. It is precisely in order to compensate for this devaluation that the (natural) rate of interest $i_h^* = \varrho_h$ has to be paid on all loans. If interests were in fact not paid, but cumulated at the end of each period with the amounts of the loans, all financial assets and liabilities would grow in time at rate ϱ_h, in terms of commodity h, but would remain constant in terms of labour. In real terms, the situation would be exactly the same as in the previous case, in which $w(t) = 1$. If, on the other hand, as is more usually the case, interest is actually paid at

169

the end of each time period, then the illusion might be created that some income is distributed to rentiers. But this is not the case. When interest is computed at the *natural* rate, the interest paid correctly compensates for the devaluation of loans in terms of labour.

Exactly the same arguments could be restated for the case in which a conventional monetary unit of account (paper money) is used as *numéraire* in terms of which all debt/credit relations are stipulated. We have seen that, in this case, the natural rate of interest is $i_M^* = \sigma_A + \varrho^*$ – see (VIII.9.4) – which is also equal to σ_w, the rate of increase of the money wage rate. And this is precisely the rate at which all financial assets and liabilities devalue through time in terms of labour. Therefore, the payment of a rate of interest equal to σ_w again takes the character of a correct compensation for the devaluation of all loans in terms of labour.

Thus, whatever the *numéraire* in terms of which loans are stipulated, the definition of a natural rate of interest, given in the previous section, allows us to say that the actual payments of natural interest on financial assets have the character of partial repayments of debts, since the debts themselves – when they are stipulated in terms of a *numéraire* other than the wage rate – devalue in terms of labour precisely by the amount that is paid as natural interest. Only the payment of natural interest will correctly compensate for this devaluation through time, thereby ensuring no distortion from the 'labour principle of income distribution'.

We can in fact go on and draw a further important conclusion. Any actual rate of interest, when it differs from the natural rate of interest, inevitably *distorts* the distribution of income from taking place in proportion to labour contributed to the production process. A higher than natural rate of interest distorts the distribution of income in favour of creditors (who would be able through time to 'command' more labour than they have contributed); and conversely a lower than natural rate of interest distorts income distribution in favour of the debtors (who would repay through time an amount which can 'command' less labour than they have been able to use). Only a *natural* rate of interest (provided of course that natural prices prevail) ensures that no distortion in income distribution takes place.

An alternative way of defining the natural rate of interest is therefore simply to say that the natural rate of interest is that particular rate of interest which ensures no distortion from the labour principle of income distribution; that is to say from the principle that national income be distributed, at any given point of time as well as through time, in proportion to labour contributed to the production process.

11. The more general case of production with labour and capital goods

The more general case in which production requires not only labour but also capital goods may now be considered rather expeditiously.

In this case, the equilibrium conditions for the economic system as a whole entail an amount of over-all savings equal to the amount of over-all investments. However, these savings do not concern single individuals. If natural prices prevail, and therefore include a natural rate of profit, each sector of the economy will receive an amount of profits precisely equal to the amount of its equilibrium investments. There is therefore no need for any borrowing or lending by the production units in a 'natural' economic system. All savings that are needed for production automatically accrue to the appropriate sectors, in the appropriate amounts, by virtue of the operation of the natural price system. This also means that productive units (the whole production section of the community) will never need to pay any interest, simply because they will never need to undertake any loan.

Borrowing and lending possibilities are, on the other hand, completely open to the single individuals, precisely in the same way as in the previous simplified case of a pure labour economy.

Note that, from what is said above, total consumption has to be equal to total wages, exactly as in the previous case of a pure labour economy. The only difference from the previous case is that total consumption for the economic system as a whole is now represented no longer by total national income, but by total national income minus the amount of equilibrium investment. The major conclusion of the previous case therefore remains unaltered: the equilibrium total amount of consumption goods cannot be transferred through time. Within each single time period, it is either produced and consumed, or it is lost (through idle productive capacity). And when it is lost, it is lost for ever.

But what is impossible for the economic system as a whole is possible for any single individual. Each single individual (and his/her family) can consume more or can consume less than the incoming wage income to any extent, *provided that* some other individuals (and their families) are prepared to do the opposite. The only constraint that is in operation is therefore the same macro-economic constraint of the previous, simpler, case. For the economic system as a whole, all personal lendings and borrowings must cancel out.

The problem then again arises of the emergence of financial assets and liabilities due to inter-personal credit/debts relations. And the related problem arises of finding *which* rate of interest is the appropriate

171

one to apply to all these inter-personal loans. Here again the conclusions of the previous analysis can be extended in a straightforward manner. We may in fact go straight to the conclusion drawn at the end of section 9 and begin by simply saying that there exists a 'natural' rate of interest which is that particular rate of interest that preserves over time the original purchasing power of all loans in terms of labour. In other words, in general, and quite independently of whether we consider an economic system that does or does not need capital goods. the natural rate of interest is equal to the percentage rate of growth of the wage rate in terms of whatever *numéraire* has been chosen.

Very little needs in fact to be added here to show the general validity of this proposition. All that is required is a re-interpretation of the symbols used to represent the structure of the own-rates of interest. To make this point clear, let us begin by supposing, for simplicity, that the rate of growth of the wage rate, in terms of the chosen *numéraire*, is exactly zero; more specifically, let us suppose that the wage rate is fixed at unity for all time (i.e. $w(t) = 1$). The actual 'natural' rate of interest, in this case, is equal to zero. But, then, the price of each commodity j in terms of the wage rate, as appears from (V.9.2), will decrease in time at a percentage rate which is a weighted average of the rate of growth of productivity in sector j and the rate of growth of productivity in sector k (the sector that produces capital goods for sector j). This weighted-average rate of growth of productivity is a rate of growth of productivity vertically integrated one further stage back, to include also the making of capital goods for consumption good j, $(j = 1, 2, \ldots, n - 1)$. We have already come across this rate of change on a previous occasion – in chapter V, section 13 – and we have denoted it by the symbol ϱ_j'. It represents the rate of growth of productivity in the vertically hyper-integrated sector for consumption good j. It clearly follows that, when $w(t) = 1$, the own-rates of interest for the $(n - 1)$ consumption goods will be:

$$(\text{VIII.11.1}) \qquad \varrho_1', \varrho_2', \ldots, \varrho_{n-1}',$$

This means that all that we need to do is to replace the $\varrho_1, \varrho_2, \ldots, \varrho_{n-1}$ of our previous analysis with the $\varrho_1', \varrho_2', \ldots, \varrho_{n-1}'$ specified above. These are the 'natural' own-rates of interest for the $n - 1$ consumption goods.

Going now over to considering the cases of all other possible *numéraires*, we may simply refer to the corresponding expressions which have been obtained in the previous sections of this chapter. Again these expressions remain valid for the general case of production with capital goods, provided only that the simple rates of growth of productivity ϱ_1,

$\varrho_2, \ldots, \varrho_{n-1}$ are replaced by the corresponding, more general, rates of growth of productivity $\varrho_1', \varrho_2', \ldots, \varrho_{n-1}'$, referring to the vertically hyper-integrated sectors for consumption goods $1, 2, \ldots, n-1$. Note that the latter include the former as a special case. We need not repeat, therefore, but simply confirm, the analysis of the previous sections 4, 5, 6, 7, 8. The introduction of *durable* capital goods into our analysis carries no complication into our previously considered relations.

As to the final analysis of section 9, there is not even any need to replace any symbol. The 'natural' structure of the own-rates of interest, as expressed by the (VIII.11.1), is precisely the one which is reproduced, in real terms, by an actual rate of interest

(VIII.11.2) $$i^* = \sigma_w,$$

where σ_w is the rate of increase of the wage rate in terms of whatever *numéraire* may have been chosen, be it a physical commodity – composite or single – labour, or any conventional monetary unit of account (paper money).

The definition of the natural rate of interest stated by (VIII.11.2) – namely that rate of interest that is equal to the rate of increase of the wage rate in terms of whatever *numéraire* has been chosen – emerges therefore as a completely general definition of the natural rate of interest.

12. Rates of interest versus rates of profit

A few further conclusions, following immediately from the foregoing analysis, may be drawn explicitly. The 'natural rate of interest', as has emerged from the analysis of the present chapter, must not be confused with the 'natural rate of profit', as has emerged from the analysis of the previous chapter. Although these concepts originate from the same theoretical scheme, they are two entirely different concepts altogether.

We have seen in the previous chapter that, in any natural economic system, there is a whole series of 'natural' rates of profit:

(VIII.12.1) $$\pi_j^* = g + r_j, \qquad j = 1, 2, \ldots, n-1,$$

which allow the required expansion of production of each commodity j to take place. In the present chapter, we have seen that, when inter-personal debt and credit relations are brought into being, there exists a whole series of 'natural' own-rates of interest

(VIII.12.2) $$\varrho_j', \qquad j = 1, 2, \ldots, n-1,$$

which allows the purchasing power of all financial transactions, expressed in terms of any specific commodity j, to remain constant in terms of labour. Since g is a rate of growth of the labour force, r_j is a rate of growth of per-capita demand and ϱ_j' is a (vertically hyper-integrated) rate of growth of productivity, it follows that the natural rates of profit (VIII.12.1) will in general be different from the natural own-rates of interest (VIII.12.2).

In fact, the whole previous analysis has been deliberately carried out in such a way as to make this contrast emerge sharply. The notion of a natural rate of interest has been made to emerge, in this chapter, from a theoretical scheme in which *ex-hypothesi* there are no capital goods and therefore there can be no rate of profit. Similarly, the notion of a natural rate of profit has been made to emerge, in chapter VII, from a theoretical scheme in which there are no interpersonal debt/credit relations, and therefore there can be no rate of interest. This shows most clearly that a natural rate of interest may indeed exist without any rate of profit, and a natural rate of profit may indeed exist without any rate of interest.

Yet, both the concept of a natural rate of profit and the concept of a natural rate of interest emerge from precisely the same approach to economic reality. The former stems from the principle that all prices be proportional to physical quantities of labour (a labour theory of value); and the latter stems from the principle that all individuals, when they engage in debt/credit relations, should obtain, at any time, an amount of purchasing power that is constant in terms of labour (a labour theory of income distribution). And the two labour theories imply each other.

The difference comes from their expressing the same basic principles within two separate spheres of economic activity. The rate of profit pertains to the sphere of production, which, in a natural economic system, is complete in itself and does not need any financial transaction to achieve self-sustained growth. The rate of interest pertains to the sphere of consumption and to the needs of individual consumers to transfer personal consumption through time. This sphere too is complete in itself, as all inter-personal borrowing and lending must cancel each other out for the economic system as a whole, quite independently of what is happening in the sphere of production.

There is no reason therefore to associate the concept of a natural rate of profit with the concept of a natural rate of interest. The two concepts are theoretically and conceptually distinct from each other. They represent two entirely different things altogether.

13. Rate of interest and rate of profit in capitalist economic systems

Misleading features, on the subject of the rate of interest and the rate of profit, come of course from the major role that interest and profits have historically played in capitalist systems.

We have seen, at the end of the previous chapter (section 15), that a structure of differentiated rates of profit – as a natural economic system would normally require – is incompatible with the institutional set-up of capitalist societies. For, free-market competition inevitably drives capital funds out of low-profit sectors and into high-profit sectors, thereby engendering a tendency towards the equalisation of the rates of profit in all sectors (actually, as we have seen, at a level necessarily higher than that of the weighted average of the natural rates of profit).

We may well add now that another inherent feature of the same institutional set-up is that financial markets are open to both individuals and firms. In other words, lendings and borrowings among individuals, in capitalist economic systems, are not separated from lendings and borrowings among firms, and between firms and individuals, and between individuals, financial intermediaries and firms. In such an institutional context, all financial transactions converge into the same financial market. The tendency becomes inevitable, not only towards the equalisation of the rates of profit all over the economic system, but also towards the equalisation (when account is taken of risk) of the real rate of interest and the over-all rate of profit.

These tendencies have always been taken so much for granted, in the economic literature (which has normally been referred, implicitly if not explicitly, to equilibrium positions of free market economies) as to engender the convention of taking the rate of interest and the rate of profit as being the same thing.

Yet the fact that particular, though important, institutional mechanisms – like those of the capitalist systems – lead to distortions from the natural features of an economic system such as to make the rate of interest and rate of profit tend to coincide should not lead us to confuse the two notions. Both theoretically and conceptually, as pointed out above, they are two distinct and different things.

Chapter IX

The accumulation of capital and related problems

1. Capital accumulation as a condition for equilibrium growth

We have just seen, in the foregoing chapter, that going over, from a simple scheme of production with labour alone, to a more complex scheme of production with capital goods does not make any difference to the theoretical foundations of the rate of interest. It only requires a re-interpretation of the concepts of rates of growth of productivity.

But, of course, from a physical point of view, the introduction of capital goods has a whole series of very conspicuous consequences.

The new investments entail the coming into existence of a whole set of stocks of capital goods – works, buildings, plants, equipment and appliances of all sorts – which are set aside for production, and are then maintained (replaced and renewed) ever after. They represent the most apparent feature of modern economies, the tangible expression of technical progress. Their *raison d'être* is technical. The technical methods of production, in order to be implemented, normally require that some commodities be set aside, kept in existence, and used as means of production.

These commodities – capital goods – are *produced* goods. They are produced by the economic system itself. As far as the technical process is concerned, they are in no economically relevant way different from consumption goods. Many commodities may in fact be used as consumption goods as well as capital goods. But there is a profound difference on the side of demand. Consumption goods are demanded for their own sake, by consumers. This demand is autonomous: it is whatever consumers like it to be. Demand for capital goods, on the other hand, is not autonomous. It is (logically) determined after demand for consumption goods has been decided already, and as a consequence of it, as a condition for equilibrium growth, according to expressions (V.4.3).

It is this *derived demand* aspect of investment goods, due to their being used as means of production, that is new and typical of production systems. There was nothing of the sort in more primitive economies.

As has already been pointed out, an economic system of the production type has additional categories of economic variables, when compared with more primitive types of economic systems. And in the field of the physical quantities, these new categories are precisely represented by the new investments. The complexity of production systems manifests itself precisely in this respect. Production requires the bringing into existence, and the maintenance, of a whole series of capital goods; it requires *a process of capital accumulation*, as a condition for equilibrium growth. In this chapter, we shall concentrate on these problems.

2. Four quantitative notions of 'capital'

It is of course understandable – and for many purposes useful – that, at any given point in time, the whole complex structure of existing capital goods should be referred to by an all inclusive collective noun: capital.

It is less understandable that to such a medley of heterogeneous things economists should have tried so often to give a single quantitative expression valid for all purposes. Not surprisingly, this has turned out to be impossible, except by making a series of almost absurd assumptions (such as those of a one-commodity type of capital, which is also a consumption good, which is malleable and adaptable to all purposes, which can absorb, instantaneously and without cost, any possible type of technical change, etc.).

But there is no reason for disappointment or dismay. One must simply realise that it is in the very nature of 'capital' to be hetero-geneous. Capital goods are economically relevant in too many different ways. Hence, to turn upside down a widespread complaint about the measurement of capital, I might say that the difficulty with capital is not that it is impossible to measure; the difficulty is that it is measurable in too many different ways. But one must specify, first of all, the purpose for which measurement is made. What is of course impossible is to find a type of measurement that can be used for all purposes.

On various occasions, in the course of the present analysis, we have in fact used already, implicitly or explicitly, at least four different quantita-tive notions of 'capital':

(a) First of all, we have talked of capital goods in terms of *physical machines*. In these terms, capital goods are a series of heterogeneous commodities, each having specific technical characteristics. There is no way of expressing all the machines and plants as a single physical entity, except when they are of the same type. In other words, we can add up the numbers of turning-lathes of the same type; but not the number of turning-lathes and the number of cranes.

(b) Secondly, we have been measuring capital goods at *current* prices. That is: the physical units of capital goods have been multiplied by the corresponding prices, expressed in terms of a particular commodity – single or composite – which has been chosen as *numéraire*. This type of measurement provides a standard in terms of which any commodity can be compared with any other. A turning-lathe and a crane may be added up, if each of them is first weighted by its price, expressed in terms of a third commodity, which is used as the common standard. This type of measurement is the most widespread in economic analysis; yet it has turned out to be more limited than was thought. It depends not only on technology, but also on income distribution at any point in time. Current relative prices change, even with a constant technique, when income distribution changes.

(c) A third way in which we have measured capital goods is again in physical terms, but in terms *of units of vertically integrated productive capacity*. A unit of vertically integrated productive capacity is, conceptually, a rather complex unit, as has been pointed out in chapter II (section 4). It is defined with reference to a physical unit of the final commodity which is going to be produced. Yet, when this commodity can be specified, the useful property of this concept is that it has an unambiguous meaning through time, no matter which type of technical change, and how much of it, may occur.[1]

(d) Fourthly, and finally, we have been measuring capital goods in terms of *physical quantities of labour* required to produce them ('embodied labour'). This type of measurement might simply appear to be a particular case of the one mentioned under (b), and of course it is, namely the particular case in which all prices are natural prices and the chosen *numéraire* is the wage rate. It has however an individuality of its own, as it expresses something physically well defined and quite independent of any *numéraire*. What must be realised is that this is not an easy type of measurement to obtain, as it requires evaluation at natural prices with the inclusion of natural rates of profit.

An approximate method of measuring capital goods in these terms consists in taking current values (whatever the rates of profit may be) and dividing them by the wage rate. This approximate type of measure-

1 This property becomes particularly useful, for example, for the problems of the replacement of worn-out equipment. With technical change going on, each machine is never replaced by an exactly similar physical machine, and this makes it impossible to say what it is that is replaced and kept intact. Measurement in terms of units of productive capacity overcomes this impossibility.

ment has been used, among others, by Keynes, who called it measure-ment in terms of wage units,[2] and by Joan Robinson, who has taken it to express what she has called 'real capital'.[3] It has also been used in our previous analysis, since the very beginning, i.e. since chapter II, where it was pointed out that, by taking physical units of productive capacity multiplied by their prices, as expressed by formulations (II.6.3) or (II.7.3), and dividing them by the wage rate, one obtains quantities of what have there been called 'labour equivalents'.

It should not be difficult to realise at this point that a distinction between these four quantitative concepts of 'capital' becomes essential in the context of a dynamic analysis. There is no ground for concentrat-ing on any particular one of them, or for calling any one of them 'superior' to any other. Each one is relevant, but for quite different purposes.[4]

3. The distinction essential for dynamic analysis

We may immediately note that, in a hypothetical world without technical progress, concepts (c) and (d), as defined above, would be superfluous. Methods of measurement (a) would coincide, or rather would have a one–one correspondence, with method (c), since more physical machines would mean more physical productive capacity in the same proportion. And methods (b) would have a one–one correspond-ence with method (d), since more capital in terms of any given commodity-*numéraire* would mean more quantities of labour, in the same proportion.

In fact, this may help to explain why traditional economic analysis has never made use of concepts (c) and (d); or rather, it has always taken concept (a) also to mean concept (c), and concept (b) also to mean concept (d). The association does not matter when the analysis refers to a stationary economic system or concerns comparisons of magnitudes at the same point in time. But the same association breaks down in comparisons through time.

Over time, technical coefficients change, and if technical coefficients change, more productive capacity – concept (c) – does not necessarily entail more machines – concept (a) – and more capital in terms of any

---

2 J. M. Keynes, *The General Theory, op. cit.*

3 Joan Robinson, *The Accumulation of Capital, op. cit.*

4 It may also be worth pointing out explicitly that the four quantitative notions of capital listed above must not be considered as exhaustive. For example, for some purposes, it might well become relevant to measure 'capital' in terms of the employment which it can provide.

given commodity-*numéraire* – concept (b) – does not necessarily entail more physical quantities of 'embodied labour' – concept (d).

Over time, therefore, each one of the four quantitative concepts of capital defined above follows its own path and must carefully be kept distinct from all the others.

4. Ambiguities in the concept of 'roundaboutness': capital intensity versus degree of mechanisation (or capital/output ratio versus capital/labour ratio)

What has just been said carries profound theoretical consequences.

When Böhm-Bawerk and then Wicksell developed their famous theories of capital, they thought – as is well known – that they could present capitalistic production in roughly the following way. It pays for society as a whole to devote its efforts (its 'factors of production') to producing 'capital' first, and then, in subsequent periods of time, to using 'capital', together with further labour, to produce the final commodities which are wanted. By this indirect process, the final commodities can often be obtained from smaller quantities of original 'factors of production' than would be the case by using direct methods. Thereby, the process of capitalistic, as opposed to primitive, production is presented as more efficient by being more *indirect* or *roundabout*.

But there is a serious ambiguity in this conception of 'indirectness' of capitalistic production – an ambiguity which does not reveal itself when one deals with a stationary economy (as both Böhm-Bawerk and Wicksell did), but breaks out strikingly as soon as one goes on to dynamics.

Indirectness or roundaboutness of a production process clearly refers to a relation between stocks and flows. A production method α is said to be 'more indirect' than a production method β if it requires a higher stock of capital goods for given flows. But here is where the ambiguity lies. Which flows are we to consider? The input flows of labour or the output flows of production? We clearly obtain two entirely different concepts altogether according to whether we express the relation between stocks and flows in terms of capital per flow of labour services (the capital/labour ratio) or in terms of capital per flow of output (the capital/output ratio). Let us examine these two concepts in turn, taking the latter first.

The capital/output ratio is the ratio of a stock of capital goods to the flow of output that in each period of time comes out of the production process. Since both stocks and flows are expressed at current prices, the wage rate appears in both of them, i.e. both in the numerator and in the denominator, and therefore cancels out – as may be seen immediately from our formulations (V.11.1), (V.11.4). This means that it does not matter whether capital and output are expressed at current prices or as physical quantities of labour; the ratio is always the same in either case. We may therefore say, that, basically, the capital/output ratio is a ratio of physical quantities of labour.[5] It expresses the physical quantity of labour that, so to speak, has to be kept 'locked up' in the stock of capital goods per unit of physical quantity of labour that in each period of time is required by the current production process. The capital/output ratio may therefore be taken to express that type of 'indirectness' or 'roundaboutness' that has been called the 'degree of capital intensity' of a production process.

It is important to be clear about the economic problems for which the concept of 'capital intensity' is relevant. There are at least two such problems, both of which are of crucial economic importance. First of all, the capital/output ratio is relevant in evaluating the effects of investment on production. That is: for any given production process, the capital/output ratio characterising it expresses the amount of investment that has to be undertaken, i.e. the amount of resources the economic system has to give up, in order to increase by one unit the flow of production. Secondly, and much more importantly, the capital/output ratio is relevant for the problem of price formation. As appears from our formulation (V.9.2), the incidence of capital in each commodity price, i.e. that component of each price which has to be charged for the use of capital, is proportional to the capital/output ratio required in that production process, quite independently of the number or the value of machines operated by each worker. The lower the capital/output ratio, the lower the charge for capital in each price, no matter whether and how much the capital/labour ratio may be changing. This is so much the case that an alternative definition of the concept of capital intensity might well be given in terms of the components of prices. We may indeed say that a process of production α is more 'capital intensive' than a process of production β, if α entails for the price of the commodity being produced a higher proportion of charges for capital (replacements plus profits) to charges for labour (wages). The definition is perfectly general, and is equivalent to the one in terms of the capital/output ratio.

The concept expressed by the capital/labour ratio is quite different.

5 The proposition refers strictly to the case of natural prices. In the case in which prices contain a uniform rate of profit, instead of the corresponding *natural* rates of profit, 'physical quantity of labour' must of course be intended as physical quantity of labour-equivalents (see section 2 above).

As may be seen immediately from our formulations (V.11.2), (V.11.3), (V.11.5), the stock of capital that appears in the numerator is expressed at current prices, while the flow of labour that appears in the denominator is expressed in physical quantities. There is no cancelling out of the wage rate, so that the capital/labour ratio will change for two quite distinct reasons: (i) because of changes in the quantities of labour embodied in the capital goods (for given current labour and wage rate); and (ii) because of changes in the wage rate (for given quantities of embodied and current labour). There is a further difficulty, represented by the fact that the wage rate depends on the *numéraire* – a difficulty that can, however, be overcome immediately by adopting formulation (V.11.3) of our analysis, where the wage rate is specifically expressed in terms of the 'dynamic standard commodity', which means in terms of a constant (average) level of prices.

Now, changes of type (i) affect both the capital/labour ratio and the capital/output ratio, but changes of type (ii) are specific to the capital/labour ratio. Hence, changes of the wage rate will indeed affect the capital/labour ratio, while leaving the capital/output ratio entirely unaffected. To put the problem the other way round, only in the particular case in which the wage rate remains constant will the changes in the capital/labour ratio go in the same direction as the changes in the capital/output ratio (i.e. in capital intensity). But when the wage rate is increasing – which is the typical case of an economy with technical progress – that will no longer be the case. Changes of type (i) and changes of type (ii) will not necessarily go in the same direction; they might well go in opposite directions and partially or totally, or more than totally, compensate and offset each other. This leads us to a first, very important, conclusion – the capital/labour ratio cannot in general be taken as an index of capital intensity. As a consequence, the type of 'indirectness' expressed by the capital/labour ratio is irrelevant for the two crucial problems mentioned above: the determination of new investment and the formation of prices.

To single out the type of 'indirectness' which the capital/labour ratio may be an expression of (as distinct from the type of 'indirectness' expressed by the capital/output ratio) one must look for what is associated with a change in the wage rate, when the proportion between 'locked-up' labour and current labour (i.e. capital intensity) remains constant. Now, an increase in the wage rate at a constant price level reflects an increase in over-all productivity, and an increase in productivity will keep the sectoral capital/output ratio constant only if there is an increase of the degree of mechanisation. We may well say, therefore, that the type of 'indirectness' or 'roundaboutness' that is represented by the capital/labour ratio is an expression of the 'degree of mechanisation' of the production process to which it is referred.

It is easy to realise, at this point, that the economic problems for which the concept of degree of mechanisation is relevant must be looked for in the sphere of employment. Indeed, the capital/labour ratio indicates the number of extra workers that will be required (the number of jobs that will be created) by an addition of one unit of investment evaluated at current prices. It follows that changes in the degree of mechanisation, as expressed by the capital/labour ratio, mean changes in the size of employment associated with any given amount of capital goods, expressed at (average) constant prices.

To conclude, the notion of 'indirectness' or 'roundaboutness' of the capitalistic process of production, which has come to us from traditional capital theory, becomes ambiguous, and hence must be abandoned, in a dynamic context. One must carefully distinguish between at least two different concepts: the concept of 'capital intensity', as expressed by the capital/output ratio, and the concept of 'degree of mechanisation', as expressed by the capital/labour ratio. Both concepts are relevant, but for different problems. The concept of capital intensity (the capital/output ratio) is relevant for the problems concerning investment and price formation; the concept of degree of mechanisation (the capital/labour ratio) is relevant for the problems concerning employment. It clearly is essential to use each one of the two concepts strictly with reference to the problems for which it is appropriate.

5. Capital intensity and degree of mechanisation in comparisons through time

It may be useful to point out straightaway how the distinction between the concepts of 'capital intensity' and 'degree of mechanisation' becomes particularly important in a dynamic context.

In a hypothetical world in which there were no technical progress, the movements of the capital/output ratio and the movements of the capital/labour ratio would have a one–one correspondence with each other. A distinction between the two would be unnecessary. Incidentally, this again may help to explain why in traditional economic analysis, which has normally relied on the assumption that technical progress is either non-existent or unimportant, the necessity for a distinction between the two concepts has never been felt.

But in a dynamic context, when comparisons are to be made through time, the distinction becomes crucial. Consider a simple example. Suppose a case in which technical progress brings about an increase of the number of physical machines operated by each worker, but in such a way as to keep the quantity of labour embodied in the increasing number of physical machines absolutely constant. An evaluation of this invariant amount of embodied labour, at current prices (supposing that the average level of prices remains constant), would yield an increasing value of the capital stock per worker, over time, because the over-all wage rate is increasing as a result of the over-all growth of productivity. This means that the ratio of physical machines to men and the ratio of capital, at current prices, to men will be increasing. In other words, the 'degree of mechanisation' will be increasing all the time. Yet, if we divide the value of capital thus obtained by the value of production coming from it, the increasing wage rate (by appearing both in the numerator and in the denominator), cancels out. The capital/output ratio (i.e. the capital intensity of the production process) remains constant, thereby representing the constant proportion of the quantity of labour which must be kept 'locked up' in the capital stock to the amount of labour employed in direct production.[6]

We thereby have a simple example where the capital/labour ratio (i.e. the degree of mechanisation) is continually increasing through time, while the capital/output ratio (i.e. the capital intensity of the production process) remains constant. A distinction between the two concepts has become absolutely essential.[7]

6. Capital intensity and degree of mechanisation in comparisons of different economic systems

The distinction considered above also becomes essential in any comparison of different economic systems.

6 Later on (in section 19) we shall see that this is a case of 'capital-intensity neutral' technical progress – a technical progress which, in the economic literature, has been called 'neutral' in the sense of Harrod.

7 An example of the contradictions into which one may fall when one fails to distinguish between the two concepts may be seen in a well-known article by R. M. Solow ('Technical Change and the Aggregate Production Function' in *The Review of Economics and Statistics*, 1957). Solow tried to estimate technical change in the United States economy from 1909 to 1949 and, after finding that capital per man increased in that period, came to the conclusion that the over-all growth of productivity could be attributed to technical progress by 87.5% and to 'increased capital intensity' by 12.5%. I had myself the opportunity of pointing out that, by using the same data and computing the over-all capital/output ratio, one finds that this ratio *decreased* from 2.75 in 1909 to 2.20 in 1949! (See my paper: 'On Concepts and Measures of Changes in Productivity' in *The Review of Economics and Statistics*, 1959, p. 274). Solow's conclusions are therefore ambiguous and contradictory. What one can simply say is that the technical change that took place in the U.S. economy, from 1909 to 1949, was accompanied by an increase in the degree of mechanisation (and not in capital intensity), and by a decrease (not an increase!) in capital intensity.

The machines and equipment which are purchased on the international market are characterised by certain technical relations, i.e. by certain degrees of mechanisation, as expressed by capital/labour ratios, which are technically given and therefore remain the same for all countries. However, the very same physical machines will in general represent different capital intensities (i.e. will entail different capital/output ratios) for different countries.

To be more specific, if a certain set of machinery is imported into a country because, for example, it cannot be made in the country itself, it must be paid for by using the proceeds coming from other goods which are exported. This means that the amount of embodied labour which the imported machinery represents for the importing country is given by the amount of labour required in the importing country to produce those commodities which are given in exchange, and not by the amount of labour which has actually been embodied in the machinery, in the country of origin. Therefore, the same technical production processes (the very same machines) have for the two countries a different *economic* meaning. In fact, they will usually entail higher capital/output ratios, i.e. more capital-intensive processes of production, in the importing country than in the exporting country, and therefore also a higher proportion of charges for capital to charges for labour in the final prices.

To give a simple example, suppose that India imports from the United States of America a certain set of machinery for an integrated chemical production process which is set up in India with exactly the same technical characteristics as it has in the United States. The physical capital per man will obviously be exactly the same in both countries, and so will be its current value, evaluated at international prices, e.g. in dollars. But suppose that the Indian industrial wage rate (at comparable efficiency and in dollars) is 1/4 of the wage rate in the U.S.: then the capital/output ratio entailed by this production process will be much greater (up to 4 times greater) in India than in the United States, despite the fact that the capital/labour ratio is exactly the same. The explanation is that the lower Indian wage rate will influence the price of final output, but not the price of the machinery (which is bought on the international market). In other words, the lower Indian wage rate will influence that part of the price of the final goods which is the charge for labour but not that part which is the charge for capital. The very same technical equipment, i.e. the very same degree of mechanisation (the same capital per man, whether in physical terms or at current prices) will entail a much greater degree of capital intensity for India than for the United States.

185

7. The so-called 'Leontief paradox', no longer a paradox in the present theoretical context

The importance of the conclusions reached in the foregoing pages is bound to emerge on any occasion in which comparisons are made through time for the same country or between countries that are at different stages of technological development. Any failure, in such comparisons, to draw a distinction between capital intensity and degree of mechanisation will inevitably lead to contradiction. In this section, as a striking example, a well-known 'paradox' will be considered that arose some years ago from comparisons of international trade carried out by Wassily Leontief.

Leontief adopted an interpretation of international trade consisting in extending to 'capital' the given-resource-endowment approach (the so called Heckscher–Ohlin model) of marginal economic theory. The traditional position is in fact very well summarised by Leontief himself at the beginning of his inquiry:

Our economic relationships with other countries are supposed to be based mainly on the export of such 'capital intensive' goods in exchange for foreign products which – if we were to make them at home – would require little capital but large quantities of American labor. Since the United States possesses a relatively large amount of capital . . . and a comparatively small amount of labour, direct domestic production of such 'labor intensive' products would be uneconomical; we can much more advantageously obtain them from abroad in exchange for our capital intensive products.[8]

Leontief then carried out an empirical study on the composition of imports and exports in the United States of America and arrived at an 'unexpected result'. He found that the proportion of labour to capital required by one million dollars of U.S. exports is higher than the proportion of labour to capital that would be required by one million dollars of U.S. competitive imports if these imports were made at home. Leontief was baffled: he had expected the opposite, since he had taken for granted – from the fact that in the United States the amount of capital per man was higher than anywhere else – that the United States was the most capital intensive economy in the world. This 'Leontief paradox', as it has been called, has then, for a good many years, become the subject of many complicated explanations and interpretations.[9]

---

8 Wassily W. Leontief, 'Domestic Production and Foreign Trade: the American Capital Position Re-examined', in *Proceedings of the American Philosophical Society*, vol. 97, no. 4, 1953, p. 333.

9 The explanation given by Leontief himself (and many others) must have sounded very pleasing to American readers: 'Let us reject the simple but tenuous postulate of comparative technological parity and make the plausible alternative assumption that in

The foregoing analysis allows us to realise that the 'Leontief paradox' is in fact no paradox at all, but precisely what should have been expected. The error which has caused the surprise lies precisely in having taken the capital/labour ratio as an index of capital intensity.

Now, it is certainly undisputable that the capital/labour ratios (either for the economy as a whole or for single processes) are generally higher in the United States than in the rest of the world. This simply means that the U.S. economy has a higher degree of mechanisation than the outside world. But the degrees of mechanisation (the capital/labour ratios) have no relevance for the problems of price formation, and therefore of comparative costs, and therefore of international trade!

To find whether the U.S. economy is more or less capital intensive than other economies, one must look at capital/output ratios. And there is no reason why capital/output ratios should be higher in the United States than in the rest of the world, while there are many reasons that make us expect the capital/output ratios to be higher in the outside world than in the United States. (Consider on this problem the arguments carried out in the previous section.[10]) And if capital/output ratios are lower in the United States than elsewhere, then we must conclude that production processes in the U.S. are less capital intensive, not more capital intensive, than in the rest of the world, in spite of the fact that they entail a higher degree of mechanisation (higher capital/labour ratios). It is therefore quite natural that the United States should import goods that – if made at home – would require production processes that would be more capital intensive than the processes employed to make the corresponding exported good.

It may perhaps be useful to underline the fact that the association of the capital/output ratio with the concept of capital intensity and of the

---

any combination with a given quantity of capital, one man-year of American labor is equivalent to, say, three man-years of foreign labor' (*Ibid.* p. 344). See the following footnote.

10 Production processes outside the United States are generally less mechanised than in the United States. But to the extent that certain machines are imported, let us say in India, and are operated in the same way as they are operated in the United States, there will indeed be 'technological parity' – the same degree of mechanisation. Hence, contrary to what Leontief says, the Indian worker operating the same physical machine is exactly as productive or as efficient as his American counterpart. However, he receives a much lower wage rate, reflecting the lower productivity of the Indian economy as a whole, as compared with the American economy as a whole. It is, therefore, the productivity of the economy as a whole that is lower in India, *not* the productivity of the worker operating the same identical machine, which is obviously the same as in the United States. This lower over-all productivity, by rendering the Indian wage rate lower, renders the capital intensity of the very same physical machines (imported from the United States) much higher in India than in the United States.

capital/labour ratio with the concept of degree of mechanisation, from which the above conclusions have been drawn, is not a mere question of definition. If it were a question of definition, one could of course choose whichever definition one preferred. But the important point to stress is that, in drawing conclusions on the composition of international trade, it is *the relative prices* of commodities that matter, and in the determination of relative prices it is the capital/output ratio which is relevant and not the capital/labour ratio. Leontief, as so many other economic theorists, has simply fallen into the trap of taking the capital/labour ratio as an index of capital intensity and then proceeding to draw conclusions *as if* the definition of capital intensity had been taken on the basis of the capital/output ratio. We should not be surprised to find paradoxes and contradictions.[11]

8. Choice of technique versus changes of technique

We are now in a position to take a fresh look at two topical problems: the problem of choice of technique and the problem of change of technique. This is a subject which traditional economic theory has been

---

11 It is important to stress these results because misunderstandings due to a confusion of the two different concepts expressed by capital/output and capital/labour ratios have been only too frequent in economic analysis. Let me mention two illustrious examples taken respectively from Ricardo and Marx.

In Ricardo's analysis, the concept of capital intensity plays a crucial role in his discussions on the theories of value and distribution. His labour theory of value holds only in the particular case of uniform capital intensity in all production processes. It is clear that, for this problem (price formation), it is the concept of capital intensity (i.e. the capital/output ratio) that is relevant. But Ricardo never realised that this was something different from the concept of degree of mechanisation, as expressed by the capital/labour ratio; and when, in the controversial chapter XXXI, 'On Machinery', of his *Principles* (3rd edition) he came to be concerned with employment (or more precisely with the unemployment generated by technical change) for which it is the concept of degree of mechanisation (i.e. the capital/labour ratio) that is relevant, he fell into well-known contradictions.

Similarly, in Marx's analysis, it is the concept of capital intensity, i.e. the capital/output ratio – or as Marx calls it, the 'organic composition of capital' – that is relevant for his discussions on value and related problems (such as the problem of the 'transformation of values into prices'). But when Marx went on to discuss the consequences of technical change on unemployment (in his terms, on generating the 'reserve army of labour'), he should have used concepts associated with the capital/labour ratio. By failing to do so he too fell into the error of thinking that the introduction of new machinery would be associated with an increase in the degree of capital intensity, or organic composition of capital (i.e. of the capital/output ratio, thereby causing a fall of the rate of profit). But this may not be so at all. New machinery may well entail an increase in the degree of mechanisation (and therefore of unemployment, at constant output) but at the same time may well be associated with a constant (or even a decreasing) organic composition of capital. The effects on the rate of profit, in Marx's own scheme, are therefore unpredictable.

dealing with for some time. Contrasts and comparisons will therefore become inevitable in the following pages.

In traditional capital theory, choice of technique and changes of technique have always been presented as two facets of the same problem. But again the association has been a consequence of dealing exclusively with stationary economic systems, which represent the special case in which the techniques which are relevant for the problem of choice happen to coincide with the techniques which are relevant in the process of change. As soon as we let time and technical progress into the picture, this coincidence disappears and two different sets of techniques become relevant for the two problems.

A problem of choice arises any time that a method of production has to be put into being and more than one alternative technical method is available. At any given point of time, therefore, a choice is open only for a small part of the technological structure of the economic system: that part which refers to new investment and replacement. The bulk of the techniques in operation at that point in time have been chosen in the past and the economic system is stuck with them.

A change of technique is an entirely different matter. It is a *process* that takes place through time. Of course, given enough time, any technical method can be changed. But the point is that, by the time the change is feasible, the old techniques may have become obsolete, and the range of possibilities open to choice may be completely new. A process of change of technique has, therefore, nothing to do with the previous problem of choice. It involves a movement towards a *different* set of possible techniques and, therefore, towards a new problem of choice.

We shall examine the two problems in turn.

9. The choice-of-technique function

The problem of choice of technique is best faced as a problem of rational choice. As has been pointed out already in chapter VII (section 14), there is no difficulty in inserting problems of rational choice into our analysis. Let us therefore specifically adopt here the hypothesis of rationality.

The problem of choice of technique is a problem that arises with reference to replacement and new investment, at the level of each single production unit, at a given point in time. This is a very practical problem: a choice has to be made between many alternative technical methods of production, each one of which is represented by a collection of organised physical machines, with well defined technical characteristics, requiring certain inputs of raw materials, intermediate commodities and man-hours, in order to produce a certain amount of final product.

As a matter of convenience, we shall here consider the entre-preneurial choice behind each final commodity X_j, $(j = 1, 2, \ldots, n - 1)$.

Suppose that, at a certain point of time, Ω alternative technical methods, $f_j^\alpha, \ldots, f_j^\omega$, are known to produce the same given quantity $\bar{X}_j$ of commodity j, i.e.

$$(IX.9.1) \quad \begin{cases} f_j^\alpha \left(K_j^\alpha, x_{nj}^\alpha \right) = \bar{X}_j, \\ \vdots \\ f_j^\omega \left(K_j^\omega, x_{nj}^\omega \right) = \bar{X}_j, \end{cases}$$

where the superscripts $\alpha, \beta, \ldots, \omega$, stand for the Ω alternative available technical methods; each K_j^k $(k = \alpha, \beta, \ldots, \omega)$ stands for the vector of all inputs of physical machines and intermediate commodities required in the whole vertically integrated sector j in order to produce physical quantity $\bar{X}_j$; and each x_{nj}^k, $(k = \alpha, \beta, \ldots, \omega)$ stands for the physical quantity of labour required in the same vertically integrated sector. Now call $p_{k_j}^\alpha$ the price vector referring to inputs K_j^α; and $p_{k_j}^\beta, \ldots, p_{k_j}^\omega$ the similar price vectors for all other $(\Omega - 1)$ technical methods of produc-tion. Moreover, call w the wage rate and π_j the rate of profit. Since we have placed ourselves at the level of the single production process, at a given point in time, all these prices are given. At least conceptually, the problem is a straightforward one.

It will be rational to choose that technical method of production which entails the minimum cost. In symbols, we may write:

$$(IX.9.2) \quad \text{Cost of the chosen method} = \text{Min} \begin{cases} p_{k_j}^\alpha K_j^\alpha + x_{nj}^\alpha w, \\ \vdots \\ p_{k_j}^\omega K_j^\omega + x_{nj}^\omega w, \end{cases}$$

$$j = 1, 2, \ldots, n - 1.$$

We shall call (IX.9.2) *the choice-of-technique function*. To yield a solution, the (IX.9.2) may well require quite complicated computational operations, for which all mathematical methods of (linear or non-linear) programming may find important applications. Moreover, in practice, many other considerations may come to complicate the picture. Methods of production may not be strictly comparable with one another because, for example, of different risk and uncertainty connected with different durability of the capital goods. Furthermore, decisions may in practice be influenced by expectations about future prices, changing scales of production, technical improvements, etc.

However if, and once, the available alternative technical methods have been reduced to a comparable basis, the problem of choice of technique becomes a straightforward one – a problem of search for a minimum, to be solved on the basis of the rational criterion of minimisation of costs.

10. The determinants of the choice of technique

We may now ask: what determines the choice of a particular technique?

It may be useful to take here, from chapter II (section 7), the more complex of our formulations for prices, namely:

$$(\text{IX.10.1}) \qquad p_{k_j} = \left[\left(\frac{T_{k_j}}{T_{k_j} - \gamma_j - \pi_{k_j}\gamma_j T_{k_j}} \right) a_{nk_j} \right] w,$$

$$j = 1, 2, \ldots, n-1.$$

Note now that all elements of costs, in the choice-of-technique function (IX.9.2), are additive, while each one of them is simply a multiplication of a price, such as (IX.10.1), by a physical quantity. Hence each line in the choice-of-technique function is in fact a sum of expressions of the same algebraic form of (IX.10.1), each of which is weighted with a given technical coefficient.

Therefore the particular features of expressions (IX.10.1) become very important and deserve careful scrutiny. We may note that the technical coefficients and the rate of profit are enclosed in the square brackets, but that the wage rate appears outside. This means that, with reference to the whole sum, the wage rate can be factored out. In other words, the wage rate is a multiplicative term that separates out from all the rest! This property has immediate remarkable implications. The technical coefficients are necessarily specific to each single technical method, but the wage rate is exactly the same for all of them. Therefore, any change in the wage rate will change the costs of all alternative technical methods, exactly in the same proportion, leaving their relative positions absolutely unchanged. Hence the choice of technique depends on the technical coefficients, but is entirely independent of the wage rate. This is the most important conclusion emerging from the present analysis of the problem of choice of technique.

When the rate of profit is uniform over all the economic system, the rate of profit also, of course – like the wage rate – becomes the same for all alternative technical methods. However the rate of profit – unlike the wage rate – appears inside the square brackets, and cannot be separated out from technology. The reason is that the profit component of each price comes from a multiplication of the rate of profit by only that part of the total labour input that is indirect. And since the proportion of direct to indirect labour (i.e. the degree of capital intensity) is in general different from one technical method to another, it follows that any change in the rate of profit will affect the cost of each alternative technical method in a different way. And this may affect the choice of technique.[12]

To conclude, the choice of technique does depend on the technical coefficients (i.e. on technology). It may also depend on the rate of profit, but is entirely independent of the wage rate.

11. Rate of profit and choice of technique

The conclusions just reached are so much at variance with those of traditional capital theory as to require some further elucidation.

For the purpose of the present analysis, we may state the results in the form of two propositions:

Proposition 1. A change in the rate of profit, *ceteris paribus* (i.e. for given technology and wage rate), will in general affect the choice of technique.

Proposition 2. A change in the wage rate, *ceteris paribus* (i.e. for given technology and rate of profit), will leave the choice of technique entirely unaffected.

Note that proposition 1, at least superficially, might sound quite in line with traditional capital theory.

As is well known, in traditional capital theory – e.g. in the theories developed by Böhm-Bawerk, Wicksell, John Bates Clark and others – the question of choice of technique has been presented as a problem of choice between alternative *proportions* of capital and labour, regulated by relative 'factor prices' (i.e. the wage rate and the rate of profit). A monotonic inverse relation has been postulated between the rate of

---

12 There is one special case in which the choice of the technical method would also be independent of any change in the rate of profit, namely the very special case in which the proportion of direct to indirect labour – i.e. the degree of capital intensity – happened to be exactly the same for all alternative methods of production (this is Ricardo's case of uniform proportion of capital to labour, or Marx's case of uniform 'organic composition' of capital).

profit and the proportion of capital to labour, so that a change in the rate of profit, from any given situation, is supposed to cause a change in the opposite direction in the degree of capital intensity of the chosen technique.

A careful analysis of our formulations reveals immediately that this conception of the problem of choice of technique is erroneous. There are absolutely no grounds for saying *a priori* in which direction a shift of technique will take place when the rate of profit is changed.[13] More specifically, if technical method f_j^α emerges as less costly than technical method f_j^β at a given rate of profit, let us say π_1; and f_j^β emerges as being less costly than f_j^α at a higher rate of profit π_2; then f_j^α might quite well come to be less costly than f_j^β at an even higher rate of profit π_3. No conclusion whatever, therefore, can be drawn when the rate of profit is changed as to the direction of change of the degree of capital intensity (or for that matter of the degree of mechanisation) of the optimum technique.[14]

To summarise, a change of the rate of profit may well affect the choice of technique, but the *way* in which it may affect it is *not* the one that traditional capital theory has postulated. More precisely, there is no systematic relation between the rate of profit and the degree of capital intensity (and for that matter the degree of mechanisation) of production processes.

Further considerations may be added. Traditional theory, by insisting on a specific relation between rate of profit and *proportions* of capital to labour has inevitably ended up by exaggerating the role of the rate of profit in the choice of technique. In a dynamic context, we can see these problems in a much better perspective. In the long run, as time goes on, the rate of profit cannot vary very much. Even from a practical point of view, therefore, there seems to be very little justification for worrying

---

13 This may be seen by simply using our unit price formulation (IX.10.1) and taking the derivative, with respect to π, of the difference between the costs required by any two machines α and β. Dropping all subscripts, for simplicity's sake, and only keeping α and β for the two techniques, we obtain:

$$\frac{d}{d\pi} \left(\frac{T_\alpha}{T_\alpha - \pi\gamma_\alpha T_\alpha - \gamma_\alpha} a_\alpha - \frac{T_\beta}{T_\beta - \pi\gamma_\beta T_\beta - \gamma_\beta} a_\beta \right) \bar{X}\bar{w} =$$

$$= \left[\frac{T_\alpha^2 \gamma_\alpha}{(T_\alpha - \gamma_\alpha - \pi\gamma_\alpha T_\alpha)^2} a_\alpha - \frac{T_\beta^2 \gamma_\beta}{(T_\beta - \gamma_\beta - \pi\gamma_\beta T_\beta)^2} a_\beta \right] \bar{X}\bar{w}.$$

As can be seen, this expression may be positive for certain values of π and negative for others.

14 These results have become widely accepted by now, following the 'reswitching-of-technique debate'. (See Luigi L. Pasinetti *et al.*, 'Paradoxes in Capital Theory: a Symposium', *The Quarterly Journal of Economics*, Nov. 1966.)

about the effects of changes in a magnitude which does not change very much. If we add to this the further consideration that, in a modern economic system, possible alternative techniques of production normally present substantial discontinuities between them, we must infer that it appears very unlikely that changes in the rate of profit may in practice play any major role in the determination of the choice of technique.

To summarise and conclude, the influence of changes in the rate of profit on the choice of technique is basically inconclusive as to the direction. In any case, whatever the direction, it is very likely in practice to be of secondary importance.

12. Wage rate and choice of technique

Of a much more striking character and importance is proposition 2 of the previous section, namely the proposition that the choice of technique, if the rate of profit is constant, is entirely independent of the level of the wage rate. This proposition appears in flat contradiction with what traditional theory has accustomed us to believe.

As is well known, it is a generally accepted traditional belief that the choice of technique crucially depends on the wage rate. But we have arrived at the opposite result and we may wonder what the explanation is. Now, the answer is that the traditional belief has originated from an unwarranted generalisation of a very special way of facing the problem of choice of technique. We shall investigate the problem in detail.

As is well known, traditional theory has always been preoccupied with what happens at the level of the individual. Oddly enough, when dealing with the problem of choice of technique (which is indeed one of individual rational choice) it has always tended to transpose the analysis to the level of the economic system as a whole, where the problem is made to appear as one of choosing between alternative *proportions* of capital to labour, for the production of just one (composite) commodity. Now, in the particular case of a one-commodity world, if the rate of profit is taken as given, the wage rate can only be one. To fix the rate of profit means *ipso facto* to determine the wage rate, and to say that there is a change in the rate of profit becomes synonymous with saying that there is a change, in the opposite direction, in the wage rate. The one implies the other. We may therefore say that, in such a case, since a change in the wage rate necessarily implies a change in the rate of profit and since a change in the rate of profit *may* influence the choice of technique, a change in the wage rate may be associated with a different choice of technique. However, we must be very careful not to be misled: we are considering a very particular case in which the wage rate is

194

changed as a consequence of a change in the *rate of profit*. In such case, the change in the wage rate may indeed be associated with a different choice of technique – not because it influences it directly but because it means a change in the rate of profit and a change in the rate of profit, as we have seen above, may influence the choice of technique.

It is precisely at this point that traditional theory has caused the mistaken belief. From the particular case sketched out above (logically correct but so limited as to be irrelevant), an entirely unwarranted generalisation has been made: the general conclusion has been drawn that the choice of technique depends on the wage rate. This conclusion is incorrect.

I should like to draw the reader's attention to this point, because the cases which in practice arise all the time are those of situations entailing roughly *the same* rate of profit and a different (sometimes a dramatically different) wage rate. It is situations of this type that have been missed completely by traditional economic theory; yet they arise continually, both through time and over space.

Consider, to begin with, a given economic system moving through time. To bring out the meaning of our results in a clear and simple way, suppose that technical progress takes place in all sectors of the economic system, except in the technical methods available for the (vertically integrated) sector j and for the sectors producing capital goods for sector j. Suppose moreover that per capita incomes grow steadily and that the rate of profit remains constant through time; so that, with reference to a constant (average) level of prices, the wage rate is growing steadily. We may ask the question: will the rising wage rate cause a change in the best technique for sector j? The answer is: no. We can see immediately, from formulation (IX.9.2) of the choice-of-technique function for commodity j, that, since the costs entailed by the alternative methods of production all take the algebraic form (IX.10.1), any change in the wage rate does not make any difference to the choice of technique. A rising wage rate simply multiplies the prices of all inputs (labour, intermediate commodities, machine wear and tear) exactly in the same proportion, and therefore leaves the choice among them entirely unaffected.[15]

Consider now the case of two different economic systems at the same

15 I realised myself, after arriving at these results, that Gerald Shove made clear hints at them in the early 1930s, at the time of the publication of Hicks' *Theory of Wages*. (See Shove's review of Hicks' book in *The Economic Journal*, 1933, pp. 460–72. The relevant passages are on p. 471, where he points out that an increase in the wage rate, when 'there is no change in the rate of interest' raises the cost of 'direct' and 'roundabout' methods in the same proportions, leaving their relative positions unaffected.) It seems to me very unfortunate that such brilliant insights should have been lost.

point in time. Call them India and the United States, and suppose that they have the same rate of profit but a different wage rate, the latter being much lower in India than in the United States, because technology in the Indian economy is by far less advanced than in the United States. However, let us suppose that, both in India and in the United States, one particular sector j has access to exactly the same (vertically integrated) technology. Again we may ask: will the enormously different wage rate cause a different choice of technique? Once more, for the same reasons as in the previous case, the answer is: no. The choice-of-technique function for India and the choice-of-technique function for the United States are exactly the same; the only exception being the item representing the wage rate. But the wage rate multiplies the costs of all alternative technical methods by the same factor and thus leaves their relative positions absolutely unaffected. The technique which is best for India turns out to be the same technique which is best for the United States.

This conclusion may sound even more striking here than in the previous case of comparisons through time. By the unwarranted generalisation pointed out above, traditional economic theory has led almost everybody to accept the belief that, given a range of equally possible technical methods of production, the best technique may be different for advanced and for underdeveloped countries because of different wage rates. This is incorrect. A different wage rate – when the rate of profit is the same and the technical possibilities are exactly the same – does not make the slightest difference to the choice of techniques![16]

An important warning, however, must be added at this point. The above conclusions are valid, provided that the two countries considered have access to *the same technical methods*. This is a big proviso, as it is seldom entirely fulfilled. In fact, it is practically impossible to find two countries where all technical methods of production which are relevant for a given (vertically integrated) sector are exactly the same. What normally happens, especially in less developed countries (this may be the case for India) is that a part of the technical method (that part which refers to the production of the machines) is carried out abroad – let us say in the United States – from where the machines are imported. In this case, that part of the technical method which refers to the production of

---

16 In the real world, of course, the traditional belief has been contradicted very often. There have been numerous examples of firms in underdeveloped countries which, in spite of very low wage rates, have applied just the same technical methods of production that are used in highly developed countries. The analysis developed above now contributes to providing an explanation.

the capital goods has a different *economic* meaning for India and for the United States (as explained in section 6 above).

To put the problem more explicitly, if the machines were made in India, by exactly the same technical method as in the United States, there would be no difference whatever. The best technique for the United States would also be the best technique for India, whatever the difference in the wage rate. But if the machines cannot be made in India, they have to be bought on the international market, and their real cost for India will be represented by the amount of inputs which must go into those goods which, at the international prices, have to be given in exchange for the imported machines. Now, in this case, it may well happen that some other production methods, which are technically more primitive but whose capital goods are made in India, may on the whole require, for India, a lower amount of direct and indirect labour (or labour-equivalent) per unit of output than the more automatic machines to be imported from the United States. In this case, the position of India with respect to the automatic machines would be comparable to the situation in which the industrially advanced countries are nowadays with respect, let us say, to nuclear reactors producing electricity: the method is technically more advanced than the traditional ones but (besides still leaving too many technical problems unsolved) its efficiency has not yet been improved sufficiently to make it less costly than the old ones. In these cases, many other considerations may of course come in – in particular, expectations as to how long it will take to improve the efficiency of internal production of the automatic methods or of the goods to be given in exchange for them. But in the normal case, when it happens that the technically more primitive machines entail a lower unit cost, they obviously are to be preferred, in India, because they entail a lower cost (i.e. a lower over-all amount of labour – or labour equivalent – per unit of output). It is precisely at this point that traditional economic theory becomes misleading. The reason why the more primitive machines may sometimes emerge as more profitable is not because of the lower wage rate. This would be quite immaterial. It is because of the lower local efficiency in making the automatic capital goods (or in making those goods which are to be given in exchange for them).[17]

[17] So often, of course, in spite of the machines being imported and paid for with goods having a higher content of local labour, the basic processes adopted in the industrially advanced countries are so efficient as to be more profitable anyhow. This does not mean that these processes, as they are operated, let us say, in the United States, should also be operated, let us say, in India, in exactly the same way. The criterion of minimum cost has to be applied independently to each one of the processes which are subsidiary to the main one (think of transporting, hoisting, etc.). Any one of these

13. The meaning of cost minimisation in the 'natural' economic system

Our analysis of the problem of choice of technique has been carried out so far in terms of a rate of profit, which has been taken as exogenously given, whatever it may be. This was done in order to make our analysis (and its conclusions) applicable to any institutional type of economic system.

It may now be useful, however, to explore briefly the meaning, for the economic system as a whole, of a rational choice of technique made in the specific case in which the rate of profit is fixed at its *natural* level.

In this case, each one of the expressions appearing in the choice-of-technique function (IX.9.1), by taking up the algebraic form of (IX.10.1), with π converted into $(g + r_i)$, contains, inside the square brackets, a sum of purely physical quantities of labour – all inputs, of all types, are simply transformed into (additive) physical quantities of (direct, indirect and hyper-indirect) labour, as we have seen in chapter VII. Each technical method is therefore simply reduced to a single physical quantity of labour multiplied by the wage rate. But the wage rate is the same for all alternative methods. Hence it follows that choosing the technical method which entails the minimum cost has, for the economic system as a whole, the meaning of choosing the technical method which requires the minimum input of physical quantities of labour.

With the natural rate of profit inserted into the price system, the principle of cost minimisation, which appears, at the level of the single production unit, as an economic principle based on prices, turns out, at the level of the economic system as a whole, to be a purely technical principle of minimisation of physical quantities of labour.

This is clearly one of the most remarkable implications of the 'natural' price system. It is this implication that gives full content to the proposition, stated in chapter VII (sections 5 and 14), that the 'natural' price system is indeed an efficient price system.

14. Asymmetry between rate of profit and wage rate mirroring the deeper asymmetry between capital and labour

It may seem rather otiose at this point to stress the asymmetrical roles

---

subsidiary processes will be conveniently replaced by local, technically more primitive, processes, any time that the actual labour to be employed through the latter is less than the (direct and indirect) labour required to produce those goods which would have to be given in exchange for the former.

played by the rate of profit and the wage rate. Yet, this asymmetry, here as elsewhere, reflects the more fundamental asymmetry that exists between capital and labour in the production process.

Note that, in the present analysis, the reduction of all capital goods to physical quantities of labour is complete. There remains no longer any profit residual, thanks to the concept of a 'natural' rate of profit; and there remains no longer any commodity residual either, thanks to our technical-progress approach to capital accumulation.

It is important to realise the extent to which these features, far from being mere analytical devices, are in fact further steps towards modelling the theory to reflect essential characteristics of the real world.

In the economic literature, the reduction of prices to physical quantities of labour has usually been shown so far with the help of infinite series going backwards in time, within the context of given technical coefficients.[18] In such time series the intermediate commodities never disappear altogether (except in the limit). But such infinite series must be correctly interpreted; they can only have a conceptual, not a real, meaning, i.e. no empirical or historical sense.

Our previous analysis, on the other hand, by making technical change play a role at each stage in time, provides a much more direct reflection of the actual process. In the real world, there can never be any *infinite* series. Today's turning-lathe was made yesterday with a less perfect turning-lathe, which was made earlier with an even less perfect turning-lathe, which was made with no turning-lathe at all, but with more primitive tools. And so on backwards in time. No machine has ever any infinite series of intermediate commodities behind it; but only a chain of successive evolving sets of more primitive tools and machines, which reduce to nothing, provided that one goes sufficiently far back. In any actual (as against any conceptual) time series, we arrive, in *finite* time, at labour alone.

To realise that this is the case, one may look at the production process in yet another way. An instant's reflection will suffice to make anyone realise that the whole structure of capital goods would not exist at all if labourers did not exist, while the contrary is not true. If we were to imagine, for a moment, that all capital goods were suddenly to vanish (let us say by the spiteful touch of a magic wand), a terrible crisis would of course ensue. But those people who could survive the crisis would start the whole process of capital accumulation all over again: from

18 See, for example, the first of Dmitriev's 'economic essays' (Moscow 1904; English translation: V. K. Dmitriev, *Economic Essays on Value, Competition and Utility*, translated by D. Fry and edited by D. M. Nuti, Cambridge 1974), or Piero Sraffa, *Production of Commodities, op. cit.*

primitive tools to atomic energy reactors! (And in a shorter time than it took in the past.) Labour alone can make all the capital goods. If we were to imagine the opposite catastrophe – the disappearance of all human beings – we can very well realise what would follow: absolutely nothing. Capital goods alone can make nothing.

15. 'Genuine' production functions

We can now move on to consider the process of *change* of technique. But since any change takes place from a given technical structure that exists and can be observed at a given point in time, it is necessary first of all to devote a few words to the existing technical structure.

At a given point in time, the existing technical structure may be represented by a series of technical *production functions*, each of which expresses the production of any particular commodity as a technical function of a whole series of physical inputs of labour, capital goods, intermediate commodities of any sort, etc. In our theoretical scheme, since we have placed ourselves at the stage of the vertically integrated sectors, production functions appear, in a compact and very simple way, as:

(IX.15.1) $$X_i = \frac{1}{a_{ni}} x_{ni}, \qquad i = 1, \ldots, (n-1),$$

where the notation is that of chapter II (section 2). Each X_i is a simple function of labour inputs. The (IX.15.1) must however be completed. Each production function for sector i requires, and thus presupposes, the existence of an appropriate stock of physical capital K_i. In other words, the functions (IX.15.1) presuppose the existence of a series of complementary stocks of physical capital goods:

(IX.15.2) $$[K_1, K_2, \ldots, K_{n-1}],$$

as defined in chapter II (section 5). Each of the (IX.15.1), coupled with the corresponding K_i in (IX.15.2), represents what we may indeed call the production function for commodity i ($i = 1, 2, \ldots, n-1$).

It is important not to confuse the production functions (IX.15.1)–(IX.15.2) with the choice-of-technique functions (IX.9.2). The (IX.15.1)–(IX.15.2) represent the *actual* production structure – what is actually in operation. Each a_{ni} and K_i, ($i = 1, 2, \ldots, n-1$), may well be made up of various 'layers' of different 'vintages' (each 'layer' representing the particular technical method actually chosen, at the corresponding time, from the choice-of-technique function of that time). In any case – whether coming from one or from various 'vintages' – the

200

(unique) technical structure represented by the (IX.15.1)–(IX.15.2) is the one that is actually in operation. On the other hand, the (IX.9.2) represent all the alternative methods of production that are known and are available at a given point in time. To put it in another way, the production functions are the ones that are relevant for actual production. On the other hand, the choice-of-technique functions are relevant for a part of future production, i.e. for that part of future production that derives from present-day new investment and replacement.

This discussion should help to make an important point clear. To represent the existing technical structure by production functions (IX.15.1)–(IX.15.2) does not mean – as almost all traditional economics textbooks have been saying – that only one technique is supposed to be known! A great number of alternative techniques may well be known at present, and a great number of alternative techniques may always have been known in the past. But this great number of alternative techniques, though relevant for the choice-of-technique functions of the corresponding times, have become irrelevant for the production functions. As far as the production functions are concerned, i.e. as far as representing the actual technical structure is concerned, only that single technique is relevant which is actually in operation.[19]

This also means that, at any given point in time, the technical structure, as represented by the production functions (IX.15.1)–(IX.15.2), *cannot be changed*. Changes may indeed come about, but through time, and, therefore, slowly. As soon as the replacement and new investment are undertaken, new methods are chosen which are different from the ones which were chosen in the past.

16. Neo-classical production functions and the irrelevance of marginal productivities

Having defined, in the previous section, what we may indeed call the 'genuine' production functions, it becomes inevitable – before going on – to open a brief digression in order to contrast the way in which they have been constructed, and hence their meaning, with the traditional way in which production functions are presented in neo-classical economic theory.

Productions functions (IX.15.1)–(IX.15.2), considered above, may be said to express the fact that, in actual production, labour and capital goods are complementary. There is therefore also an alternative way of

---

19 In other words, to use a widespread terminology, the 'fixed-coefficient case' does not mean, and must not be confused with, the case in which only one technique is known.

expressing the same technical relations, which consists in defining the output technical coefficients with reference to the capital goods. These coefficients would take the place of (IX.15.1), with the specification that such functions presuppose the employment of appropriate physical amounts of labour, to be represented by a vector similar to (IX.15.2). This would simply be another way of expressing the same thing.

But it seems almost inevitable, among economic theorists, to think of such a way of representing production as unnecessarily asymmetrical and 'inelegant', and to think that one can avoid all asymmetries by writing the production functions as:

$$(IX.16.1) \qquad X_i = F_i(K_i, x_{ni}),$$

$$i = 1, 2, \ldots, n - 1,$$

which means that each physical quantity X_i of commodity i is a technical function of a physical stock of capital K_i and of a physical amount of labour x_{ni}; with the specification that the shapes of such functions are such that:

$$(IX.16.2) \qquad \frac{\partial X_i}{\partial K_i} = 0, \quad \text{and} \quad \frac{\partial X_i}{\partial x_{ni}} = 0,$$

$$i = 1, 2, \ldots, (n - 1),$$

which is itself another way of saying that labour and capital goods are complementary in production.

One must say immediately that, if things simply remained at this point, there would be no harm in using such formal representations. Expressions (IX.16.1), with specifications (IX.16.2), would simply be another way (more 'elegant', but also more complicated), of presenting the same things as expressions (IX.15.1) with specifications (IX.15.2). But the difficulty precisely is that usually things will not stop here. A century of exposure to neo-classical economic thinking will normally lead almost any economist to think of (IX.16.2) as only 'one particular way' of defining the shape of functions (IX.16.1), and to think of another 'more general' way of re-interpreting them as functions in which the partial derivatives (to be called 'marginal productivities') are not necessarily equal to zero. Almost inevitably, one will actually be induced to go on to think also of the case in which they are exactly equal to the corresponding prices, i.e.:

$$(IX.16.3) \qquad \frac{\partial X_i}{\partial K_i} = p_{k_i}, \qquad \frac{\partial X_i}{\partial x_{ni}} = w,$$

$$i = 1, 2, \ldots, n - 1,$$

where p_{k_i} and w are expressed in terms of commodity i. And, at this point, it takes a small step to go on to say that shape (IX.16.2) would define perfect complementarity and shape (IX.16.3) would define perfect substitutability between the various inputs. Functions (IX.16.1) would thus be turned, by way of a chain of re-interpretations, into standard neo-classical production functions.

This is the point where the analysis has become, not only misleading, but actually incorrect. For *the meaning* we gave to functions (IX.16.1), when they were written down as an alternative way of representing (IX.15.1)–(IX.15.2), has been altered completely. We have in fact come to represent – no longer the (unique) technique we intended to represent – but all alternative techniques, *on the very particular* and very restrictive *assumption* that these techniques can in fact be used in the place of the one that has actually been chosen. This means introducing precisely those particular assumptions – i.e. stationary technical knowledge – that make the techniques which are relevant for the problem of choice coincide with the techniques which are relevant for a process of change. As has been pointed out already, this means frustrating any possibility of a dynamic analysis. Note moreover that – in spite of the superficially more elegant formulation – to *assume* coincidence of phenomena that are in general not coincidental is precisely the opposite of what is meant by 'generalisation'.

For all these reasons, in order to avoid deceptive features, the formulation (IX.16.1)–(IX.16.2) has nowhere been used in the present work.

Incidentally, an implication of this analysis also is that the main analytical tool that has emerged from a neo-classical re-interpretation of (IX.16.1), namely the concept of marginal productivity, is itself rather misleading, as it is bound to generate ambiguities; the basic reason being that the partial derivatives $\partial X_i/\partial K_i$, $\partial X_i/\partial x_{ni}$, $i = 1, 2, \ldots, n-1$, will come to mean different things in different contexts. It may actually be useful to examine these meanings in at least three different contexts.

First of all, partial derivatives $\partial X_i/\partial K_i$, $\partial X_i/x_{ni}$, $i = 1, 2, \ldots, n-1$, may be referred to the production structure at a given point of time, as was done when they were first written down in (IX.16.1), (IX.16.2). In this context, they can only be equal to zero, or near zero. At any given point of time, machines are what they are; they cannot be changed. The traditional textbooks normally (and mistakenly) refer to this as a 'particular' case. But this is not so. Given the context we have considered, this is the *general* case. For, at a given point of time, to talk of substitutability makes no sense. Machines and labour are inherently

203

complementary, without implying by that the existence of only one technique.[20]

Secondly, one might write down functions (IX.16.1) as expressing all the techniques that *ex-ante* are available for the choice of technique problem. As we have pointed out, this is the neo-classical re-interpretation of the meaning of (IX.16.1). Unfortunately, in this case, there is absolutely no reason to expect that the partial derivatives will actually exist. The physical inputs characterising the various techniques may well be completely different, or exhibit big discontinuities. In any case, quite apart from discontinuities, there is no reason to expect that the changes of prices should go in the direction opposite to the direction of change of the corresponding physical quantity.[21] There is, of course, one way of making sense out of the partial derivatives and that is to *assume* that functions (IX.16.1) are continuous, differentiable, 'well-behaved' etc., i.e. to *assume* that they possess in fact that shape which neo-classical economic theory has always assumed them to have (the so called 'neo-classical production functions'). But this particular case can obviously claim no generality. Of course, if, in a particular industry and at a particular time, the technical methods available happened to satisfy all the neo-classical assumptions (continuity, differentiability, 'good behaviour', etc.) then equalities (IX.16.3) would obviously be realised at the equilibrium point, simply as a consequence of the choice of the optimum technique. Yet, even in this case, since only that production process would satisfy the neo-classical assumptions, the marginal productivities would simply be passively determined by all the rest, so that the concept of marginal productivity itself would carry no relevance. It would not be the marginal productivities that determine, or contribute to determining, the corresponding factor prices, but exactly the opposite: it would be the input prices that determine (through the choice of the optimum technique) what the marginal productivities are going to be.[22]

Thirdly, yet another context in which the partial derivatives $\partial X_i/\partial K_i$, $\partial X_i/x_{ni}$, $i = 1, 2, \ldots, n-1$, might be re-interpreted is that of the changes which actually take place when the technical methods are slowly changed through time, owing to technical progress embodied in new investment and replacement. In this context, clearly, there is absolutely no relation one can envisage between these partial deriva-

20 See footnote 19 above.
21 On these problems, see my own article: 'On Non-substitution in Production Models', *Cambridge Journal of Economics*, 1977.
22 Note the similarity of these conclusions with those arrived at in chapter VII (section 7) with reference to the 'marginal utilities'.

tives and the corresponding input prices. They might be higher, or lower, or zero, or have no meaning at all, depending on the technical characteristics of the new methods of production.

To conclude, therefore, in no one of the three contexts considered above does the concept of marginal productivity deserve that prominent theoretical role that neo-classical economic theory has always attributed to it. The partial derivatives – which express that concept – are always zero, or near zero, in the first context, and hence have no relevance. They might not even exist in the second context, and even when they are assumed to exist and to be equal to the corresponding input prices, they turn out to have no causal relevance. Finally, they have no relation to the corresponding prices in the third context we have considered. It is hard to think of any justification for the central role that has traditionally been attributed to such a theoretically irrelevant analytical tool.

17. The process of change of technique

We may resume at last our analysis of the process of change of technique.

As time goes on, new and better technical methods of production are invented. But to put them into operation takes time; in each period the new methods can only affect a part of the production structure.

In our theoretical framework, this process of technical change emerges as the result of an interplay between the choice-of-technique functions and the production functions.

Over time, each choice-of-technique function is continually being enriched by new, previously unknown, technical methods. By itself, this involves no change in production. But, when an actual decision is to be taken regarding either replacement and/or new investment, the new technical methods become relevant. If they are put into operation, the corresponding sector will undergo a change in at least part of its production process. Thus, over time, the coefficients of production will change, as they will represent production methods coming, in succession through time, from different choice-of-technique functions.

This means that technical innovations have two quite different effects on the two types of function we have considered. In the choice-of-technique functions (IX.9.2), they simply add new alternative technical methods to the previously known ones – the list of available technical methods becomes longer and longer. In the production functions (IX.15.1), on the other hand, some components of the technical coefficients change over time. These changes through time, at the vertically integrated level of each production sector, have been approximated in our analysis by exponential functions of time. There is of course no way of telling *a priori* the time path of these movements, as they will generally be quite different from one sector to another (as was pointed out in chapter IV). However, some definite statements on their over-all effect will become possible after drawing up a classification of the various types of technical change.

18. The meaning of technical progress

The term 'technical change' is a very general one. But we may now ask more specifically: when is it that technical 'change' actually means technical 'progress'?

First of all, there obviously is 'progress' when technical change takes the form of invention of entirely new, previously unknown, goods.

But we are concerned here with that type of technical change which consists of improvements in the production of already known goods. In this case, the answer to the above question is no longer so straightforward. To begin with, one may say that there is 'progress' when, for the production of any given unit of output, a decrease takes place in the amounts of required inputs. This definition is not very helpful, however. Or rather, it may be helpful only in those particular cases in which no one of the inputs has increased. But, in general, some inputs decrease and others increase, over time, and a standard is needed on the basis of which to assess, and set against one another, positive and negative changes of heterogeneous inputs.

It is here that, by going at the vertically integrated level, our formulations come to help. By taking the simplest of our price formulations (from section 6 of chapter II) and by using the wage rate as the *numéraire* (i.e. $w(t) = 1$), the unit price of each commodity i may be written as:

$$(\text{IX.18.1}) \qquad p_i(t) = a_{ni}(t) + (\pi_i + 1/T)a_{nk_i}(t),$$

$$i = 1, 2, \ldots, n - 1.$$

We may now say that, for any given rate of profit $\bar{\pi}_i$, there is technical progress in the production of commodity i, when, through time,

$$(\text{IX.18.2}) \qquad \frac{dp_i(t)}{dt} < 0, \qquad\qquad i = 1, 2, \ldots, n - 1.$$

Note that the qualification 'for any given rate of profit' is absolutely necessary. The diminution of inputs (technical progress) implied by (IX.18.2) is assessed in terms of 'labour equivalents', and therefore has a sense only *relative* to a given rate of profit. This means that it is not yet completely unambiguous. In general, cases cannot be excluded in which $(dp_i(t)/dt) < 0$ for certain rates of profit and $(dp_i(t)/dt) > 0$ for other rates of profit. Yet, this is as far as one can go in the context of a uniform rate of profit.

We can go further by going over to the 'natural' price system. When the rate of profit is fixed at its 'natural' level $\pi_i = g_i + r_i$, (IX.18.1) becomes:

$$(IX.18.3) \qquad p_i(t) = a_{ni}(t) + (1/T)a_{nk_i}(t) + (g_i + r_i)a_{nk_i}(t)$$
$$i = 1, 2, \ldots, n-1.$$

This is indeed a purely technical formulation. All ambiguities have here disappeared, as (IX.18.3) has become a sum of purely physical quantities of labour: direct labour plus indirect labour, plus hyper-indirect labour. Let us therefore write:

$$(IX.18.4) \qquad l_i(t) = a_{n_i}(t) + (1/T)a_{nk_i}(t) + (g_i + r_i)a_{nk_i}(t)$$
$$i = 1, 2, \ldots, n-1,$$

where $l_i(t)$ defines what we have earlier called the vertically hyper-integrated labour coefficient for commodity i ($i = 1, 2, \ldots, n-1$).

Now we are indeed in a position to make unambiguous statements. When, through time, there is a diminution of $l_i(t)$, and therefore of $p_i(t)$ as expressed by (IX.18.3), we know that somewhere in the economic system there has been a saving of labour requirements. More precisely, when, through time,

$$(IX.18.5) \qquad \frac{dl_i(t)}{dt} < 0, \qquad\qquad i = 1, 2, \ldots, n-1,$$

we can say, without any ambiguity, that there is technical progress in the production of commodity i.

This is a remarkable conclusion. It represents yet another aspect of the pure-labour character of the natural prices, which allowed us to present their efficiency property in terms of minimisation of physical quantities of labour (see section 13 above and sections 5 and 14 of chapter VII).

The major implication is very clear. Technical progress is ultimately revealed to be a diminution of labour inputs. To put it in another way, all technical progress is, in the end, labour-saving.

In a production system, saving labour is the ultimate meaning of technical progress.

19. A classification of technical progress

All technical progress is ultimately labour-saving, as we have just concluded, but according as to whether it takes place in the production of consumption goods or in the production of capital goods its effects on the production structure are quite different. By using the two concepts of degree of capital intensity and degree of mechanisation developed earlier in this chapter, a classification of the various types of technical progress can now be made by looking at their effects on the capital/output ratios and on the capital/labour ratios. For clarity, the 'natural' price system will be used throughout; and thus the particular 'natural' rate of profit appropriate to each sector will be inserted into the corresponding ratio. But the results can obviously be extended to all other cases as well, provided only that they are considered *relative* to any externally given rate of profit.

Let us first resume our formulations for the sectoral capital/output ratio ($\varkappa_i$) and capital/labour ratio (χ_i), from chapter V (section 11):

$$(IX.19.1) \quad \varkappa_i(t) = \frac{p_{k_i}(t)K_i(t)}{p_i(t)X_i(t)} = \frac{a_{nk_i}(0)e^{-\varrho_{k_i}t}}{a_{ni}(0)e^{-\varrho_i t} + (g_i + r_i + 1/T_i)a_{nk_i}(0)e^{-\varrho_{k_i}t}}$$

$$(IX.19.2) \quad \chi_i(t) = \frac{p_{k_i}(t)K_i(t)}{a_{ni}(t)X_i(t)} = \frac{a_{nk_i}(0)e^{-\varrho_{k_i}t}}{a_{ni}(0)e^{-\varrho_i t}}w(0)e^{\varrho^* t},$$

$$i = 1, 2, \ldots, n-1,$$

where the symbols are those defined in chapter V; and ϱ^*, which appears only in the capital/labour ratios, is the standard rate of productivity growth, i.e. the (weighted average) rate of growth of productivity in the economic system as a whole. This means that the wage rate is being expressed in terms of a constant (weighted average) price level.

We may now first distinguish three basic cases of technical progress, to be indicated under headings (a), (b), (c).

(a) *'Capital-intensity neutral' technical progress*

When technical progress takes place at exactly the same rate in the production of commodity i and in the production of capital goods for commodity i, i.e. when

$$(IX.19.3) \qquad\qquad \varrho_i = \varrho_{k_i},$$

the numerator and the denominator of (IX.19.1) change through time at exactly the same rate. The sectoral capital output/ratio, $\varkappa_i(t)$, remains constant, although the technical coefficients are changing all the time. This is the type of technical progress which, in the economic literature, has been called 'neutral' in the sense of Harrod.[23] Technical progress is 'neutral' with reference to the capital intensity of the production process. The quantity of labour to be used directly and the quantity of labour to be kept locked up into capital goods maintain the same proportion to each other through time. Note now, from (IX.19.2), that the capital/labour ratio is increasing all the time at rate ϱ^*, since the wage rate is increasing, in real terms, as a reflection of the growth of productivity in the economic system as a whole. Each worker will be using more and more expensive machines. Assuming – as we have been assuming – that more capital per man, at current (constant) prices, means more *physical* capital per man, i.e. more mechanised machines, the degree of mechanisation in the production of commodity i is increasing all the time. 'Capital-intensity neutral' technical progress thus always entails the use of more physical capital per man: it always is 'physical-capital using'.

(b) 'Capital-intensity increasing' technical progress

When

$$(IX.19.4) \qquad \varrho_i > \varrho_{k_i},$$

both the capital/output ratio and the capital/labour ratio are increasing through time. Both the degree of capital intensity and the degree of mechanisation are increasing. This is 'capital-intensity increasing' technical progress. 'Capital-intensity increasing' technical progress is always *a fortiori* 'physical-capital using'.

(c) 'Capital-intensity decreasing' technical progress

When

$$(IX.19.5) \qquad \varrho_i < \varrho_{k_i},$$

the capital/output ratio (i.e. the degree of capital intensity) is decreasing through time. Technical progress is 'capital-intensity decreasing'. However the capital/labour ratio (i.e. the degree of mechanisation) may increase or decrease. As we can see from (IX.19.2), that part of the ratio which refers to the technical coefficients is decreasing through time – as is the case for (IX.19.1). However, as opposed to what happens to

---

23 See Roy F. Harrod, *Towards a Dynamic Economics*, op. cit., pp. 22–3.

the capital/output ratio, the capital/labour ratio also contains the wage rate, which is increasing through time at the over-all rate of growth of productivity. To sort out what may happen, we must further distinguish three sub-cases; to be listed under headings (c, i), (c, ii), (c, iii).

(c, i) *'Physical-capital neutral' technical progress*

If it were to happen that the over-all rate of growth of productivity ϱ^* were exactly to balance the excess of the productivity growth in the capital good sector over the productivity growth in the consumption good sector, i.e. if

$$(\text{IX.19.6}) \qquad \varrho_{k_i} = \varrho_i + \varrho^*,$$

then, as may be seen from (IX.19.2), the capital/labour ratio would remain constant through time, although the capital/output ratio would be decreasing. A technical change that leaves the capital/labour ratio constant was called 'neutral' by Hicks.[24] As we may now see clearly, technical progress is, in this case, 'neutral' with reference to the degree of mechanisation of the production process. It is 'neutral' with respect to the use of *physical* capital per man (to the extent that changes in capital goods at constant (average) prices reflect changes in *physical* capital, as we have assumed). However it is not neutral with respect to the degree of capital intensity, which is decreasing all the time.

(c, ii) *'Physical-capital using' technical progress*

When

$$(\text{IX.19.7}) \qquad \varrho_{k_i} < \varrho_i + \varrho^*,$$

the capital/labour ratio (i.e. degree of mechanisation) is increasing, even though the capital/output ratio (i.e. the degree of capital intensity) is decreasing. Technical progress, though being capital-intensity decreasing, is physical-capital using.

---

24 J. R. Hicks, *The Theory of Wages*, Macmillan, London 1932, pp. 121–2. To be precise, Hicks' definition is in terms of a constancy of the capital/labour ratio and also of an increase of the 'marginal productivities' of labour and capital in the same proportions. In our context, the concepts of 'marginal productivities' make no sense (see section 16 above). In their place, one might refer to constancy of the income shares. But it is clear that (IX.19.6) does not necessarily keep income shares constant. Therefore, physical-capital neutral technical progress, as defined by (IX.19.6), does not exactly coincide with Hicks' definition of neutrality. It takes, however, the same bench-mark for neutrality (constancy of the capital/labour ratio).

(c, iii) *'Physical-capital saving' technical progress*

When

$$(IX.19.8) \qquad \varrho_{k_i} > \varrho_i + \varrho^*,$$

technical progress is so strong in the capital goods producing sector as to overcome the effects of productivity growth both in the consumption goods sector and in the economic system as a whole. Hence, the capital/labour ratio also (as well as the capital/output ratio) decreases through time. In this case, technical progress is both capital-intensity decreasing and physical-capital saving.

To complete the classification, with reference to the terminology that has been used in the economic literature, it may be useful to mention that Solow has shown special concern precisely with this type of technical progress. Those inventions that increase the efficiency of physical capital, he has called 'capital augmenting' technical progress.[25] Thereby yet another criterion of 'neutrality' has been used. To cover this criterion as well, we may sub-distinguish case (c, iii) into three further subcases, to be indicated by headings (c, iii, a), (c, iii, b), (c, iii, c).

(c, iii, a) *'Direct-labour neutral' technical progress*

When, the (IX.19.8) being satisfied, $\varrho_{k_i} > 0$, but

$$(IX.19.9) \qquad \varrho_i = 0,$$

both the capital/output ratio and the capital/labour ratio decrease, but the ratio of output to labour remains absolutely constant. A technical progress that leaves the output/labour ratio constant has been called 'neutral' in the sense of Solow.[26] In this case, technical progress is 'neutral' with respect to the output/labour ratio. This simply means that there is no technical progress in the consumption goods sector. All improvements in productivity take place in the capital goods sector. It

---

25 Robert M. Solow, *Capital Theory and the Rate of Return*. North Holland, Amsterdam 1963, p. 59.
26 See, for example, F. H. Hahn and R. C. O. Matthews, 'The Theory of Economic Growth: a Survey', in *The Economic Journal*, 1964, pp. 830; R. G. D. Allen, *Macro-Economic Theory*, London 1967, p. 239. Here again one must repeat the same *caveat* expressed in footnote 24 with reference to Hicks. Direct-labour neutral technical progress, as expressed by (IX.19.9), does not keep the income shares constant. Hence it does not exactly coincide with the definition of Solow neutrality given by Hahn–Matthews and by Allen. However, it takes the same neutrality bench-mark (constancy of the output/labour ratio).

becomes particularly clear, from our analysis, that Solow's 'capital-augmenting' technical progress (i.e. all 'physical-capital saving' technical progress) ultimately expresses an increase of labour productivity (i.e. a saving of labour) in the capital goods producing sector.

(c, iii, b) *'Direct-labour saving' technical progress*

When (in addition to $\varrho_{k_i} > 0$)

$$(IX.19.10) \qquad \varrho_i > 0,$$

then the ratio of output to labour is increasing through time, as always happens in cases (a), (b), (c, i), (c, ii).

(c, iii, c) *'Direct-labour using' technical progress*

When

$$(IX.19.11) \qquad \varrho_i < 0,$$

(while of course, $\varrho_{k_i} > 0$ to such an extent as to ensure $(dl_i(t)/dt) < 0$, for otherwise there would not be technical progress) the ratio of output to labour is decreasing through time. In this case there is in fact technical regress in the consumption goods producing sector but technical progress in the capital goods producing sector is strong enough as to more than compensate for it.

Our classification is now complete. Table IX.1 summarises the results. Note that using the more complex formulations (III.4.6n), (III.4.10n) would lead to exactly the same results.

Before finishing, it seems important to stress that in *all* cases considered – namely in cases (a), (b), (c, i), (c, ii), (c, iii, a), (c, iii, b), (c, iii, c) – technical progress *always* is ultimately labour-saving.[27]

20. Alternative criteria of 'neutrality' of technical progress and their information contents

We may note that the three alternative criteria of 'neutrality' of technical progress mentioned above, referring to constancy respectively of the capital/output ratio, the capital/labour ratio and the output/labour

---

27 It should be quite clear, at this point, how misleading the macro-economic growth literature has been when it has taken the term 'labour saving' as equivalent to 'capital using' and the term 'labour using' as equivalent to 'capital saving'. The present analysis shows that there is no equivalence between these terms. Whether capital-intensity increasing, neutral, or decreasing, whether physical-capital using, neutral or saving, whether 'labour augmenting' or 'capital augmenting', technical progress is always ultimately labour saving.

Table IX.1 Classification of technical progress

Capital-intensity classification	Physical-capital classification	Direct-labour classification
Capital-intensity increasing, when $\varrho_i > \varrho_{k_i}$		
Capital-intensity neutral, i.e. 'neutral in the sense of Harrod', when $\varrho_i = \varrho_{k_i}$	*always physical-capital using*	
Capital-intensity decreasing, when $\varrho_i < \varrho_{k_i}$		
	Physical-capital using when $\varrho_{k_i} < \varrho_i + \varrho^*$	
	Physical-capital neutral when $\varrho_{k_i} = \varrho_i + \varrho^*$	*always direct-labour saving*
	Physical-capital saving when $\varrho_{k_i} > \varrho_i + \varrho^*$	
		Direct-labour saving when $\varrho_i > 0$
		Direct-labour neutral when $\varrho_i = 0$
		Direct-labour using when $\varrho_i < 0$ (and yet $(dl_i/dt) < 0$)

213

ratio, have quite different information contents. The third criterion – which takes constancy of the output/labour ratio as the bench-mark for neutrality – is in fact rather poor in this respect. It only conveys the information that technical progress takes place exclusively in the capital goods producing sector. In terms of information content, the second criterion – which refers to constancy of the capital/labour ratio – is a little better. It conveys the information that the degree of mechanisation remains constant in spite of technical change. As we have seen, this information is relevant for problems concerning employment.

The richest of the three criteria of 'neutrality' – in terms of information content – seems therefore to be the first one – the one originally proposed by Harrod – which conveys information on the effects of technical progress on capital-intensity, i.e. on the proportion between the labour which must be kept locked-up in the means of production and the labour which is currently required. Harrod's criterion of 'neutrality' emerges as the only one to be relevant for all the problems concerning prices, income distribution and international trade.

It should also be noted that all classification of technical change has been made at the sectoral level, simply because it is only at the sectoral level that capital/output or capital/labour ratios have a purely technical meaning. As was pointed out in chapter V (section 11), the over-all capital/output and capital/labour ratios are more complex concepts, as they depend not only on technology but also on the composition of output (except in the trivial case of a one-commodity world). Any extension of the concepts examined above to macro-economic magnitudes must therefore be made with great care.

There is no doubt that there still is a sense in taking the over-all capital/output ratio as an expression of the capital intensity of the production process in the economic system as a whole, as it expresses, for the whole system, the proportion between the total labour that must be kept 'locked up' in the means of production and the total labour that is currently required. Similarly, there still is a sense in taking the over-all capital/labour ratio as an indication of the degree of mechanisation of the production process in the economic system as a whole. But it would clearly be illegitimate to take *changes* in the over-all capital/output and capital/labour ratios as indicating any particular type of technical change. They might well indicate changes in the composition of output, and thus of demand, or – more likely – compensations of various changes both in technology and in demand. Confirmation is thus obtained of the earlier proposition (see chapter V, section 11) that the macro-economic capital/output and capital/labour ratios cannot be used for any classification of technical change.

214

21. Increase in the degree of mechanisation, appearing as a process of 'substitution' of capital for labour

An interesting question that might be asked at this point is: which type of technical change is more likely to take place in the real world, and therefore which one of the three criteria of neutrality is more likely to be near to the actual process of capital accumulation? One cannot of course fully answer this question, except by empirical research. Yet one can make a few definite and important remarks.

Clearly, *all* types of technical change will be observed in practice, sometimes and somewhere. Yet experience seems to indicate that, by and large, in the industrial world in which we live, most technical progress – though not each single technical change – takes the external form of an increase in the degree of mechanisation. We have seen that this does not necessarily mean an increase in capital intensity. In fact, in spite of the continually increasing degree of mechanisation, the proportion of labour embodied in the capital goods to current labour has not anywhere shown any definite tendency either to increase or decrease. This makes neutrality in the sense of Harrod appear to be, from among the three types of neutrality, also the one that comes nearest, on average, to the actual process.

To the extent that this is so, it is interesting to note that a process of continual increase of the capital/labour ratios (at roughly constant capital/output ratios) will appear as the normal pattern of technical change in industrial systems. Each worker will be operating more, and more complex, and more expensive, machinery – i.e. will actually be using more and more capital, both in physical terms and at current (constant) prices – in spite of the fact that the labour directly and indirectly embodied in such machinery remains roughly constant. Note now that this is precisely the usual pattern of technical change, which in common parlance is referred to as 'substitution of capital for labour'.

It is important to stress this point, as we can see most clearly here that the usual process of increasing mechanisation, which to any external observer will appear as one of substitution of physical capital for labour, has nothing to do with the 'substitution process' which has been presented by neo-classical economic theory. As is well known, neo-classical economics has presented the process of substitution of capital for labour as being generated by a 'movement along the (neo-classical) production function' – a movement which is necessarily associated with an increase in the wage rate, a decrease in the rate of profit and a move to more 'roundabout' (more capital intensive) processes of production. But there is nothing of the sort in what emerges as the usual pattern of

215

technical change. 'Roundaboutness', if we take it in the sense of degree of capital intensity, need not change at all; the rate of profit need not change either; and yet the degree of mechanisation (the 'substitution of physical capital for labour') may be increasing all the time. The wage rate will also increase, but as an effect, not a cause, of technical change![28]

In a production system – we may conclude – the process of a continually increasing degree of mechanisation, which for all practical purposes will appear as one of 'substitution of physical capital for labour', emerges as the normal expression of the process of change of techniques – the normal pattern of technical progress.[29]

22. The determinants of capital intensity

An interesting implication of the foregoing analysis, worth underlining explicitly, is that – contrary to what neo-classical economics has always maintained – neither the problem of choice of techniques nor the process of substitution of physical capital for labour, and thus none of the problems related to changes in the degree of capital intensity of the production processes, can in any relevant way be linked up with changes in the rate of profit.

What then determines the degree of capital intensity? Rigorously speaking, this question has been implicitly answered already in our previous analysis, but it may be useful to make this answer explicit here.

At the sectoral level, each capital/output ratio is essentially determined by *technology*. In more practical terms, if, at any given point of time, the capital/output ratio in a sector such as 'house renting' is of the order of 100 times larger than in a sector such as 'clothing', the reason simply is that *technology* is such that the minimum-cost production processes requires, in the house renting sector, a capital/output ratio

28 It is quite easy to be misled on these matters. If we notice, for example, that in a certain branch of industry the process of increasing wages – which reflects the general increase of productivity – determines at a certain point the replacement of some workers by a machine (whose price has remained constant or has increased less than the wage rate) this does not mean at all that the shift of technique has been caused by the fact that the higher wage rate has made 'labour relatively more expensive than capital'. The wage rate has increased for the process of making the machine as well! What the substitution simply means is that improvements in productivity must have taken place in the machine producing industry so that the cost of the machines has increased less than the wage rate. In this way, in the new situation, it takes a lower total (direct and indirect) amount of labour inputs per unit of output to make the new machines and then to operate them with fewer workers than to employ the replaced workers with the old machines.

29 Cf. my own 'Substitution in the Real World', an appendix to 'On "Non-Substitution" in Production Models', *Cambridge Journal of Economics*, 1977, pp. 393–4.

which is 100 times larger than in the clothing sector.[30] Clearly, no change in the rate of profit (or in the rate of interest) will appreciably change this proportion. Similarly if, in any production process, at a certain point of time, machines are substituted for labour, the reason simply is that productivity in the machine producing sector is increasing faster than the over-all wage rate. This process, again, is entirely independent of any change in the rate of profit (or in the rate of interest).

At the level of the economic system as a whole, the picture becomes more complex, because the aggregate capital/output ratio also contains the demand coefficients. This means that both technology and demand contribute to determining the degree of capital intensity of the economic system as a whole, and both the evolution of technology and the evolution of demand govern its movement through time. But no relevant role on these matters can be attributed to the rate of profit.

23. Rate of interest and total investments in capitalist systems

One final point deserves to be brought out explicitly. The finding that changes in the rate of profit have no role whatever to play in the process of substitution of physical capital for labour and in the determination of the degree of capital intensity, either in any single sector or in the economic system as a whole, does not mean that, in any given economic system, the rate of interest has no role to play in the determination of the total amount of investment. This is an entirely different matter.

The point is important to stress, especially with reference to the institutions of the capitalist systems, where the real rate of interest and the general rate of profit are pushed towards equalisation.

To clarify the problems involved, one must go back to consider the decisions for investment projects at the level of the single enterprise. At this level, entrepreneurs will have, on the one side, a certain set of expectations about future developments of demand and prices, referring to the various products which are within their technological reach. And, on the other side, they will have many plans (technical projects) before them, of which they know the cost (based on current and expected

---

30 This proportion is taken from R. N. Grosse ('*The Capital Structure of the American Economy*', pp. 185–242, in *Studies in the Structure of the American Economy*, ed. by W. W. Leontief, New York, 1953). The statements made in the text are so plain that they would not even require mentioning were it not for the fact that traditional economic theory, by its emphasis on the rate of profit, has led us to overlook them – namely to neglect the role played by factors accounting for differences of the order of 1 to 100 – and to concentrate on factors of uncertain influence and in any case of negligible importance.

prices). On the basis of these two sets of data the obvious way to proceed is to rank all the technical projects in order of profitability.[31] Let me stress that the order in which the projects come into this ranking depends on their present cost (i.e. the relative prices of machines, of intermediate commodities, the wage rate and rate of interest) and on future expectations about expansion of demand, quite independently of the degree of capital intensity of each single project. Then a rational procedure will be to carry out these projects in the order in which they are ranked and to stop at the point where the available financial funds, if they are limited, have been exhausted. If financial funds are available in a practically unlimited amount at the market rate of interest, then the projects will be carried out up to that point where the expected profitability of the last project is slightly higher than, or at least equal to, the rate of interest.

It thus follows that, in any actual economic system, changes in credit facilities and/or in the rate of interest will indeed influence the total amount of investment. If, for example, at a certain point in time, the Central Bank, or the monetary or credit authority, decides to make more favourable terms for loans or to cut down the rate of interest at which financial funds may be borrowed, an increase in the total amount of investment is to be expected. The point to stress is that this increase has nothing to do with any 'substitution' of physical capital for labour or with any change in capital intensity. The increase is simply due to the fact that some extra projects are carried out. These extra projects might quite well be the least capital intensive of all.[32]

---

31 This is nothing but Keynes' 'marginal efficiency of capital' schedule. (*The General Theory, op. cit.*, chapter 11.)
32 Cf. my own *Growth and Income Distribution, op. cit.* p. 43.

Chapter X

The structural dynamics of a growing economic system

1. Technical change as a decision-generating process

The time has now come to inquire into the structural dynamics of an industrial economic system, and into the manifold decision problems that such structural dynamics impose on the individual members of the community.

The obvious point of departure for an analysis of this type is represented by equilibrium condition (V.7.1). We have seen that this condition would pose no decision problem if there were no technical progress; for, in such a case, its fulfilment would simply require a once-for-all gearing up of all sectors of the economic system to a uniform rate of growth.

But if there is technical change, then each technical coefficient decreases in its own way over time. As a consequence, the structure of prices and of employment will change, while condition (V.7.1) will steadily tend to become under-satisfied. Unemployment will steadily be generated, unless compensating upward movements take place in the coefficients of *demand*. On average, per capita demand will have continually to increase, as a necessary condition for keeping the economic system in equilibrium growth. It is this requirement that becomes of crucial importance, as it comes to impose a whole series of *new* decisions about consumption and investment.

More specifically, a whole process of decision-making is necessarily imposed on the members of the community by the very existence of technical progress. This is a characteristic of any progressive industrial society, quite independent of its institutional set-up.

2. Structural dynamics of prices and the movement of the general price level

The most immediate impact of technical change can be observed on the structure of costs, and consequently, if efficiency is to be maintained in the economic system, on the structure of prices.

This process of change may be looked at in two successive steps. The first step consists in considering the movements over time of the wage rate and of the average of commodity prices. Suppose, for the sake of simplicity, an economic system in which the over-all rate of profit remains roughly constant over time. Then the *real* wage rate will have to increase at the standard (i.e. average) rate of productivity growth. This means that, in equilibrium growth, the movements in time of the wage rate and of the average price level are linked to each other by a very definite dynamic relation. Whatever the movement of prices, if efficiency is to be kept through time, the wage rate must increase at a percentage rate of change that exceeds the percentage rate of increase of the price level (or 'rate of inflation') by the standard rate of productivity growth.

The second step that we may take is to consider the changing structure of prices themselves. Since productivity is moving at a different rate of change in each sector, the cost of each commodity is changing over time relative to the cost of any other. Therefore, the price of each commodity *must* also change over time relative to the price of any of the others. Were this not to happen, the price structure would become distorted and cease to perform one of its two functions – the function of efficiency – which has been discussed in chapter VII. The important result that emerges from this analysis is that the price structure *must change* over time. A price structure which is efficient at any given point of time is no longer efficient in the subsequent time period, if kept invariant in spite of the variation of the structure of technology, and thus of costs. In practice, this means that, in a modern economic system, a price structure which is kept constant over time is a price structure which is cumulatively becoming more and more distorted.

Let me stress that these propositions are valid whatever the movement of the *average* price level may be. To understand this better, it may be useful to consider an economic system in which a conventional unit of account, the monetary unit – rather than any particular physical commodity, e.g. gold – is used as the *numéraire* for the price system. If the central monetary authority concentrates its attention on trying to govern the average level of prices, then it must be realised that such an authority will not be able to fix the absolute level of *any* price. Suppose, more specifically, that the aim of the central monetary authority is stated as that of keeping a *stable* level of prices, while letting the wage rate increase at the same rate as the over-all (i.e. 'standard') rate of productivity growth. This means that the *average* price level must be kept constant. But if the average of prices is to remain constant over time, then – except by a fluke – no single price can actually remain constant over time. Half of the prices on average (on a weighted average) must increase and the other half *must* decrease. These results should be stressed because we have not yet become accustomed to the idea that relative prices *must* change over time. We have not yet become fully aware of the fact that constant relative prices from one period to another mean a cumulative distortion of the price system, if meanwhile technical progress is taking place at different rates in different sectors.

A regrettable consequence of this failure to understand the requirements of an appropriate structural dynamics of prices can be very widely observed today. And it may well be useful to refer briefly to the specific institutional set-up of the market economies. It is a well-known and proud claim of many large industrial concerns in the Western industrial countries that they have maintained prices constant over long periods of time or have slightly decreased them, in spite of wage increases. The fact has even impressed many economists (so much accustomed to thinking in terms of a static world) as a remarkable performance. But if these large concerns are precisely those which enjoy productivity increases above average – as is normally the case – the performance may in fact not be good at all. The aim of price stability would require that they should *decrease* their prices. If they do not cut their prices, or even if they cut them by less than the excess over average of their increases in productivity, then the Trade Unions cannot be blamed for pressing to obtain a general wages increase *above* the average increase of productivity. In fact, Trade Unions should be encouraged to do so in order to maintain efficiency in the economic system. Of course, this will cause those branches of the production system where productivity is increasing less than average to put their prices up even more, which means that the general price level will rise. A 'creeping' inflationary process, as it has been called, will follow as a consequence. Yet the increase in the price level, in these circumstances, is the only way in which a distortion of the price structure can be avoided, or sometimes even only contained within tolerable limits. In other words, if prices do not fall in those branches where productivity increases above average, then creeping inflation is the only way in which the economic system can maintain or try to maintain an efficient price structure.

The conclusion is very simple. When there are institutional obstacles to cutting prices in those branches of production where productivity is growing above average, a corresponding rise in the general level of prices (creeping inflation) must be allowed in order to restore, or at least to move towards the restoration of, the natural (efficient) structure of the price system. In the same way as it has by now been acknowledged that the general level of prices and the level of wages cannot both be kept constant, if productivity is increasing, it also must be acknowledged that the general price level, and, we may say, most of the industrial prices, cannot both be kept constant if, in most of the industrial branches – as is normally the case – productivity increases at a rate above average. Constancy of these (industrial) prices and avoidance of inflation is a contradiction, if efficiency is to be kept in the economic system as a whole. It follows that, in such situations, any attempt by the central monetary authority to prevent the average price level from increasing (by limitations on credit or on the available quantity of money) can only result in putting the economic system under strain. These attempts may sometimes give the appearance of attaining the purpose of slowing down the process of creeping inflation, but this is only a temporary illusion. They can only succeed to the extent that they make a price distortion permanent, thereby generating inefficiencies, or, even worse, to the extent that, by discouraging investments, they slow down the whole process of increase in productivity and therefore of economic growth.[1]

3. Structural dynamics of production and the organisational necessity of aiming at steady growth

There is another aspect – the demand aspect, as we know – of technical progress, and as a consequence there is another complex dynamic

---

1 It is rather interesting to note that many large industrial concerns of the Western countries have been much quicker than Governments, or economists, to find a way out of this *impasse*. Unwilling on the one side to cut prices, and faced on the other with the necessity of containing a too marked price distortion, they have often preferred to give out a substantial part of their productivity gains in the form of wage increases *to their own workers*, well above the increase of the general wage level. In this way, a distorted wage structure is substituted for a too markedly distorted price structure (which would arouse the anger of Trade Unions and of public opinion), with the consequence of creating privileges for the workers who happen to be in progressive industries. The policy is of course more advantageous to the single firm than a policy of decreasing prices, because it concentrates the benefits of technical progress among the firm's workers, instead of spreading them out impersonally over all consumers. In this way the policy: (a) links the workers much more closely to the firm; (b) makes them feel less solidarity towards the other (less well paid) workers, thereby weakening their loyalty to the Trade Unions; (c) allows the firm itself to make a better selection of its personnel; (d) increases the personal incomes of the workers and therefore their demand for industrial goods. Whether this state of affairs may be tolerated, *faute de mieux*, especially in developing countries, for the sake of not hitting progressive firms which are producing 'economic miracles' is another matter. But the process itself cannot be considered a normal one in a full employment economic system; nor can it go on cumulatively.

process, 'dual' to that of prices – the dynamics of the structure of production. As productivity increases, per capita incomes rise: the increments of demand will cluster in succession around different goods. This means that the rate of change of demand for each commodity will be continually changing over time and will normally be different from the rate of change of demand for any other commodity. The actual production of each sector will follow a growth path of its own, at a *non-steady* rate of change.

This process has been described in chapters IV and V. Now we can go a step further, or rather deeper. A process of structural change of production imposes a very specific type of difficulty, and therefore of decision to take, on any administrative unit in which production is organised. Clearly, a pattern of growth requiring unsteady rates of change for the production of each commodity is not the best one from a purely organisational standpoint. Especially if we imagine production organised into large enterprises – which is a pattern that technology very often imposes – it is quite easy to realise how the financial means at the disposal of each enterprise, the possibilities of training new personnel, the outflow of new ideas, the abilities of the managers to face new situations, etc., take the shape of rather steady flows over time. Within each period of time, these possibilities have a definite upper limit (or at least an upward rapidly stiffening limit). And on the other hand, most of them, if not utilised within the time period, can hardly be reserved for the following one; they simply go to waste. This means that an efficient way, from a purely organisational point of view, of pushing for a long-run expansion of plants, technical and administrative structures, trained personnel, etc., is that of gearing up expansion to a rate of growth which is roughly steady or at least not too unsteady. Now, if the pattern of expansion of demand, on the other hand, is *necessarily* non-steady, a great deal of organisational difficulties and inefficiencies may arise. When demand overcomes the steady rate to which the enterprise is geared up, at least a part of it will remain unsatisfied, and when it falls below that steady rate, the enterprise will remain with idle productive capacities or with unexploited organisational or research possibilities. There is a further aspect of this problem in connection with employment, as will be shown in further detail in the following section 5. When, in a certain sector, demand becomes saturated and fails to increase as fast as productivity, the number of jobs in that sector will begin to be reduced. But, in any enterprise, the actual dismissal of workers is, on efficiency and organisational grounds, a rather painful step to take. It entails wastage of skills and many re-adaptation problems on the side of the workers; and the dismantling of organisational structures and waste of experience and ideas behind them on the side of the employers.

There is here an interesting contrast that represents perhaps one of the most problematical aspects of any policy of economic growth in modern industrial societies. The contrast is between the steady possibilities of efficient growth of the single organisational units of production and the necessarily unsteady nature of the expansion of demand for each commodity. (Economic development would become so much easier if production of all commodities were to expand proportionately!)

This contrast is inevitable. Actually, the stronger technical progress, the more striking this contrast will turn out to be. The immediate inference that we may make is that, in practice, the dynamics of the production structure must indeed be exerting an enormous pressure on the single enterprises to place themselves, so to speak, across the process of structural change, in order to catch the directions in which demand is expanding. In fact, each production organisational unit will turn out to be the more successful in avoiding inefficiencies and therefore in keeping costs down and potential growth up, the more it is able to shape its over–all expansion as closely as possible to a pattern of steady growth, in spite of the necessarily unsteady growth of demand for each commodity. There are at least four ways in which a pattern of steady growth can be aimed at. The first and most obvious one is to try to utilise the existing physical appliances, personnel, organisational and financial structure, technical know-how, etc. to enter new fields of production, where demand is expanding, or to introduce entirely new products. A second way is to keep a reservoir, or backlog, of ideas about new products and new investment projects, in order to smooth out prospective difficulties and ensure a potentially steady expansion. A third way is to try to manipulate consumers' decisions through advertising. A fourth way, finally, is to find out new outlets abroad or directly to develop new markets abroad.[2]

2 As a corollary to this discussion, some new light may also be shed on the dispute on 'balanced' and 'unbalanced' growth, which took place some years ago (see, for example, R. Nurkse, *Problems of Capital Formation in Underdeveloped Countries*, Oxford 1953; A. Q. Hirschman, *The Strategy of Economic Development*, New Haven, 1958; P. Streeten, 'Unbalanced Growth', in *Oxford Economic Papers*, 1959). In a strictly closed economic system, especially when full employment has already been reached, balanced growth (namely an expansion of each production branch according to the elasticity of demand with respect to income) is clearly the ideal pattern of economic growth. The proponents of the concept, however, did not originally realise the implications of such a pattern of growth, namely a series of unsteady rates of expansion for the production of each commodity. Organisationally, this is a very difficult (and in many respects wasteful) pattern of growth to plan. Therefore, to the extent to which – through exports,

All these are, after all, rather familiar features of a modern industrial society. Multi-product firms, the continuous marketing of new products, advertising, export drives, and the establishment of branches abroad have by now become in any industrial country the normal pattern of operation of expanding and successful enterprises, especially of those which are very near to the final consumers. But even those enterprises which are in the earlier stages of production – like iron, steel, coal, etc. – find themselves inevitably inserted into the same process, by a continuous change in the composition of their customers, which takes for them the place of the structural change in the composition of the products.

The deep motivating factors of these all too familiar features, however, have hardly ever penetrated traditional economic theory. In particular, the traditional theoretical framework of marginal economic theory makes it almost impossible to realise that the efficient organisation of the single units of production is not something which can be investigated in isolation from the structural dynamics of the economic system as a whole.

4. A digression on the relevant decisions at the level of the single production units

It may be useful to follow up the foregoing remarks and open a short digression to point out more explicitly how the relevant decisions which are imposed on the entrepreneurs by the structural dynamics of production lie a very long way away from those on which traditional economic analysis has accustomed us to concentrate our attention.

The traditional image of the producer is that of an 'agent' intent on finding the optimum *proportion* in which 'labour and capital' are to be combined. No other problem is supposed to exist for him. Technology is supposed to be fixed, the commodity to be produced is supposed to be well-defined, and the quantities which can be sold at any price are supposed to be known and given. The producer only has to watch carefully any relative change of the wage rate and the rate of interest that may occur, in order promptly to modify the existing technique so as to reach the new optimum 'proportion of labour to capital'.

This picture, besides distorting the whole problem of choice of technique, as has been argued already in the previous chapter, now

---

prohibition of certain imports, etc. – it is possible to abandon such a pattern and specialise in the direction of a more steadily expanding production of a limited number of commodities (this is in fact what 'unbalanced growth' has been taken to mean) a higher over-all rate of growth may be achieved.

appears to be misleading also in the selection of the factors which are relevant in entrepreneurial decisions. Surely, in a dynamic environment, the most predictable factors, even for rather long periods of time, are just those that the marginalist approach considers to be the variables of the problem – the wage rate and the rate of interest. On the other hand, those elements which are most uncertain and which in practice are most susceptible of changes are just those that the marginalist approach considers as fixed – technology and demand.

In practice, there is very little that the single producer has to decide on the question of proportions of labour to capital. The requirements of an efficient-growth organisation will induce him (her) to tend to gear up expansion to steady (though not necessarily uniform) rates of growth of capital investment, sales, trained personnel, etc. The aim will then be to try *not* to change the proportions in which labour and financial funds tend to flow in, whatever the use that the enterprise is going to make of them. At given prices, decisions will mainly concern technical methods and the composition of production. On the side of technology, expectations on the comparative possibilities of improvements of different technical methods of production may sometimes cause a technique to be preferred simply because its technology is improving very fast, even when its relative efficiency is not the optimum one at the time the choice is made. On the side of the composition of output, very important may become the expectations on: (a) the length of time required before the growth rate of demand falls below the growth rate of productivity; (b) the possibilities of inducing fresh demand for new products which fall into the technological range of the existing experience and productive capacity; (c) prospects of entering or opening up new markets at home or abroad, and so on.

To conclude, in a process of economic growth with rapid technical change, it is not on problems of varying the proportions of inputs for a given output that major decisions are required, but on problems of finding out – through diversification of products and markets – an appropriate and ever changing composition of outputs to be obtained from fairly steady inflows of inputs.

5. Technological unemployment and labour mobility as a consequence of technical progress

There is a third type of structural dynamics, which follows as an inevitable consequence of the two previously discussed – the dynamics of the structure of employment. Although, fortunately, less marked than the others, structural changes in employment deserve particularly careful attention because they concern the individual members of the community themselves.

In chapter V, these structural changes are represented by expressions (V.10.1), which show the time evolution of employment required by each single sector, and by (V.7.1), which expresses a necessary over-all condition for maintaining full employment. A discussion on the economic meaning of these mathematical expressions has been anticipated already in chapter V (section 10), but it must now be resumed and brought to yield all the implications it contains.

Consider equilibrium condition (V.7.1). It consists of a sum, where each term is the product of a labour coefficient and the corresponding consumption coefficient. Each product $a_{in}a_{ni}$ represents the relative amount of labour (i.e. the proportion of total employment) required for the production of each commodity i ($i = 1, 2, \ldots, n-1$). Over time, each of the technical coefficients (i.e. each a_{ni}) decreases; and this means that, unless the corresponding demand coefficient (the a_{in}) increases at a rate of change higher or at least equal to it, the percentage of total employment required by the production of commodity i ($i = 1, 2, \ldots, n-1$) will decrease, even if production itself may be increasing.

Therefore if – as must normally be the case – the binomials $a_{ni}a_{in}$s continually change over time, condition (V.7.1) will be kept satisfied, i.e. over-all full employment will be maintained, only if the economic system is able to carry out successfully a continuous process of structural redistribution of employment from one sector to another, in accordance with the pattern shaped by the structural dynamics of technology and demand. It should be stressed that this is an unavoidable process. It cannot be stopped, unless technical progress itself is stopped. Therefore, over time, half of the production processes, on average and *in relative terms* (i.e. as a percentage of total employment), will be pushing out redundant labour and the other half will have to absorb it, if total over-all employment is to be successfully kept.

A structural process of this type evidently poses innumerable problems, owing to the fact that labour is inseparable from people and division of labour and specialisation are inseparable from technical progress. The structural dynamics of employment therefore pose grave problems both to the firm and to individuals. It takes time and investment for a firm to train personnel. If a man is to be transferred from one job to another, most of his previous training is lost, potential efficiency is wasted and fresh training, i.e. supplementary capital funds and time, are required. For individuals there are all the psychological and social difficulties of re-adaptation, especially strong when structural

227

redistribution of employment also implies geographical redistribution of population.

Fortunately, the relevant consequences of this structural dynamics are connected with *absolute* rather than relative changes. In other words, it is the number of people actually to be transferred from one job to another that matters and not the variation of the *proportion* of total employment in each industrial branch. And the actual transfers of people are substantially less marked than the variations in percentage terms. There are at least four factors working in this direction (two of which have been hinted at already in chapter V):

(i) First of all, the working population is continually renewing itself through the natural biological process of life. Old people retire and are replaced by the younger generation. By taking advantage of this natural process, it is possible to direct the young to jobs which are different from those the old performed.

(ii) Population is normally growing, and the higher the rate of population growth, the easier it is to operate a relative redistribution, without actually transferring people from one job to another. A growing population means both a higher proportion of inflow of young people into the working population; and a *proportional* expansion of demand in all sectors.

(iii) Another most powerful stabilising factor is represented by the operation of the multi-product enterprises. This factor is quite distinct from the previous two, because it can be built up by the economic system itself, and therefore represents yet another aspect of the responses of the production organisation to the requirements of 'natural' structural dynamics. The multi-product enterprises, by turning the same organisational unit into the production of a continually changing range of products, are able to provide a remarkable stability of employment. By a continuous change in the composition of their production, they may carry on efficiently (because they are able to choose their new branches according to their experience and know-how) and inside their own organisation, that process of structural change of employment which would otherwise cause so many difficulties to the economic system as a whole. This function of the multi-product enterprises does not seem to have been noticed so far. Yet, multi-product enterprises are playing in our industrial societies a stabilising role which no group of small firms, however flexible they might be, could ever perform.

(iv) A fourth stabilising factor is represented by the extent to which single or multi-product firms succeed, through a successful export policy, in substituting foreign demand for a declining internal demand.

To realise the importance of these four factors, it is enough to reflect that, if it were not for their combined operation, the number of firms dismissing workers, over time, would be no less than half (on average) of the total number of firms. Owing to these four factors, the actual situation is much improved. We shall find, in practice, that half the sectors are expanding both in relative and in absolute terms and are therefore absorbing new workers. The other half will inevitably have decreasing possibilities of providing employment, in relative terms, but not necessarily in absolute terms. In fact some sectors, although reducing the percentage of the total labour force which they employ, may still be increasing the number of their workers. Some other sectors will be decreasing the number of jobs they can offer, although still expanding the physical amount of production. And, finally, some sectors may even be compelled to reduce the absolute amount of production (and *a fortiori* the number of workers) over time. The last two groups of sectors will be dismissing workers. However, since people undertake to work for administrative units of production (business enterprises) and not for abstract 'sectors', the number of actual dismissals may be further narrowed down if the shrinking sectors succeed in finding some outlets for their products outside the economic system (through exports), and/or are operated by multi-product enterprises that simultaneously also operate expanding sectors, where the labour redundancies of the former may be absorbed.

Yet, in spite of all these compensating processes, there may still remain quite a few industrial branches where employment is genuinely decreasing in absolute terms. These industrial branches, which are declining as an effect of technical progress, form a particularly interesting and important category: the declining industries in a process of economic growth.

6. Declining industries in a process of economic growth

As must have become clear by now, there is nothing irrational or undesirable about the existence of declining industries in a process of economic growth. They represent yet another aspect of technical progress and of the structural dynamics that it entails.

In the real world, of course, the phenomenon of declining industries is very well known. It has constantly – and we may well say, inevitably – been with us since the inception of the industrial revolution. In the nineteenth century, it aroused the anger of the workers even to the pitch of destroying the machines which, by increasing productivity more than the possibility of expansion of demand, caused their dismissal (remember the 'Luddite' riots).

Unfortunately, economic theorists have never been adequately equipped to deal with this problem, although, of course, they have not been able to avoid it, owing to its enormous practical relevance in an industrial society. Ricardo was drawn to face it in the controversial chapter 'On Machinery' which he added in the 3rd edition of his *Principles*. As is well known, he was compelled there to concede an exception to his previous full employment theoretical model, by admitting, without being able to give a satisfactory explanation, that the introduction of machines (technical progress) may cause unemployment. Later on, the marginalist economists, despite the elegance of their theories, were even worse equipped than the Classical economists to understand the process behind the declining industries. Suffice it to mention, as an example, the argument used by Wicksell,[3] when trying to refute Ricardo's analysis of technological unemployment. For Wicksell, technical improvements and the introduction of machines may cause unemployment, but this unemployment is immediately re-absorbed because the wage rate will fall, and entrepreneurs will 'substitute' labour for capital, i.e. shift to more labour-intensive methods of production, so that more labour will be needed. If one follows this argument logically, one comes to the conclusion that a continuous process of technical progress is accompanied by a continuous process of decreasing wage rates! The conclusion is so absurd that it requires no comment.[4] Perhaps, the economist who perceived this process more clearly than anybody else was Schumpeter. Unfortunately, he had no clear theoretical scheme in which to put it. But he gave at least a descriptive analysis, which he tried to epitomise in a famous expression: 'creative destruction',[5] applied to the disruptive effects of technical progress on some sections of the economic system.

In the theoretical framework which has been provided in the present work, the phenomenon of declining industries appears, in all its clarity and simplicity, as the logical counterpart of the expanding industries. We must say that, fortunately, owing to population growth, retirements,

3 Knut Wicksell, *Lectures on Political Economy, op. cit.*, vol. I, pp. 133 and ff.
4 We have seen already how important the phenomenon of substitution of capital for labour may become (see previous chapter). But, as we have seen, such a phenomenon has a quite different explanation from the one insisted upon by the marginalist economists.
5 Joseph A. Schumpeter, *Capitalism, Socialism and Democracy*, New York [1942] 1950, chapter VII.

the existence of multi-product enterprises and sometimes also to successful export policies, the process is not as marked as potentially it might be. Nevertheless, to have industries which are reducing their employment, and even industries which are compelled to shrink their production, is a necessary consequence of technical progress. In order to understand the process correctly, it is essential to look at it in the framework of the structural dynamics of the economic system as a whole.

If a machine is introduced in an industrial sector because the indirect labour it embodies is less than the direct labour it replaces, and if production – owing to saturated demand – does not expand (or expands at a lower rate than the rate of the increase in productivity), then workers will be pushed out of that sector. But this is what technical progress is. It means producing the same amount of goods with a smaller quantity of labour; in other words, it means that a lower percentage of the working population are able to provide the economic system with the same amount of production as before. Understandably enough, the redundant workers may create serious problems of adaptation, yet they have become redundant. Society as a whole can obtain the same quantities of goods as before without their 'toil and trouble'. The solution to these difficulties clearly cannot be that of preventing the introduction of the machines, as the 'Luddite' workers thought in the nineteenth century. This would mean arresting the application of technical progress. Nor can the solution be that of decreasing wages, as the marginalist economists advocated with the supposed purpose of decreasing costs and prices and thus of stimulating demand. Decreasing wages would produce precisely the opposite result; namely a diminution of personal incomes, which would reduce, not stimulate, demand. The correct answer to the problem is clearly that of introducing the machines, of producing with them the same physical quantities as before with fewer workers, and of employing the workers that have become redundant in the production of *other* commodities, old and new. Or, alternatively, to increase for all the proportion of leisure time to total time. In this way productivity and total production and leisure time will increase; which will mean an increase in the real per capita incomes of the whole community.

Of course, a process of growth with structural change, in order to take place while maintaining full employment through time – i.e. while keeping permanently satisfied the two conditions for dynamic equilibrium, (V.4.3) and (V.7.1) – requires that the decision makers in the economic system always succeed in correctly finding out the new sectors that are to be expanded. This is not always an easy problem to solve. We

231

come in fact to face here a process of decision making which is imposed by technical progress and which represents one of the most crucial aspects of the process of economic growth in a full employment economic system.

7. The periodic recurrence of short-run difficulties to full employment

Our analysis has brought us back to the problem hinted at at the very beginning of the chapter. A series of new decisions about consumption and investments are continually and inevitably imposed on the individual members of the community by the structural dynamics of a growing economic system. The crucial point is that these decisions must take place within an over-all framework, which is fixed by the condition of maintaining full employment. A failure to carry them out to their full extent entails a failure to keep macroeconomic condition (V.7.1) satisfied, which means that total effective demand will fail to increase as fast as total potential demand, and unemployment will appear.

As will be realised, we come across a problem here which has been widely discussed in the economic literature, following upon the publication of Keynes' *General Theory*; a problem which has kept a whole host of trade-cycle theorists busy for decades. Keynes had given an explanation of the possibility of a drop in effective demand causing unemployment by formulating two separate behavioural theories – for total consumption and for total investment. His analysis was elaborated in macroeconomic terms – an approach which was justified in his case, since he was only concerned with the short run. (And in the short run, as we have seen earlier, the composition of demand does not matter.) But, in this way, he was only able to pose the problem in a hypothetical and negative form: if, from one time period to the next, total investment falls, because expectations drop, then total demand becomes insufficient and the economic system plunges into a depression. He was not able to give an explanation of why expectations and investment, and therefore total demand and employment, should *periodically* fall.

The task of giving an explanation was taken up only after Keynes, by those economic theorists who elaborated the macro-dynamic models of the trade cycle. I have had the opportunity of showing elsewhere that all these macro-economic models have failed in their purpose.[6] I shall not

6 See 'Cyclical Fluctuations and Economic Growth', *Oxford Economic Papers*, 1960, reprinted in my *Growth and Income Distribution, op. cit.* In this essay, to which the reader is referred also for the bibliography, my purpose was to show that the logic of all macro-dynamic models is such as to explain either fluctuation or growth, but not both. But the arguments of the present section will enable us to carry the conclusions one crucial step further (see also the following footnote).

herefore repeat that critique here. I shall concentrate instead on the positive task of presenting an alternative explanation; a task which is made possible by the disaggregated analysis developed in the previous pages.

The starting point is provided by the demand coefficients in the macro-economic equilibrium condition (V.7.1). There are two different groups of such demand coefficients: the consumption coefficients and the investment coefficients. Each coefficient moves at a particular rate of change, but the way in which consumption coefficients and investment coefficients are decided upon is essentially different. The former are decided upon by consumers, according to their likings and preferences, however determined, and therefore move – so to speak – in an autonomous way. On the other hand, the latter *must* move at the same rate as the corresponding coefficients of the first group. Of course, they also are the outcome of a decision, but not of an autonomous one. For, the decision on each investment coefficient will be successful only if the movement of the corresponding consumption coefficients is exactly detected. Moreover, consumption coefficients may come from breaking down a decision which was previously taken in the aggregate, while the investment coefficients cannot but be decided upon independently of any aggregate magnitude. In other words, especially when per capita incomes are rather high, an individual may well decide first of all how to divide his personal income between consumption and savings (for future needs or anything else) and then decide how to distribute his (her) total consumption among single items. On the other hand, investment decision makers cannot but consider single types of investment. Total investment will then simply result as a sum. It requires a conscious and *ad hoc* decision (by a Central Planning Authority, or by the managing Boards of large enterprises), which by itself is not implied by the process of investment decision, to keep a certain aggregate amount of investment from one time period to another.

For these reasons, we must expect the decisions concerning investment, as a proportion of total national income, to be much more unstable over time than the decisions concerning consumption. Not because of any lack of ability of the investment decision makers to scrutinise consumers' preferences, but simply because investment in each sector has to be made in anticipation of the expected future growth of demand, and at any given point of time consumers themselves may be uncertain about the directions in which their demand is going to develop. It is in this respect that the process of consumers' learning discussed in chapter IV becomes relevant. When per capita incomes are increasing, consumers are pushed into new and previously unexperi-

233

enced fields of consumption, in which they are compelled to make their choices; and it may from time to time become very difficult for the investors to detect clearly which are the directions in which consumers choices are going to expand (or may be induced to expand). When this happens, and some uncertainty falls over the future direction of expansion, *the simple attitude of waiting* or of postponing the actual undertaking of investment, will cause the weighted sum of the investment coefficients to fall. This will make condition (V.7.1) under satisfied.

Unemployment will inevitably appear, and it will be unemployment *both* of productive capacity *and* of labour force.

But why – we may ask – should these falls happen *periodically*? This question can be answered if we recall the contrast, which has been discussed earlier, between the necessarily unsteady rate of expansion of demand and the steadier character, imposed by technological and organisational factors, of the expansion of productive capacity. When some new lines of expansion have been found, i.e. when consumers have learnt their new preferences and are therefore able to decide in which direction to spend their increments of income, the rates of growth of demand are likely soon to become rather high. The rates of expansion of investment cannot be as high, because it takes time to build new plant and also because investors must take a longer-run view of the expansion pattern. There will therefore be a (boom) period in which demand remains partially unsatisfied. But, over time, demand begins to saturate and the rates of expansion of demand inevitably flatten down. Since the rate of inflow of funds for investment, on the other hand, will more or less remain steady, the two rates are bound to meet at a certain point. This may look as if investment has caught up, but in fact most of the catching up is facilitated by demand flattening down. Sooner or later, the investors will realise that they are investing too much, with respect to the rate of expansion of demand. This is a crucial point; and at the same time an inevitable one, because of the very nature of consumers' preferences. When it comes, investors will be compelled to stop or slow down investment, unless they are able to find new outlets – for example by selling abroad, or by devoting the existing productive capacity to making new models or new products for which they can promote demand.

We may notice that, although there is no inevitability about the slowing down of investment and the appearance of unemployment (new outlets may be discovered after all), there is indeed an inevitability about the *periodic* emergence of the *necessity to find new outlets*. This is sufficient to cause the periodicity of slumps, as can easily be realised.

The very nature of the process of structural growth – i.e. of consumers' preferences and of producers' organisational requirements – *imposes periodically* on the economic system, both on the part of consumers and on the part of producers, the necessity of *speeding up the rate of learning*, if unemployment is to be avoided. Unfortunately the rate of learning is not something which can be manipulated at will. Here again multi-product large firms may be of help in increasing the stability of the economic system, by keeping backlogs of ideas to be used when needed. However, the natural consequence will clearly be that, periodically, the direction of expansion will indeed become rather uncertain, that new outlets will not immediately be at hand and that the rate of investment will inevitably flatten down. The effect is that macro-economic condition (V.7.1) will tend to become under-satisfied. Some unemployment will begin to appear and the economic system will at least enter a period, so to speak, 'of pause', until new types of products for expansion or new interests in old products are found (which is a learning process that may take quite some time). Only then will expansion be started all over again.

To conclude, the growth of an economic system with technical progress is normally, though not inevitably, bound to take place by an alternating succession of expansion waves and pauses. I say 'pauses' because this is what comes out of our analysis so far. These 'pauses' are periods in which the rate of growth of effective demand tends to fall short of the rate of growth of the production potential. They are not necessarily depressions (i.e. sharp falls of demand and of employment). Whether they will develop into large scale depressions or not depends on further factors, mainly on the existing type of institutional arrangements, as will be further investigated in the following section.

It is rather important to realise for the moment that the alternating leaps and pauses are inseparably and inevitably linked with the structural dynamics of the economic system; they are – in other words – an *effect of technical progress*. In a hypothetical stationary economic system, or in an economic system expanding only as a result of population growth, with constant coefficients, there would be no difficulty of this sort. No fluctuation of demand, and employment, would arise![7] The only exception would be represented by external

---

7 Note that this is enough to render all the macro-dynamic models inherently incapable of giving any explanation of the recurrence of slumps. The very macro-economic nature of these models implies the assumption of a constant composition of total production through time, as was shown in chapter IV. This means that the equilibrium growth path corresponding to all macro-economic models is such that all sectors are required to expand in the same proportion. But a growth path of this type would entail no learning difficulty whatever! And if no learning difficulty is entailed then there is no reason to

events, entirely outside the process of economic production (such a
military, or economic, wars, natural calamities, etc.).

It is also interesting to note that when economic growth is, as i
normal circumstances, the product of both technical progress an
population growth, the likelihood and the hardship of the difficultie.
discussed above will be the stronger the higher is the proportion o
technical progress with respect to population in determining the over-a
rate of economic growth. Technical progress and population growth
emerge, therefore, as influencing the fluctuating character of economi
growth in *opposite* directions. The former inevitably carries with it al
the difficulties mentioned above. The latter makes it easier for the
economic system to overcome them.

8. Fluctuations in a process of economic growth

There are many consequences that follow from the foregoing analysis
and it may be useful to single out at least a few interesting ones.

The first simple result that may explicitly be pointed out is that the
alternating succession of booms and pauses which has been described
above is necessarily different, quantitatively and qualitatively, *in each
successive recurrence*. This might sound almost a trivial and obvious
remark were it not for the fact that this aspect has necessarily been
missed by the whole macro-economic literature on trade cycles. Yet, i
is one of the most essential features of the process. If, each time, the
level of income and of technology is different, the sectors leading the
expansion will be different; the way and the reasons why the 'pauses'
come about will be different; the difficulties themselves of learning and
finding out new channels of development, and therefore the structural

---

expect any fluctuation at all. In other words, in a hypothetical economic system, where
the composition of production always remains the same, the only problem that each
producer would have to solve, in order to avoid fluctuations, is that of finding the
growth rate to which to gear up the expansion of his (her) enterprise. This is a
once-for-all learning problem, and a very easy one to solve (as the growth rate would be
exactly the same for all sectors). We may also look at the same problem from the point
of view of the economic system as a whole. Here again the only problem to be solved
would appear to be that of learning those particular values of the parameters of the
consumption and investment relations that produce steady growth. It emerges clearly
that this is a *once-for-all* learning problem. It might well require some time to be solved
but once this problem is solved, no other learning would be required any more, and the
economic system would therefore grow smoothly and steadily for all time.

The final conclusion is clear: if the real world were of the type that macro-economic
trade-cycle theorists have assumed it to be, there would be no cycle, but only steady
growth.

character of the *impasse*, will be different as well. This means that there can be no once-for-all *récipe* that solves all the structural difficulties, because these difficulties are new from each time to the next. If they were the same, there would be no recurrence of slumps! Each time, the way in which an economic system can resume full-employment growth is clearly by a structural dynamics appropriate to the level of real per capita income and of technology which has been reached at that time.

A second series of results is the following. Since the alternating successions of booms and pauses (as all processes discussed in the present chapter) are an effect of structural dynamics, i.e. of the interplay of technical improvements and demand evolution, they are typical of an industrial society as such, whatever its institutional organisation may be. Whether, for example, an industrial society is capitalist or socialist will be immaterial to the source of the problems. However, what will indeed be different in a capitalist or in a socialist economy is *the way* in which the economic system reacts to the emergence of the difficulties, so that the same initial difficulties may give rise to different consequences.

On this score a capitalist system may be at a serious disadvantage. During the booms, when part of expanding demand is not satisfied, since decisions are taken by many entrepreneurs with imperfect or no knowledge of what the others are doing, there may easily be investment in excess of the amount which is justified on a long-term basis. Then, when the difficulties mentioned above come about, and a period of pause is entered, the economic system will not be able to stay where it is. If demand is tapering off in some branches and workers are dismissed without being immediately reabsorbed elsewhere, then total demand will drop even more, because it will drop also in sectors where it would not drop had full employment been maintained. A downward cumulative movement will ensue and the economic system will plunge into a slump. Another way of putting this problem is to say that a capitalist economy with technical progress cannot afford to stay still because, if it stops expanding, it falls back. This feature has become all too well known and need not be insisted upon. Historically, the actual economic growth of the most advanced capitalist countries has come about only by passing through serious and prolonged depressions.

Until Keynes, the nature of economic depression had not even been understood. After Keynes, we have understood that they are due to falls in effective demand and we have learnt how to provide remedies. Demand needs to be stimulated and all available means will do: easy credit, cheap money policies, tax reductions, direct public expenditure. We must note, however, that all these provisions are indeed helpful but only in order to overcome the *negative* part of the phenomenon: the slump. They *will not*, by themselves, put the economic system back on a growth path. In other words, a successful Government policy in keeping up demand will help the economic system to avoid setbacks and *to stay where it is*, but it will not, as such, cause a resumption of economic growth.

If this analysis is correct, then quite a new view of the whole process of fluctuations and growth in a capitalist economy has here emerged. The Keynesian theory and the Keynesian anti-cyclical policies come out themselves as drastically reappraised, and their effects and limits clearly defined; the important point being that both Keynesian theories and Keynesian anti-cyclical remedies only refer to the negative aspect of the whole problem of fluctuations in a process of economic growth. Had this been correctly understood many recent disillusionments with Keynesian theories and policies might have been avoided. We cannot expect from the Keynesian theories and policies what they cannot give. We have gained from them the avoidance of large scale unemployment and this has been a notable achievement. But the resumption of growth is another matter. The economic system still has to solve the much deeper problems which have been discussed above – the structural problems of learning the appropriate ways to expand.

But let us now have a look into the opposite camp. The deeper structural problems just mentioned are clearly common to *any* growing economy with technical progress. This means that they will periodically emerge also in a socialist economic system. One might immediately ask why it is that, historically, no periodic growth difficulties have strikingly appeared in socialist countries. But the answer is at hand. No socialist country has so far reached the levels of per capita incomes experienced by the most advanced capitalist countries. It has been possible therefore to take advantage of all the previous experience accumulated in capitalist countries, not only in technology but also – an aspect which has passed unnoticed – in consumption. By scrutinising the previous development of the most advanced economies in the Western world, the socialist countries have been in a much better position to avoid mistakes and to select criteria of priority among the different goods to produce.

However, if it should ever happen that a socialist country overtakes the capitalist West in the level of per capita incomes, then that country will have to find out, for itself and anew, the types of goods to produce. Owing to these reasons, it is very likely that a leading socialist country too would periodically face the same structural problems discussed above, and periodically come to a standstill after periods of expansion. Of course, the way in which a socialist economy would react to the situation would be different. Total investment and employment are more easily maintained if decisions are centralised. This may well help avoid severe setbacks, namely the negative and most painful aspect of capitalist depressions, and at least enable the economic system to stand still. (In other words, a socialist country would not need Keynesian provisions to fight *cumulative* falls in effective demand and therefore depressions.) Some adverse effects seem nevertheless to be likely. The keeping of full employment might imply over-production in some branches of the economy, a phenomenon which might quite well emerge as the socialist counterpart of the waste that in a capitalist economy manifests itself in the form of unutilised productive capacity and under-employment. However, when faced with these difficulties, a socialist – as much as a capitalist country – could not resume expansion until it had itself solved the structural dynamics problems of finding out the new channels into which to direct the increasing efficiency of the economic system (or how to make a proper division between more production and more leisure). And there is no reason to believe that the process of learning which is required would be faster or easier in a socialist than it is in a capitalist economy.

There are two further corollaries which follow directly. The first one is that in the same way as socialist countries nowadays, by looking at the most advanced capitalist countries, can more easily learn the pattern of production and of consumption, and thereby avoid forced pauses in the process of growth, so can the other capitalist countries too (provided of course that they have solved the other problem of capital accumulation and growth). In fact, all the foregoing analysis about structural difficulties as the initiating cause of slumps is to be referred to the leading capitalist country (or countries). In other words, the source of depressions in a process of growth emerges as lying typically in that capitalist country, or in those capitalist countries, which find themselves in the vanguard of technical progress and per capita incomes. The other (less industrially advanced) countries will suffer indirectly – from the repercussions due to the drop in trade with the advanced countries. But, as far as the structural dynamics difficulties are concerned, they can follow much better, by taking advantage of the experience of the leading countries. This does not mean of course that, in the less developed countries, difficulties as to the composition of production (let alone other types of difficulties) do not exist: nor does it mean that the consumption pattern of the most advanced countries may automatically be imitated. The task of looking at, and imitating, what others have done may itself entail no easy process of learning, and moreover it must respect local or traditional tastes. There is no doubt, however, that to

239

learn patterns already experienced elsewhere is much easier than to invent them anew.[8]

The second corollary is of a far more speculative character but no less exciting. If it were to happen, in the future, that a socialist country should jump to the vanguard of progress and per capita incomes, that fact would also automatically have the effect of easing the periodic difficulties of the leading capitalist countries, as the latter would be able to take advantage of the experiences and discoveries of the leading socialist country. In other words, the leading capitalist countries can benefit and even see their periodic difficulties eased by a socialist country being in the lead of per capita incomes and being the first to try out types of mass production and mass consumption that can be imitated later on, only if they have proved successful.

9. Say's law and under-consumption theories – a reappraisal

It seems impossible to close this chapter without examining explicitly the bearing of our results on the old controversy about the possibility of market gluts, under-consumption and over-production, which has been going on for almost two centuries in economic theory. The controversy goes back to the early times of the Industrial Revolution when some economists expressed the fear that the society which was emerging might not be able to develop sufficient demand to absorb the increasing production that technical progress was bringing about. This view, very forcibly expressed by Simonde de Sismondi on the continent at the beginning of the nineteenth century, was strongly supported by Malthus in England, and later revived and further developed by Marx. But the leading economists of the time rejected the fear. As is well known, Jean-Baptiste Say answered these preoccupations with his famous *lois des debouchés*, later to become known as *Say's law*; simply stating that in an economic system there can never be a situation of over-production

---

8 This corollary, in addition to the previous remarks about population, may go quite a long way in explaining, for example, the smooth and remarkable development of West European countries immediately after the Second World War. It may be useful to recall an empirical inquiry into the composition of consumption in Western Europe and in the U.S.A. carried out by Milton Gilbert on behalf of O.E.E.C. with reference to the year 1950. The result was that all divergences of composition between Western Europe and the United States were explained up to 90% by differences in per capita incomes and relative prices and only up to 10% by other factors (among which different tastes!). In other words, the European countries had done nothing but basically imitate and follow the patterns of consumption which, at the same levels of per capita incomes and relative prices, had been experienced previously in the United States of America. (See M. Gilbert and Associates, *Comparative National Products and Price Levels: A study of Western Europe and the United States*, O.E.E.C., Paris, 1958).

or under-consumption (market gluts) because production itself creates its own demand. Say's view was accepted and wholeheartedly defended in England by Ricardo, and soon became one of the foundation stones of all economic theory that followed. In fact, with the exception of the Marxian stream of thought, the view remained virtually undisputed until the publication of Keynes's *General Theory*.[9]

We may now consider the whole controversy in the light of the foregoing analysis.

On the one side, the under-consumption theorists have really been touching on a crucial problem, which, incidentally, as we have seen, is not linked to any particular institutional set-up, but is a characteristic of an industrial society as such. In order to understand it, one must look at production in terms of *increments*, rather than in terms of absolute values, and, of course, one must consider a monetary economy, i.e. an economy in which individuals are in a position to hoard abstract purchasing power. Clearly, an increment of production, contrary to Say's contention, does not, by itself, create its own demand. What Say could have said is that any increase of production automatically creates a corresponding equal increase of *potential* demand. In our theoretical model, this proposition directly follows from the distributional aspect of the price system discussed in chapter VII, whereby, to any amount of production, at current prices, there corresponds an exactly equal amount of wages and profits, i.e. of potential demand. But this does not mean that any increase of potential demand is automatically transformed into an increase in *effective* demand. In order that it may be so, the increments of wages and profits must actually be spent; and in order that this may happen consumers must know *how* to spend their extra income and producers must have perceived (or have contributed to the shaping of) consumers' likings, so as to make the increments to total production take up *the correct composition*.

Let us notice, to understand Say's followers, that in a hypothetical stationary economic system, a statement of this kind would have no relevance. For, in a stationary economy, increments to production and to consumption would be zero. Both technology and consumers' preferences would always have been perfectly known and total produc-

---

9 The essential terms of the controversy can be seen in J. C. L. Simonde de Sismondi, *Nouveaux Principes d'Economie Politique*, Paris 1819; T. R. Malthus, *Principles of Political Economy*, London 1820, and letters to Ricardo (see especially the letters quoted in the biographical essay on Malthus by J. M. Keynes, *Essays in Biography*, London 1933); J. B. Say, *Traité d'Economie politique, op. cit.*, book I, chapter 'Des débouchés'; David Ricardo, *Principles*, Sraffa edition, *op. cit.*, chapter 21; K. Marx, *Das Kapital*, especially vol. II, Hamburg 1885; J. M. Keynes, *The General Theory, op. cit.*, chapter 23.

tion would always have been of the correct composition. Hence, a stationary economic system presents no structural problem. But in an economic system in which productivity is increasing, consumers' preferences evolve, and the problem of making the increments to production correspond to the evolution of consumers' preferences is by no means a trivial one. As already discussed at length, the consumption decisions concerning increments to expenditure are necessarily different from the previous ones as they concern preferences that have to be learnt, i.e. found out for the first time. But the amount that can be learnt within each period of time is not infinite; which means that, although the process of learning itself can go on *ad infinitum*, the *rate* at which it can go on is limited. And when it happens – as is periodically bound to happen – that a sudden jump is required in the rate of consumers' learning, in order to keep up with technological discoveries, there is no reason to expect an immediate response. In these cases, investment decisions will tend to be postponed, which means that the total amount of actual investment will drop and cause total effective demand to fall short of the technical possibilities of production. The economic system will indeed remain unable to take advantage of all its technologically possible production, until it succeeds in finding an appropriate structural re-distribution of demand, employment and productive capacity.

Yet, on the opposite side, Say, Ricardo and the rest have been right in rejecting the gloomy view of the under-consumptionists about the future of a progressively industrialising society. Provided that enough time is allowed for learning how to make the best use of the technologically potential production, there is no reason to fear any limit to the *level* of consumption. What the under-consumptionists did not realise is that the difficulty of increasing total effective demand is one of finding out, and achieving, at a sufficient speed, its appropriate structural composition and not one of reaching any absolute level. It seems important to stress that this proposition does not depend on the belief that human possibilities and imagination for new types of consumption can increase indefinitely. Even if the absolute amount of consumption had a limit, the alternative would always be open of devoting the continually increasing productivity to reducing labour time (and increasing leisure time), instead of increasing production. The point is that this process is not one to be expected automatically. The learning process it entails can by no means be taken for granted, although there is no inherent impossibility in human nature of carrying it on. Difficulties do arise because periodic *accelerations* of this process of learning are required. More specifically, the maintenance of full employment requires a speeding up periodically in the rate at which technical improvements are, so to speak, to be digested. But of course there is no impossibility in the process itself. In other words, with an appropriate structural dynamics, an economic system can indeed grow indefinitely, though through periodical difficulties. In the end, it can indeed take advantage of whatever increase in potential production technical improvements may bring along, with per capita consumption indefinitely increasing in quantity and quality, or alternatively with leisure time increasing.

If this analysis is correct, then even the way in which the two sides of the controversy agreed to settle their differences becomes unacceptable. To take the side of the optimists first, let me quote Ricardo in a well known letter to Malthus of 24 January 1817:

It appears to me that one great cause of our difference in opinion on the subjects which we have so often discussed is that you have always in your mind the immediate and temporary effects of particular changes, whereas I put these immediate and temporary effects quite aside, and fix my whole attention on the permanent state of things which will result from them. Perhaps you estimate these temporary effects too highly, whilst I am too much disposed to undervalue them.[10]

A century later, Keynes quoted this passage with whole-hearted approval, and, on exactly the same ground but for opposite reasons, came down on the other side.[11] For Keynes, the short-run difficulties had to be taken as much more important than the long-run problems, as 'in the long run we are all dead'.[12]

But, in this way, each side declares itself unable to look at the opponents' arguments. The long run and the short run become sorts of analytical blinkers which prevent each side from looking beyond the narrow aspect it has chosen to analyse. And the main question of whether an economic system is or is not able to take full advantage of all the possibilities that technology makes available is avoided instead of being answered.

It is only with a comprehensive analysis of the structural evolution of the economic system that the barren separation of the short from the long run yields to a more fruitful understanding of the inter-connections between the two. The relevant point is that *the very nature* of the process of long-run growth requires a structural dynamics which leads to difficulties in the short run. The one implies the other; therefore the whole process has to be accepted and tackled in its entirety. It is no use

10 *The Works and Correspondence of David Ricardo*, vol. VII, edited by Piero Sraffa, Cambridge, 1953, p. 120.
11 J. M. Keynes, 'Robert Malthus' in *Essays in Biography*, London 1933, p. 116.
12 This oft-quoted sentence is actually contained in J. M. Keynes, *A Tract on Monetary Reform*, London 1923, p. 80.

complaining about short-run difficulties, since they are the inevitable effect of long-run technical and social evolution. Nor is it useful to rely on long-run full employment growth-paths, for they will never be achieved, unless an appropriate process of structural change is continually carried out in the short run.

From this approach, the more constructive attitude emerges of singling out first the fundamental structural dynamics which must take place and then of trying to facilitate them. When this is done without prejudice, it becomes much easier to work in the direction of shaping the institutions themselves so as to enhance economic growth and progress, instead of sacrificing these aims – as only too often happens – for the sake of institutional arrangements which the inexorable pace of progress is from time to time rendering obsolete.

Chapter XI

International economic relations

1. Limited international mobility

The foregoing analysis has been carried out with reference to a single, and closed, economic system. All prices and the wage rate have been supposed to be the same everywhere. On many occasions, we have also considered a uniform rate of profit. This has meant supposing that commodities, capital funds, labourers and technical knowledge are all mobile, at least at such a speed (i.e. at such a rate of change) as not to interfere with the structural dynamics required by the process of economic growth.

But such a degree of mobility, though a reasonable aim to pursue within the boundaries of a single country, becomes a practical impossibility on an international scale. Several obstacles to mobility are inherent in the character of the magnitudes concerned; many others are imposed artificially by the Governments of the various countries.

It seems therefore necessary, at this point, to go on to considering *different* economic systems, corresponding to different countries co-existing side by side with one another. Within each country, we shall continue to suppose that commodities, capital funds, labourers and technical knowledge are sufficiently mobile as to justify aiming at the achievement of the 'natural features' with the exception of the rate of profit, which, for convenience, will be supposed to be uniform within each country (and not necessarily at its 'natural' level). But, between countries, mobility will be considered to be much lower, and our purpose will be to investigate consequences and implications of such a limited mobility.

2. International comparisons at the same structure of commodity prices

We may begin our analysis with a hypothetical and analytically simple, but extremely useful, case.

Let us suppose that there are two countries (i.e. two economic

245

systems) which we may call A (for advanced) and U (for under-developed). Technical knowledge of the average person is such that per capita productivity in country A is ten times greater than in country U, *for each single consumption good*, so that the structure of costs (in spite of their absolute levels being different) is exactly the same in both countries. We may also suppose, for the sake of simplicity, that the two economic systems are growing at exactly the same over-all steady rate, that they both have a uniform rate of profit (in other words, we are in the situation described in section 15 of chapter VII), and that the over-all capital/output ratio is exactly the same in both countries, although of course the methods of production, and therefore the physical capital goods used (the actual machines), will be entirely different.

Suppose, moreover, again for the sake of simplicity, that in both countries the medium of exchange (money) is anchored to gold, so that the exchange rate of the two currencies is fixed by the ratio of gold contents of the two monetary units. At this rate of exchange, both currencies have exactly the same purchasing power, in both countries, in terms of any physical commodity. However, since all commodities (gold included) can be produced in A with 1/10th of the labour they require in U, the amount of physical production per worker, and therefore the amount of real per capita income (i.e. of purchasing power) at the disposal of the average person is ten times greater in A than in U.

By applying our previous analysis, we can say immediately that the relative prices of commodities – let us say commodity prices in terms of gold – are exactly the same in the two countries. If the relation between rate of growth and rate of profit were the same, as we may suppose for simplicity to be the case, the over-all rate of profit will also be the same, but the wage rate, in terms of real purchasing power, i.e. in terms of the physical commodities it can buy, is ten times greater in A than in U.

In spite of the real wage rate being ten times greater in A than in U, the shares of total wages and total profits in national income are exactly the same. For, the amount of capital per man – i.e. the capital/labour ratio – evaluated at current prices, i.e. in terms of any arbitrarily chosen commodity, is ten times greater in A than in U, while the capital/output ratio is the same in both countries. This means that methods of production are ten times more mechanised in country A than in country U. (They actually entail a higher number of machines per worker, both in physical terms and in terms of productive capacity.) In other words, the degree of mechanisation is ten times greater in A than in U, while the degree of capital intensity of the methods of production (i.e. the proportion of charges for capital in the final prices, or alternatively the proportion of the labour force engaged in producing capital goods) is exactly the same in both countries.

The first important thing that this hypothetical case shows immediately is that, across countries, the principle of 'embodied labour' as a regulator of commodity prices no longer holds. In our case, all prices, in terms of gold, or in terms of any arbitrarily chosen physical commodity, are exactly the same in both countries; and they would clearly remain the same if exchange was allowed across borders. But the quantity of embodied labour (or labour-equivalent) that each price represents in the two countries is dramatically different: in U it is ten times greater than in A. This means that relative quantities of embodied labour (or labour-equivalent) will continue to regulate relative commodity prices *within the boundaries of each country*, but not across countries. A bushel of wheat is a bushel of wheat, wherever it is produced. Nobody will be prepared to give 10 bushels of wheat produced in A in exchange for 1 bushel of wheat produced in U just because these two quantities have been produced with the same quantity of labour.

These propositions crudely evince the fact that, when communities are separated from one another by political borders, any exchange across the borders cannot but take place on the basis of *physical commodity comparisons*. To look at the matter in another way, international exchanges are bound to be 'unequal', if assessed in terms of embodied labour. It is physical comparison that is bound to prevail. More precisely, it is the comparison of physical commodities that will determine how many units of embodied labour of one country will exchange for one unit of embodied labour of another country.[1]

3. A fallacy arising from the Heckscher–Ohlin model

An interesting feature of the simple case discussed in the previous

1 David Ricardo nearly completely stated this principle in his treatment of 'foreign trade' (See his *Principles*, Sraffa edition, *op cit.*, pp. 128 and ff.). He failed, however, as all Classical economists did, to distinguish between two different concepts of measurement (denoted here by (b) and (d); see section 2, chapter IX), namely between (b) measurement of commodities at current prices, i.e. in terms of any physical commodity which has been arbitrarily chosen as *numéraire*; and (d) measurement in terms of embodied labour. Classical economists generally associated the term *value* with both concepts. This association is harmless when used for comparisons at the same moment of time and within the same economic system (where the two concepts coincide) but represents a confusion of concepts when used over time and/or in international comparisons, where the two concepts become divorced from each other. Of course one is free to define by 'value' either concept (b) or concept (d), but not both.

Marx was more accurate on this point. He definitely associated the term 'value' with concept (d), i.e. with 'labour embodied'. But then, as a consequence, his arguments could not be applied across countries.

section is that it brings to the fore, clearly and without any minor complication, the primary factor accounting for the different wealth of countries A and U, and thus also the primary source of gains from their possible international economic relations, namely: technical knowledge.

In general, economic inquiries into international relations have been prompted by the simple question: granted that various countries, with different characteristics, exist side by side with one another, are there ways in which one country may take advantage from the existence of the others, without the others being put at any disadvantage? It becomes quite clear, in our hypothetical case, that this question has a different answer according as it is posited from the point of view of country A or from the point of view of country U.

Let us consider first of all the position of country A – the industrially advanced country. From the point of view of this country, the situation appears entirely uninteresting. There is nothing that country A can learn from country U. Moreover no gain (but actually losses) would accrue to people migrating from A to U. The price structure is exactly the same across the borders, so that there would be no gain whatever from any exchange of commodities, i.e. absolutely no gain from international trade (except in times of temporary shortage).

There is one field, however, for which it might appear, from traditional theory, that country A ought to be able to obtain gains from international exchange; and that is the field of international movement of capital funds. But this is a fallacy, which we are now in a position to expose. As is well-known, the marginalist scheme of optimum allocation of given resources – which has become known as the Heckscher-Ohlin model when applied to international trade – would approach the case of an industrially advanced and of an underdeveloped country as a case in which the two countries have different 'endowments of labour and capital'. In the case we are considering, country A is 'endowed' with an amount of capital per man, which is ten times greater than the similar 'endowment' of country U. Traditional theory would predict a higher 'marginal productivity of capital', and a higher rate of profit, in country U than in country A, and therefore a flow of capital funds – if such flow were allowed – from country A to country U.

Our theoretical construction shows clearly that there would be absolutely no movement of capital funds, even if perfect mobility of funds were allowed. In fact, if the rate of growth, and thus the rate of profit, in country U were to be lower than in country A, there might even be a flow of capital funds from the underdeveloped to the industrially advanced country, i.e. in the direction opposite to the one which traditional theory would lead us to expect.

There is an important practical conclusion that can already be drawn. If underdeveloped countries want to attract foreign capital – or, even more importantly, if they want to discourage their own savings from flowing abroad – there is no hope they can put in the fact that they have a low degree of mechanisation and a low stock of capital goods. They shall have to speed up their rates of economic growth.

4. The primary source of international gains

But let us now consider the question stated in the previous section from the point of view of country U.

Keeping strictly to the features of our hypothetical case, one must immediately say of course that, for country U as much as for country A, there is no possibility of any gain whatever either from international trade of commodities or from movements of capital funds. But, from the point of view of country U, this now emerges as only a very minor part of the whole picture.

Consider, first of all, population movements. From a strictly individual point of view, workers from country U would gain substantially if they could move to country A, where the per capita incomes (and per capita wages) are ten times as large. There is, therefore, for single individuals, an enormous inducement to emigrate to country A, an inducement that will especially apply to the more educated and more skilled part of the U population (as they will normally encounter fewer difficulties in being accepted in country A). It must be added immediately that this is a great danger for country U as a whole. A 'brain drain', as it has become known, though advantageous to the single individuals concerned, is extremely harmful to country U taken as a whole, as it lowers the average 'stock of knowledge' of its people, while its needs would lie in precisely the opposite direction. In any case, the single individuals of the industrially advanced country, especially the less educated and less skilled ones, fearing competition for jobs, are likely to exert strong pressure for the introduction of limitations to immigration. In practice, nowadays, we must admit that these pressures are successful (however badly we may disapprove of them). Movements of population due to migrations account for a very minor proportion of population growth anywhere, except in a few countries; and, even in these countries, immigration has become very selective. It seems, therefore, reasonable to proceed here on the assumption that migrations of people from country to country are negligible.

Yet, even if migrations were forbidden altogether, people in country U have at their disposal a most fundamental way of taking advantage of the existence of country A, and of increasing their wealth. They can *learn* the methods of production which are being used already in country A.

The inhabitants of A may be very little interested in this. They may not even think that such possibilities of learning are open to country U, for no advantage can accrue to them.[2] But for country U as a whole, this is the greatest of all means available to increase the nation's wealth. Just because methods of production are in operation already in A, it is actually possible in U (simply by learning to do what other people do already) to improve productivity at such a rate of change as could never be achieved in A. In other words, it is actually possible for U to grow at a faster rate than A. There can be no doubt that, for country U, international learning represents the major source of international gains.

It must be added that, in general, for any country – whether industrially advanced or underdeveloped, whether in practice it can take enormous advantage from international learning or no advantage at all – any increase in knowledge represents a gain for the country, *unconditionally*, i.e. without any requirement or proviso at all being satisfied first. It will be seen in a moment that this is not true of other sources of international gains. In this sense, international learning can indeed be said to represent the primary source of international gains.

5. The order of priority in the expansion of demand as a strict limitation to international learning

The possibility of international learning just considered is not as wide as it might appear at first sight. For, although accumulated technical knowledge may cover a wide range of fields, the part of this technical knowledge which an underdeveloped country can draw from, at any particular point of time, is only a small percentage of the total.

This point is important and deserves being stressed. In our simple case, the assumption has been made that relative prices are the same in both countries. But nothing has been said about the structure of production. Now, even if relative prices are the same, the structures of production and of employment cannot be the same in A and U, because

2 It may not be without interest to point out that the foundations of the traditional theory of international trade have been laid by economists who lived in the economically advanced countries. Quite understandably, their attention has been attracted by those problems – and by those ways of obtaining gains from international relations – that were relevant for the countries in which they lived. As a consequence, very little attention has been paid so far to what emerges here as the major source of international gains.

of the tenfold difference in real per capita incomes. The physical quantity of each single commodity to be produced is determined by demand, as was shown earlier (chapter VII), but we have also seen (in chapters IV and X) that the nature of human needs and preferences gives rise to entirely different compositions of demand, and, therefore, different structures of production and employment, at the various levels of real per capita income.

In our case, where real per capita income in A is ten times greater than in U, the structures of production and employment must be very different indeed. If, for example, annual per capita incomes are on average of the order of 500 dollars in country U, and of the order of 5,000 dollars in country A, demand in U will almost entirely be concentrated on food, while, in A, demand for food will represent only, let us say, 10% of total income. And since productivity in U is 1/10th of what it is in A, most probably a percentage of the order of 80–90% of the labour force of U will have to be concentrated in agriculture, while in A this branch of production – though giving a higher physical output – will only account for, let us say, roughly 10% of total employment.

Most likely, all types of commodities which we find in U will also be produced in A, but not all types of commodities which are made in A – in fact only a small fraction of them, let us say only 1/5th of them – will also be produced in U. Thus, production in A is much more differentiated and concerned with a much greater range and variety of commodities than in U. Which ones of all these commodities produced in A will also be produced in U clearly depends on the needs of the U-consumers at their lower level of per capita incomes. But the point is that, whatever the choices of the U-consumers, the number of types of commodities demanded by them can only be a small fraction of the number of types of commodities which are produced in A.[3]

3 This fact is seldom kept in mind in international comparisons of national incomes. One normally forgets that the average billion dollars of, let us say, India's gross national product is, in real terms, i.e. in terms of its *physical* composition, something almost entirely different from the average billion dollars of, let us say, the United States' gross national product.

A related point, arising from the Heckscher–Ohlin model, is the widespread view that low-income countries enjoy comparative cost advantages in agricultural production, a view drawn too hastily and uncritically from the fact that, in underdeveloped countries, the great majority of people are working in agriculture. But this is another fallacy of traditional economics. Our analysis shows clearly how in country U, for example, almost all people may indeed be concentrated in the production of agricultural goods, without any comparative advantage at all existing for any country. (Relative prices have been supposed to be the same everywhere!) The explanation is of course much simpler. Productivity in U is so low that the great majority of people can afford no time to produce anything else but the very basic goods necessary to their survival.

Of course, as time and economic growth go on, country U will be able to enlarge the variety of its production. But this process will have to follow a very strict order. At any given point of time, producers in U are not free to pick up any type of commodity they like from among the 4/5ths of all types which are not produced. They will have to start production only of those commodities for which demand is expanding. Our simple case brings this phenomenon out clearly and without secondary complications, owing to the assumption of precisely the same commodity prices in both countries and thus of no international trade. There is a definite order in which the various production processes can be introduced in U, strictly fixed by the order in which demand for each commodity is expanding as income increases.

But a fixed order in which the production process can be enlarged also represents a fixed order in which the various methods of production can be learnt. Thus, however big the stock of accumulated technical knowledge may be in A, country U can take advantage only of that small part of it which refers to the few products for which demand is expanding and for those commodities (in our case only 1/5th of the total) which are produced already. This also means that people in U are not free to draw as they please from the existent pool of technical knowledge. They have to follow a very definite order. And if they do not follow this order, their increase of technical knowledge will simply have no effect on their incomes. To give an example, if any increment of productivity, and thus of per capita income, that takes place in U translates itself into more demand for food, the learning activity will have to be concentrated on increasing productivity in food production. It would be no use to learn how to make, let us say, refrigerators because very few people would want them. Demand for refrigerators will come later on, but only at higher levels of income, which will never be reached if productivity is not increased in food production to begin with.

There is a stringent conclusion that follows. If country U is incapable to learn in the particular 1/5th of the total field of technical knowledge for which it can provide demand, it will never grow at all, whatever its possibilities of learning may be in the other 4/5ths of the total field of technical knowledge. These other vast 4/5ths of the total field of technical knowledge may well be easy to acquire but will remain for the time being, entirely irrelevant. (As far as the possibilities of increasing production are concerned, it is as if they did not exist!)

These are severe restrictions indeed to the process of international

252

learning.[4] And they are the stricter, in each particular country, the lower its level of per capita income. For any underdeveloped country, therefore, a process of economic growth also represents a way of widening continually the field in which advantage can be taken of the stock of technical knowledge that has accumulated in the outside world.

6. Trade – a secondary source of international gains

The assumption that both country A and country U of our example have exactly the same structure of costs, and of prices, is of course unrealistic, and has been made so far only in order to isolate the problems we wanted to investigate from secondary complications. But we are now ready to drop that assumption.

In practice, relative costs cannot be the same in all countries. Particular geographical positions, climates, endowments of natural resources, etc., may put some countries in a better position than others to produce certain commodities. In some countries certain particular commodities may not be producible at all. Other, important, reasons are connected with the different stages of economic development. There are certain products and services, for which productivity can be increased only at a much smaller rate than for the average of all other commodities. (Many services, especially, come into this category.) Thus, within each economic system, the costs of these commodities and services inevitably become greater and greater, relative to the costs of all the others, as economic growth continues. Between countries which are at different stages of economic development, these differences in relative costs may reach quite striking magnitudes. Furthermore, especially in manufactures, there are products which can be made at low costs only on a large scale, or only with the complicated complementary organisation of many other branches of production. These products can be made efficiently in countries with high levels of demand, but not in low income countries, where, to develop the necessary organisation to produce only a few of them per year would make them prohibitively expensive.

We shall therefore now enlarge our analysis to the case in which the two countries we are investigating, A and U, have different structures of costs (and prices). We shall suppose that *average* over-all productivity and thus also the real wage rate are, as before, ten times greater in A than in U. But sectoral productivities in the two countries are now supposed to differ according to a much wider range: in some sectors

---

Some relaxation of these restrictions is provided by the possibilities of international trade, when this is possible. See footnote 5 below.

productivity may be in A, let us say, twice as great as in U, and, in others, it may be up to twenty times as great. Since, within the same country, the wage rate is uniform *ex hypothesi* over all sectors, relative prices will now differ between the two countries. We may still suppose, for simplicity's sake, that the two monetary units are linked to gold and that productivity in the gold producing industry is equal to average, i.e. it is ten times greater in A than in U. Then, we can say unambiguously that those goods for which differences in productivity are smaller than tenfold will have a lower price in U than in A and those goods for which differences in productivity are greater than tenfold will have a lower price in A than in U. As opposed to the previous case, this is a case in which, if international trade were allowed, goods would be induced to move between the two countries. People in A would buy goods of the first type in U, where they are cheaper; and similarly people in U would buy goods of the second type in A. Country U would be induced to specialise in producing, and then exporting, the first type of commodities, and country A would be induced to specialise in producing, and then exporting, the second type of commodities.[5]

The question that now arises is the following: should international trade be allowed? Are movements of commodities across the borders going to be beneficial to the two countries? The question has become relevant, this time, for *both* countries, but the answer has become a conditional one. International trade is going to be beneficial to both countries, *provided that* two conditions are satisfied.

The first condition is that, at the particular point in time when exchanges take place, the existing structure of costs be the best one which can be obtained for the time being. For, if this were not so, i.e. if it were easy to learn quickly (let us say, from abroad) how to bring costs (and prices) down to the international level, then it would obviously be more advantageous for each country to produce the commodities concerned at home, by increasing internal productivity. This proviso is worth stressing because it is likely to be overlooked, owing to the fact that it normally will not be relevant for the advanced countries. Yet, it is obviously very important for the underdeveloped countries. It is only when all possible efforts to learn have been made that an under-developed country can hope for further gains to be obtained from international trade. In other words, possible benefits from international trade are subordinated to the benefits from international learning. We

---

5 Another important consequence, for the underdeveloped country, of the opening up of the possibility of international trade, brought about by the different price structure is represented by the widening of the possibility of learning, beyond the narrow range of the goods required by internal demand.

can therefore conclude that international trade emerges as a subordinate, and thus, in the sense discussed in the previous section, a secondary source of international gains.

The second condition to be satisfied is that the trading countries be actually able to specialise in production, in the sense of being able to transfer labour and invested capital from the less to the more favoured branches of production, without suffering a drop in the level of employment. During this process, if production were disrupted, in the sense that labour and capital equipment remained idle, the country as a whole would lose the physical amount of commodities which would have been produced by the unemployed labour and capital, had they not remained unemployed. These might well be temporary losses only, and when the chances for a quick re-absorption of unemployment are reasonable, a country may well accept some short-run disruption in view of the longer-run advantages. Yet the short-run losses have to be taken into account. There is, moreover, an important aspect of this proviso, which again is particularly relevant for any country (most likely the underdeveloped country) which had unemployment to start with. In this case, clearly, the importation of any commodity which, by having a lower price than that possible at home, prevents an increase of local employment (which would otherwise take place) entails a net loss for the country. For, although some particular people (those who buy the imported commodity and at the same time do not lose their jobs) might well gain by paying the lower international price, the workers who would otherwise produce that commodity remain unemployed and produce nothing. So that the country as a whole would suffer a net loss which is represented by the entire amount of all those physical goods which are given in exchange for the imported commodity. In such a situation, it would clearly be advantageous to the country not to import that commodity at all and to produce it at home, in spite of the internal higher cost (and price).

But of course when, at any particular point of time, these two provisos are both satisfied, i.e. when all possible efforts have been made to improve productivity, and when employment is being preserved (or unemployment is prevented from increasing), international trade will bring real gains to both countries. Country A, by being induced to concentrate on producing (for both countries) those commodities for which it has been able to secure the higher levels of productivity, rather than on those for which its productivity lead is the least, will be able to increase for both countries the physical quantity of those commodities in the production of which it specialises. And, conversely, country U, by being induced to concentrate on producing (for both countries) those

255

commodities for which it least lags behind A, will similarly be able to increase for both countries the physical quantities of these commodities.

As the reader will realise, this is nothing but the well-known *principle of comparative cost advantage*, of which David Ricardo gave a celebrated and perhaps yet unsurpassed exposition in his *Principles*,[6] more than a century and a half ago.

7. The effects of international trade

Let us suppose that for both countries A and U, with different cost (and price) structures, the two provisos just stated are fulfilled, and let us suppose that, at a certain point of time, international trade is actually allowed to take place, starting from a situation in which there was no trade. We may now examine in greater detail the effects that will follow.

First of all, there are many commodities – those commodities which cannot move outside the country where they are produced – for which nothing at all will happen. Almost all services, after all, come into this category: they cannot be exported separately from the people who provide them (and we are supposing that there is no emigration). Many other commodities, moreover, are so quickly perishable as to be subject to a very limited geographical mobility. Even for those commodities that can move, not *any* comparative cost difference will induce trade, but only those differences that are large enough as to cover the costs of transport, storage, and risk insurance.[7] When all these factors are taken into account, the number of types of commodities which can actually be traded may not emerge, in the end, as a great percentage of the total.

But for those commodities which can move and for which the comparative cost differences are bigger than transport, storage and risk insurance costs, trade will begin. In both countries, those branches of production which operate at a comparative cost disadvantage will be faced with the prospects of closing down. Some firms may respond with exceptional efforts to the challenge, and learn quickly how to bring costs down, at least to the international level, in which case they would put themselves back into the category of those firms whose production is not affected. This means that, even in branches of industry which, on the whole, are compelled to close down, some firms might still be able to survive. All other firms, incapable of responding to the challenge, will be compelled to close down, and their labour and invested capital will

6 David Ricardo, *Principles, op. cit.*, chapter VII.
7 In the present analysis, however, costs of transport, storage and risk insurance will normally be neglected, for simplicity's sake.

have (when possible) to be transferred to those branches of production that operate at a comparative cost advantage. These latter branches will expand. Eventually, for each single commodity which is traded internationally, the price prevailing in that country which produces it at the lower comparative cost (i.e. the lower of the two original prices, corrected by effects due to economies or diseconomies coming from a larger scale of production) will become the price prevailing in both countries. The physical quantity of each tradeable commodity to be produced (by the firms in the country that specialises in producing it, but also by those firms in the other country which manage to survive) will then be determined by the sum of the demands of both countries.

But the most important effects of all this process is clearly on real incomes. In each country, prices of imported goods will begin to fall, relative to other prices, either as an effect of increased internal productivity in response to international trade competition or as an effect of taking advantage of the lower foreign price. In the latter case, it is exactly *as if* technical progress had suddenly brought down costs to the comparative level of the other country. Real per capita incomes and therefore total demand increase correspondingly. This means that an increase takes place in physical production of *all* commodities, whether they are internationally traded or not. It is precisely this increase, in physical terms, that represents the net gain from international trade.

The necessary modifications can now be made to the results obtained in section 2, where the assumption was made of exactly the same price structures.

If the currencies of both countries are anchored to gold, as we are supposing (see the previous section), the rate of exchange between the two currencies again coincides with the ratio of gold contents of the two monetary units. But, in order to assess their purchasing power, a distinction must now be made between the goods that are traded and those that are not traded internationally.

For those commodities which cannot move, and hence are not internationally traded, prices remain different in the two countries. Therefore, if assessed in terms of any one of these commodities, the purchasing power of either currency will be different in the two countries. With reference to any specific commodity, this purchasing power will be higher (or lower) in that country where the commodity is produced at a comparative cost advantage (or disadvantage).

But for those commodities which can move and are internationally traded, relative prices in A and U become the same. In terms of these commodities, the purchasing power of either currency becomes the same in both countries. In other words, for these commodities, we are back to the results that have emerged from our analysis in section 2. Relative prices are determined by the relative amount of 'embodied labour' *within* each country. But the same physical quantity of any internationally traded commodity, evaluated at the current (common) price, expressed in either currency, represents a different quantity of 'embodied labour' in the two countries; the physical quantity of labour required in A and in U, to produce the same commodity, being different.[8]

Here is therefore a principle that emerges as one of general validity. *Relative* prices of internationally traded commodities continue to be determined by relative amounts of embodied labour inside each of the trading countries. But the absolute quantities of embodied labour will be different from country to country so that exchanges of commodities across countries will be 'unequal' in terms of labour, as was seen in the previous case. The only complication, with respect to the simpler case of section 2, is that some (internationally traded) commodities may not be produced any more in one of the two countries. For these commodities the quantities of embodied labour must be intended as the quantities of labour embodied in those commodities that are given in exchange. Therefore, for these commodities, relative amounts of embodied labour can be arrived at through an intermediate comparison; i.e. through the relative price with respect to one of those (internationally traded) commodities which are produced in *both* countries.

8. Correcting two widespread views

We may pause for a moment here and use the foregoing analysis to correct two widespread views.

A generally accepted conclusion of traditional marginal economics theory, drawn on the basis of its usual assumptions of fixed natural resources and thus decreasing returns to scale, is that the cost (and thus the price) of each single commodity which is internationally traded will gradually increase in the exporting country (where it was originally lower), and decrease in the importing country (where it was originally higher). When the two prices come to coincide, change will stop. At that point, specialisation in one of the two countries in production may not yet be complete. This argument is used in order to explain two things:

8 Here and in the following pages, we are simply using the term 'embodied labour', without adding any qualification, for simplicity's sake. It goes without saying that, if the rate of profit is uniform in each of the two countries, as we are supposing in the whole of the present analysis, the term 'labour' must be intended in the sense of 'labour equivalent', as defined in chapter II (section 6).

(a) that the international price of any commodity, after trade has taken place, will be higher than it was at the beginning in the country that had a comparative cost advantage; (b) that not always will complete international specialisation take place.

On the basis of the foregoing analysis, we can assert that on neither of these two statements can marginal economic theory be accepted. Proposition (a), as a general statement, is simply false. There is nothing that can be said in general and *a priori* as to whether costs will increase or decrease in the exporting country, as an effect of international trade and a larger scale of production. Even if no improvement takes place in technical knowledge, the consequences on cost depend on the technical methods available. In practice, especially in manufactures, it is actually much more likely that costs – and thus prices – will decrease (not increase) in the exporting country, owing to economies from larger scales of production.

Proposition (b), on the other hand, is simply a statement of a well known fact. But the explanation given by marginal economic theory is incorrect. Indeed, if this explanation were correct we would find in practice complete international specialisation in those fields (mainly manufacturing), where decreasing costs to scale represent the general rule, and international non-specialisation in those fields (mainly agriculture and mining) where increasing costs to scale are more likely. In the real world, we find exactly the opposite.

A much more satisfactory explanation is the one that emerges from the present analysis. Namely: the primary source of international gains is international learning (not international trade). When firms in one country are challenged by lower priced products from abroad, they will either learn how to cut down costs or close down. Some of them, at least, may learn and survive. Furthermore, when a new product is invented in one country, the very first thing that all other countries will try to do is to learn how to make the product themselves (by buying licences and paying royalties, if necessary). Only in the temporary learning period, or in the period – which may sometimes be quite long – in which internal demand is not yet big enough to allow the minimum scale required by the new methods, will each country import that product from abroad. This means that manufactured products, though internationally traded, will normally be produced in all countries considered. The case of agriculture and mining is quite different. In these fields, there are indeed many products for which the methods of production cannot be applied (even if they can be learnt) because, for example, they come from crops, or from mineral deposits, that are specific to particular geographical areas. In these cases – contrary to what traditional theory, on the basis of decreasing returns, would make us expect – international specialisation becomes inevitable.

9. The once-for-all character of the gains from international trade

We are now in a position to take a further step. On the assumption of different price structures in the two countries A and U, which we are considering, we shall go on to investigate movements through time. To begin with, for simplicity's sake, it will be useful to assume a uniform rate of growth of productivity. In other words, we consider *different* relative prices in the two countries A and U, but we suppose that, at least for those commodities which can move and are internationally traded, productivity is increasing at exactly the same rate in all sectors of the same country, although not necessarily at the same rate in the two countries. Thus international trade, granted that it has been allowed to begin with, will go on all the time, because the two different price structures, whatever their differences may be, remain unchanged over time.

We may ask: which effects can be detected through time? There are two important propositions that may be stated immediately.

Proposition (i). After the gains which international trade brought about when it started, no *further* increases in real per capita incomes will be obtained any more by either country, over time, from the continuation of the international trade which is taking place.

Indeed, international trade may well have brought about a big jump in the real per capita incomes of either or both countries at the time when it was first allowed. But those increases have come once for all. Further (once-for-all) increases can only come from the *expansion* of international trade, i.e. from new international trade. But the continuation of the international trade which is already taking place will bring no increase of real per capita income any more to either countries. The situation – unlike that for productivity increases – is in fact reversible. The once-for-all increases obtained in the past, when international trade was started, would be lost if international trade were now to stop. In other words, in the same way that the commencement of international trade brought about once-for-all increases in per capita incomes in the past, so the stopping of international trade would bring about once-for-all losses of per capita incomes now. Continuation of international trade thus emerges as a condition for avoiding the loss now of the once-for-all gains obtained in the past.

This once-for-all character of the gains from international trade is yet another aspect of the subordinate role played by trade as against learning in economic development. In the present work, this simply emerges as yet another implication of the general principles sketched out since the very beginning (see chapter I).

10. The remarkable closedness of economic systems as regards productivity gains

The second proposition is even more important. It may be stated as follows.

Proposition (ii). There is no sharing whatever that either country can take in the increases in productivity that take place in the other country, no matter how much international trade is taking place between the two countries. In other words, the gains coming from productivity growth are not leaked abroad by international trade.

This proposition is so important as to require some expansion. If, in each country, the relative prices remain unchanged over time, each country continues to pay, for each physical unit of imported commodity, with the same physical units of exported commodities. Thus no gain whatever will ever come to the country considered from any diminution of the physical labour embodied into the imported physical amounts of goods. On the other hand, the country will gain from all diminutions of labour embodied in the physical amounts of goods which are given in exchange. This means that all productivity increases that take place in A remain inside A, and all productivity increases that take place in U remain inside U. It follows that the rate of growth of real per capita income in each single country – and thus the rate of growth of the natural wage rate – is determined by the rate of over-all growth of productivity in the production processes which are operated inside the country, whether the goods are then consumed at home or exported abroad.

To put this matter in another way, there is no part whatever that people in U can take in the productivity gains which are achieved in A, and there is no part whatever that people in A can take in the productivity gains achieved in U. In either country, people are able to increase their per capita incomes only to the extent – and indeed to the full extent – that they succeed in increasing productivity *inside their own country*.

All this does not mean of course that absolutely no advantage whatever can come, let us say to country U, from the fact that there is growth of productivity in country A. Some *indirect* gains are possible. If productivity increases, in country A, this means that also its total national income, and thus its total demand, will increase. And an increase of total demand in A will normally bring with it also an increase in demand for the products of country U. This may have beneficial effects for U, since expansion of international trade brings once-for-all gains for both countries. Moreover if in country U there is unemployment, an increase in external demand may generate increases in employment and in production, that otherwise would not take place. And, as was pointed out above (though in a different context, in section 6), increases in production that require employment of previously unemployed people are a net gain for country U. It must be noted, however, that these are secondary and indirect gains. They have nothing to do with sharing in the gains of productivity that take place in country A. These latter gains remain entirely in country A.

We must conclude that economic systems are indeed remarkably closed, as regards the gains coming from the growth of productivity. If international relative prices remain unchanged (but we shall examine in a moment the case in which they change) *all* technical improvements within a country translate themselves into higher *internal* per capita incomes. No one and no part of these gains are spread abroad, whatever the size attained by international trade, although foreign countries may obtain some indirect benefits from the increase in the size of international total demand.

The practical relevance of this conclusion is so enormous as hardly to need being emphasised. To have an idea of what it means, it is enough to have a look at the world's situation as it appears today. After barely 200 years from the inception of the industrial revolution, i.e. from the time when a few nations began the cumulative process of improving their methods of production (and thus keeping to themselves the corresponding gains of productivity), average per capita incomes in the various countries of the world have reached disparities which are unprecedented and almost fantastic, ranging from an order of magnitude of 200 dollars in India to an order of magnitude of 10,000 dollars in the United States.[9]

11. International movements of workers and exploitation

The subject of international disparities in per capita national incomes raises the problems of disparities in population densities and migrations.

9 The precise figures of per-capita G.N.P.s in 1978, as given by the World Bank are $180 for India and $9,590 for the United States. (See: World Development Report 1980, World Bank, Washington 1980.)

These are very complex problems that go beyond the scope of the present work. Yet a couple of points may very briefly be made.

First of all, to the extent that geographical movements of people are deemed to be desirable but do not take place, no movements of commodities can be a substitute for them.

Secondly, when migrations from one country to another do take place, the only acceptable frame of reference into which they can be inserted appears that of a process of expansion of an economic system at a rate that goes beyond the one allowed – at the existing technology – by the natural growth of internal population. This means migrations on a *permanent* basis. It is hard to conceive of any other acceptable form of migration, except in exceptional circumstances. More specifically, it is hard to conceive of any acceptable form of temporary migrations, such as the regular movements of commuting workers across the political borders of countries with different per capita incomes. As we have seen, international trade is bound to be 'unequal' in terms of labour. If labour itself is made the subject of international trade, one cannot but open it up to the widest forms of abuses and discriminations.[10]

12. A 'general' principle of comparative productivity-change advantage

We are now going to take our last analytical step and drop the assumption of constancy through time of the price structures of tradeable commodities.

As has emerged from the foregoing analysis, what a country obtains from abroad, through international trade, is a certain collection of *physical commodities*, in exchange for a certain amount of *physical labour* embodied in the physical collection of commodities that are exported. Hence the normal and primary way of obtaining increases in the physical collection of imported goods is through a diminution of the quantity of labour embodied in each physical unit of exported goods. This is what we have considered in the previous sections.

There is, however, also another way, which consists in a change (an increase) of the physical amounts of goods which are imported per given physical amounts of goods which are exported, i.e. an improvement of what has been called 'the terms of trade', or ratio of the (weighted) average prices of exports to the (weighted) average prices of imports.

10 Migrations have always been the source of social discrimination and exploitation. It seems therefore the more important to avoid built-in institutional mechanisms that encourage them. Unfortunately this is not being done. The recent widespread practice, in some industrially advanced countries, of accepting foreign workers in times of booms and expelling them in times of slumps appears as one of the clearest examples of international exploitation.

When this happens, clearly, the country will be able, through international trade, to absorb some benefits from the rest of the world. The opposite will happen to the country whose terms of trade are worsening (i.e. the country for which the ratio of export prices to import prices falls). This country will lose some of its productivity gains, leaking them to the rest of the world.

Two interesting questions may now be asked; namely (i) what is it that determines the dynamics of the terms of trade? And (ii) what is the relation of these dynamics to the economic growth of the countries concerned?

The answers to these questions (on the hypothesis, which we are using in the whole of our analysis, that 'natural' prices tend to be realised inside each country, with the only modification of a uniform rate of profit) can be given by applying the analysis of sections 2 and 7 above. As has been shown there, international relative prices are determined by the relative quantities of labour required to produce the commodities concerned *inside* each country. And if one of the commodites to be compared is not produced in the country concerned, the relative amount of 'embodied labour' it represents can be obtained by an intermediate comparison with any one of those (internationally traded) commodities which are produced in both countries.

Therefore, in our case, whether the prices of exports from A, relative to the prices of exports from U (i.e. the terms of trade between the two countries), will change through time depends on changes in productivity in the industries in which each of the two countries has specialised, *relative* to changes in productivity in the other industries. To be more precise, let us call R_A and R_U the (weighted) average rates of change of productivity in A and in U respectively, for those commodities which are produced in both countries (and are mobile, so that they have the same price both in A and in U) and let us call ϱ_A and ϱ_U the (weighted) average rates of change of productivity for those commodities in the production of which country A and country U, respectively, have specialised. Then, the prices of exports from A, relative to the prices of imports from U, i.e. the terms of trade for country A, will worsen, improve, or remain unchanged over time (and conversely the terms of trade for country U will improve, worsen or remain unchanged) according as to whether:

(XI.12.1)
$$\frac{\varrho_A}{R_A} > \frac{\varrho_U}{R_U},$$

or

(XI.12.2)
$$\frac{\varrho_A}{R_A} < \frac{\varrho_U}{R_U},$$

264

or

(XI.12.3)
$$\frac{\varrho_A}{R_A} = \frac{\varrho_U}{R_U}.$$

Correspondingly, over time, international trade:

(i) will cause leakages of some productivity gains from country A to country U in case (IX.12.1),
(ii) will cause leakages of some productivity gains from country U to country A in case (IX.12.2),
(iii) will keep all productivity gains inside the country in which they have taken place (as in the case considered in the previous section) in case (IX.12.3).

All this means – to answer now the second question set out above – that there is no necessary relation between the direction in which productivity may be leaking and the absolute level of the rate of growth of productivity in countries A or U. Whether country A is growing faster or slower than country U is immaterial to the problem of possible international leakages of productivity gains. The dynamics of the terms of trade, and thus the direction in which productivity may be leaking, depends on *ratios* of rates of change, no matter how large or how small the rates of change themselves may be. It depends on *comparative rates of change of productivity* in the two countries, the terms of reference being the industries that have specialised in producing for export and the others.

To look at the matter the other way round, we can also say that no judgment at all can be passed on whether a country is doing better or worse than another simply from the movements of the terms of trade: it all depends on the level at which these movements are going on in the two countries. Take for example case (IX.12.3), in which the terms of trade remain absolutely constant over time. Yet, for any given structure of costs of the other commodities (those that are not internationally traded), per capita incomes will be growing in country A: faster than, slower than, or exactly at the same rate as, in country U, according to whether equality (XI.12.3) is the result of the rates of change, ϱs and Rs, being:

(a) both higher in A than in U;
(b) both lower in A than in U;
(c) both the same in A and in U.

Exactly the same three cases *mutatis mutandis* can be repeated for inequalities (XI.12.1) and (XI.12.2).

We must conclude that the results of the previous section 10 must be modified, when the price structures of the two countries concerned are changing through time in a different way, to the extent that there is a consequent change in the terms of trade. As has been shown, the changes in the terms of trade depend on the comparative speed with which, in each country, productivity in the industries that specialise for export proceeds with respect to productivity in the other industries. This is what we may call the (general) *principle of comparative productivity-change* advantage.

It will be noticed that, as opposed to the gains that come from productivity growth, the gains that come from improvements in the terms of trade can only be obtained at the expense of equal losses by other countries. While international learning can be pursued simultaneously by all countries all the time, any improvement of the terms of trade for any one country can only mean a corresponding loss for other countries. On average – i.e. for all countries taken together – all the changes in the terms of trade cancel each other out completely. For the world as a whole, changes in the terms of trade cannot bring any gain at all.

13. Terms of trade between primary products and manufactures – a digression

There is a corollary to the conclusions reached in the previous section that deserves to be brought out explicitly. Improvement or worsening of the terms of trade between any two countries (A and U) depends on *comparative* international changes in productivity. It has nothing to do with the *level* of the rates of change. In other words, they have no relation to the fact that in one country over-all productivity may be growing faster or slower than in another country. This means, for example, that the faster growing country might well be the one that, besides keeping to itself all its productivity increases, also absorbs some of the scantier productivity increases achieved in the other countries!

The practical importance of this is great enough to deserve a brief digression on at least one of its applications, concerning the topical question of the terms of trade between primary products (normally exported by underdeveloped countries) and manufactured products (normally exported by advanced industrial countries).

As is well known, there has been much speculation, during the past thirty years, on why the terms of trade have been worsening – as it seems they have been – for the primary product producing countries (normally underdeveloped countries), at a time when the largest increases in productivity are taking place in the manufactured product producing countries (the industrially advanced countries).[11]

Our analysis shows that there is no relation whatever between these two things. If, in the underdeveloped countries, productivity growth in the export industries *relative* to productivity growth in the home-market industries happens to be larger than in industrial countries – as in fact it is very likely to be – the terms of trade will worsen for the former. To put the matter in a simple analytical way, suppose that productivity is increasing at exactly the same rate in all export industries, both in industrial and in underdeveloped countries. Yet, the industrial countries – where productivity in their *other* industries may be increasing at roughly the same rate – will be able to keep their relative prices constant and will thereby keep all productivity increases to themselves. On the other hand, the underdeveloped countries – if their economies are otherwise technologically stagnant – will inevitably experience tendencies towards decreasing prices in the technically progressive sectors, relative to the others. When this happens, they will transfer abroad – through decreasing prices – even those productivity increases (those in the exporting industries) that they can obtain. And the terms of trade will worsen for them the more, the heavier their concentration of technical improvements in the export industries. In the short run, there is an easy way out, and that is to let the economy take a 'dualistic' structure, with wage rates in the export (high productivity) industries becoming higher than elsewhere. But in the long run this will only make the situation worse. If the trend is to be reversed, productivity will have to be speeded up in the *non-exporting* industries. In this way, the underdeveloped countries would gain not only from these technical improvements, but also from becoming able to retain inside the country the productivity increases that take place in the exporting industries and are now leaked abroad.

---

11 The question was first raised by Raul Prebisch in a United Nations publication (*The Economic Development of Latin America and its Principal Problems,* United Nations, New York 1949. See also: 'Commercial Policy in the Underdeveloped Countries', Supplement to *The American Economic Review,* 1959, pp. 251–73). It has since given rise to a long debate. Prebisch's own explanation was a rather complicated one, based on a mixture of structural features, facts and events (different elasticities of demand with respect to income, different behaviour of manufactured and primary product firms, different responses of prices and incomes to the trade cycle, different bargaining power of the Trade Unions, etc.). The explanation given here goes much deeper and is much simpler.

14. A 'special' principle of comparative productivity-change advantage, and the structural dynamics of international trade

We may now go on to consider the changing composition of trade between various countries that are trading among themselves.

Over time, the structural dynamics of international prices are obviously determined by the comparative evolution of productivity in the various countries. But the structural dynamics of international production have a more complex determining process behind them. First of all, we may notice that *total* international production of any specific commodity is clearly determined by the evolution of total demand. There is very little influence that the dynamics of prices can exert on this. At any particular point of time, a higher or a lower price can only postpone or anticipate a growth pattern of demand which is going to take place anyhow. So that, for any single physical (internationally traded) commodity, the rate of change of total demand will depend almost exclusively on the growth of national incomes (i.e. on the economic development) of those countries where that commodity has a high elasticity of demand with respect to income.[12]

However, while *total* international demand of any specific commodity depends on the levels of incomes, the international distribution of its production, or, as we may say more effectively, *which particular country or countries* will be able to produce it at a given point of time, will mainly depend on prices. Other things being equal, those countries will be able to export a specific commodity which are able to achieve and then maintain the lowest comparative cost (and price). This is crucial to the whole pattern of international trade.

Let us consider the dynamic implications. When there are many countries exporting the same commodity, a fall in price caused by a speeding up of comparative productivity in only one country will improve the international competitive position of the industry producing that commodity in that single country (in the sense that the industry concerned will be able either progressively to increase its share of total production, or to reap extra profits, or to do both). It does not necessarily follow, however, that this change will be advantageous also to that single country as a whole. The previous analysis puts us in a position to investigate this problem in detail.

12 There are some important practical implications of this conclusion for those countries that have become the suppliers of a substantial part of world consumption of a particular commodity (the case of sugar, cocoa, etc.). Whatever these countries may do (in terms of improvements in technology and thus of prices) they will always be unable to exert any appreciable influence on total demand for their products. Their production will depend almost entirely on the economic growth of the importing countries in the rest of the world.

In the notation of section 12, we may formulate a second (special) principle of comparative productivity-change advantage. This special principle on comparative productivity refers, no longer to the country as a whole as the 'general' principle does, but to a particular industry – let us say to industry η in country H, as against the same industry in the rest of the world, to be called W. (We shall denote by $\varrho_{\eta H}$ the rate of growth of productivity of industry η in country H, and by $\varrho_{\eta W}$ the rate of growth of productivity of industry η in the rest of the world.)

Clearly, over time, industry η from H will improve, worsen, or maintain unchanged its international competitive position, according to whether:

(XI.14.1)
$$\frac{\varrho_{\eta H}}{R_H} > \frac{\varrho_{\eta W}}{R_W},$$

or

(XI.14.2)
$$\frac{\varrho_{\eta H}}{R_H} < \frac{\varrho_{\eta W}}{R_W},$$

or

(XI.14.3)
$$\frac{\varrho_{\eta H}}{R_H} = \frac{\varrho_{\eta W}}{R_W},$$

i.e. exactly in reverse order to its influence on the terms of trade of its own country (and, incidentally also of all countries exporting η). It does not follow, however, that (XI.14.1) and (IX.14.2) will also be advantageous and disadvantageous, respectively, to country H as a whole. That will depend on whether the two inequalities have been caused by a speeding-up and slowing-down, respectively, of the productivity rates that appear in the numerators or by a slowing-down and speeding-up, respectively, of the productivity rates that appear in the denominators.

In more precise terms, suppose that equality (XI.14.3) has prevailed for some time (whatever the way in which it has been fulfilled; i.e. whether owing to the numerator and denominator of the first ratio being both higher than, both lower than, or both equal to, those of the second ratio). Then, suppose that, at a certain point in time, a change takes place in country H and equality (XI.14.3) is converted into an inequality. Four cases are possible:

(a) (XI.14.3) is converted into (IX.14.1) by an increase in $\varrho_{\eta H}$;
(b) (XI.14.3) is converted into (IX.14.1) by a decrease in R_H;
(c) (XI.14.3) is converted into (XI.14.2) by a decrease in $\varrho_{\eta H}$;
(d) (XI.14.3) is converted into (XI.14.2) by an increase in R_H.

Now, from the point of view of *any one* of the industries and the countries belonging to the rest of the world, where no change (or rather no change in the rates of change) has taken place, the assessment of advantages or disadvantages is quite straightforward. Cases (a) and (b) entail a worsening of the competitive positions of all industries η in W and at the same time, a worsening of the terms of trade for any country exporting η. Therefore (a) and (b) are disadvantageous both to all industries η in W and to all countries exporting η in W. Conversely, (c) and (d) entail an improvement of the competitive positions of all industries η in W and at the same time an improvement of the terms of trade for any country exporting η. Therefore cases (c) and (d) are advantageous both to all industries η in W and to all countries exporting η in W.

But the situation is more complex from the point of view of country H. Here, both (a) and (b) represent cases in which the international competitive position of industry η has improved; and both (c) and (d) represent cases in which the international competitive position of industry η has worsened. However, in case (a) the improvement for industry η comes from a speeding up of productivity in η – and thus denotes a clear improvement also for country H as a whole – while in case (b) it comes from a slowing down of the rate R_H, and thus denotes a worsened position for country H as a whole. Conversely, in case (c) the worsening for industry η comes from a slowing down of productivity in η – and thus denotes a worsening also for country H as a whole – while in case (d) it comes from a speeding up of productivity in all other industries, and thus denotes an improved position for country H as a whole. Thus, cases (a) and (d) denote an improvement for the country (although case (d) is disadvantageous to the single industry η), while cases (b) and (c) denote a worsened position for the country (although case (b) is advantageous to the single industry η).

The important distinction that emerges from these conclusions is again between the factors determining the growth of real per capita income in a country and those determining changes in its competitive international position (and terms of trade). The former depend on absolute levels of rates of growth of productivity, while the latter depend on *comparative* rates of changes in productivity. This means that, although the prosperity of a country (the speed at which it is able to increase its per capita income) will be higher the greater the rates of change in productivity, the success of a particular industry in international exchange – let us say of industry η from country H – does not depend exclusively on the rate of growth of productivity that this industry is able to achieve. It also depends on the rates of growth of productivity which are achieved: (i) by industry η in the rest of the

270

world; (ii) by all other industries producing internationally traded commodities in H; (iii) by all other industries producing internationally traded commodities in the rest of the world.

The practical relevance of all these conclusions is so great as hardly to need being emphasised. In practice, this practical relevance is evinced by the continually changing pattern of world international trade. Whenever, in countries which may not be much advanced, some particular branches of industry succeed, simply by learning and introducing technical methods which are currently used abroad, in achieving high rates of growth of productivity, they immediately become much more competitive than the similar industries of the industrially advanced countries, where such high rates of change are impossible to achieve. The latter may find themselves unable to expand their exports, and even to keep at home the purchasing power of their internal customers, in spite of their higher technical efficiency (on absolute standards). This is clearly a situation of which, for example, so many Japanese, and continental European, firms have widely taken advantage in the post-war period. Many firms in less industrially advanced countries might well do the same in the near future.

15. Economic policy implications

We may now try to gather the threads of the foregoing analysis and concentrate on some of its major logical implications for economic policy.

We may well say, to begin with, that there seems to have been, in the past, a widespread failure to realise that the primary source of international gains is not mobility of goods, but mobility of knowledge. In fact, if technical knowledge were perfectly mobile, international mobility of goods would be made unnecessary, except for those goods that can only be produced, or found, in particular geographical areas. On the other hand, no mobility of goods – however extended or perfect it may be – will ever fulfil the function of spreading productivity gains across borders. Productivity gains may indeed be leaked abroad, sometimes, but for other reasons, as we have seen. In any case they may go either way, and in the aggregate they cancel out entirely.

International learning must therefore remain, for any country, the major and primary aim. This principle of economic policy is one of general and unconditional validity.[13] Its generality comes from its

---

13 This principle is not incompatible with the fact that some small countries may find it useful to concentrate their technological efforts (and technological learning) on some branches of production. Modern technology often requires minimum scales of

coincidence with the primary aim (learning) of any international policy. It thereby is a principle subject to no condition, internal or external, and subordinated to no equilibrium or disequilibrium situation; it is valid for all economic systems – for industrially advanced countries (which can always learn new methods developed abroad) as well as, and in practice of course much more, for underdeveloped countries.

The real difficulty is that technical knowledge is far less mobile, or rather by far less quickly mobile, than goods, so that – when all possible efforts have been made to improve technical knowledge, and only when all such efforts have been made – a country can obtain further gains by expansion of international trade. But these will not be *further* gains, unless – as we have seen in detail earlier – the importation of goods: (i) is not going to hamper the process of learning, or to deplete the accumulated stock of technical knowledge; and (ii) is not going to increase the number of unemployed, transitory situations being taken into account. On these two provisos the discussion of section 6 now simply needs to be completed with the results emerging from the dynamic analysis of the foregoing pages.

Proviso (i) – one must admit – is often not fulfilled, especially in underdeveloped countries, when an industry, just in order to be set up and for its costs to be brought down to an internationally competitive level, needs a certain period of time in which to learn and accumulate experience. This situation has been so important in practice as to lead traditional economists to making of it an exception to their free-trade *récipe* and to calling it the 'infant industry case' for protection. The interesting thing that emerges from the foregoing dynamic analysis is that there is also a corresponding case for industrially advanced countries. As we have seen, efficient industries – on absolute technical standards – may be displaced from their own home market by technically less efficient firms from less advanced (i.e. lower wages) countries when these succeed in achieving much higher *rates* of productivity growth. In this case, the industrially advanced country may actually give up production of those commodities for the time being, if accumulated technical knowledge can be kept, even without being used. But if a net loss of technical knowledge is inevitable, then protection might become advisable. (This case has always been perceived, of course, in the practice of industrially advanced countries, but traditional economists

---

operation, which may be larger than the country's demand requirements. In these cases, a choice has obviously to be made on which commodities to import and which commodities to produce at home in larger quantities than required by internal needs (the excess production having to be exported).

have never been able to explain it. They might have made of it another exception: the 'mature industry case' for protection.)

Proviso (ii) is much harder in practice to assess, within a dynamic context. The general attitude in the past has been to consider unemployment losses as transitory and gains from trade as permanent. But when comparative costs, and prices, are changing all the time, gains from trade may become as transitory as unemployment losses. The question is not one of weighing up temporary losses as against permanent gains, but a more complex one of evaluating how temporary and how permanent losses and gains may be; a question of evaluating rates of change and thus the relative dynamism of the various sectors.[14]

The practical importance of having clear ideas about these two provisos is hardly in need of being emphasised, especially if one thinks that both of them are in practice so easily open to abuses.[15]

But when these two provisos are satisfied and international trade is allowed, the obvious policy problem arises of achieving the highest possible gains from trade. As is well known, the recommendation that traditional economic theory – both Classical and Marginalist – has unanimously been giving, for almost two centuries, is: in order to maximise gains from trade, a country should specialise in producing those commodities for which it enjoys a comparative cost advantage.

Our analysis has shown that this policy recommendation is, strictly, incorrect. In any case it is incomplete. Comparative cost advantages are changing all the time. And in those few fields where they are permanent – i.e. for those particular goods which can only be produced in certain geographical areas – specialisation is inevitable anyhow. The essential point to stress is that policies of specialisation in production cannot be stated independently of dynamic trends; more specifically, they cannot be stated independently of the rates at which productivity is changing over time. As we have seen, comparative cost advantages, at a given point of time, are not enough to justify specialisation: they are not even necessary, if they can be achieved quickly.

---

14 This goes much deeper than the usual explanation in terms of strategic reasons (risks of war) used to account for, e.g., the heavy protection of agriculture, in almost all countries. The complex problems of training labourers coming from an agricultural environment for industrial jobs have made agricultural unemployment, from among all types of unemployment, the slowest and most difficult one to re-absorb.

15 Industries compelled to close down will always exert pressures on Governments to obtain protection, even when labour and capital can be transferred elsewhere reasonably quickly; or when losses of technical knowledge and skill are negligible; or when the effects of international trade are in fact to compel them to devise ways to cut their costs – thereby stimulating, rather than hampering, productivity increases. Moreover, industries which used to be 'infant' may insist on protection even after having grown up.

Perhaps the nearest we can get to a general policy recommendation on international trade, if we want one to replace the traditional one, is to say: in order to obtain the highest possible gains from international trade, a country should specialise in producing those commodities for which it can achieve, over the relevant period of time, the highest comparative rates of growth of productivity.

There are cases, of course, in which comparative advantages from the present levels of costs and comparative advantages from productivity rates of change coincide: and in these cases the traditional *récipe* may lead to the correct results, after all. This was the case of England in the last century, when the traditional conclusion was used to advocate specialisation in the production of manufactures. But there are cases – or stages of development – in which this coincidence does not take place, and in which therefore the traditional *récipe*, if it were to be followed, might lead to disastrous results. By and large, this seems to be the case for the majority of underdeveloped countries today.

16. The wealth of nations

It is clearly the entire topic of international economic relations that is in need of a change of outlook, at this point, with a shift of focus in our attention from the narrow subject of international trade to the basic problem of lack of international mobility of technical knowledge. For, when technical knowledge does not spread, the benefits and gains arising from its continuous improvements are all kept inside those countries where it is actually applied to production.

Historically, the result of all this has been the enormous disparities in the wealth of the various nations that can nowadays be observed on the face of the earth. They have become so wide (see the hints given at the end of section 10 above) that one cannot but feel a strong emotional sense of repugnance, and rebellion, against the social injustice which they express. After the foregoing analysis, one might even be induced to consider economic systems as a sort of modern invention made in order to retain for their internal members all the gains coming from productivity growth. And of course, to a certain extent, economic systems are such inventions.

But we must not harbour illusions on this. The time is very far away, and perhaps will never come, when political borders will be considered artificial and the right of anybody to move freely anywhere he (she) pleases be recognized. The fragmentation of the world into numerous, separate economic systems being a fact that has to be accepted, we must be consistent and recognise that the wealth of the industrially advanced countries is something that is rooted in them and is not something of which they are depriving the poor countries.[16] There is nothing that can be 'restored' by 'redistribution' of material goods. And if we were to believe – as is only too widely mistakenly asserted – that all that needs to be done today is a huge redistribution of material goods from the rich to the poor countries, we would simply fall into another tragic trap of traditional thought. We may indeed all agree that average per capita incomes of the order of 200 dollars per year in India, and of the order of 10,000 dollars per year in the United States are differences repugnant to the most elementary sense of human justice. Yet it is not by a redistribution of materials goods, at a given point of time, that anything will be accomplished. Even if, as an extreme hypothesis, the average American, in a certain year, were heroically to deprive himself (or herself) of 5,000 dollars' worth of his (her) income to be *distributed freely* to Indians, no *permanent* change at all would take place in the wealth of the two nations. Or rather, it would take place only to the extent that the transfer of goods would bring with it a spread of technical knowledge. This is the essential and crucial point. If only goods, and no knowledge, were distributed, the average Indian, in the following year, would continue to produce his (her) 200 dollars' worth amount of production and the average American would continue to produce his (her) 10,000 dollars' worth of per capita income.

It is only by absorbing technical knowledge that the poor countries will be able permanently to increase their wealth. It should not be surprising that all these concepts have remained so unclear so far. The modern industrial age has brought to us a new type of wealth, of which perhaps we have not yet become fully aware, although the original insights into the matter go back as far as Adam Smith. We have not yet fully realised that the very concept of wealth, in a modern society, has changed in its own content.[17]

In a pre-industrial society, wealth is mainly a stock of material goods – something that people have inherited from the past or have appropriated from 'nature'. (This is incidentally the concept on which the whole marginal economic theory was built.) The more some people or countries have of this type of wealth, the less remains at the disposal of

16 There is, of course, plenty of justification for accusing the richer countries of selfishness; but, if the ground were only that of the existing disparities of per capita incomes, there would be no justification for accusing them of exploitation. International exploitation does, unfortunately, take place, but for other reasons (see, as an example, section 11 above). See also footnote 19 below.
17 For further details on these concepts, see my own *Lectures, op. cit.*, pp. 2–4.

others.[18] The less rich some people are made, the less poor others become.

But the wealth of an industrial nation is something quite different, or rather it is something deeper. It is not so much the material goods that people have; it is the technical knowledge of how to make them. There may be some conceptual difficulties in grasping these concepts, because technical knowledge is often incorporated into material goods, and because of what appears at the level of the single individuals. But material goods are not to be confused with the technical knowledge which is behind them, and ways of increasing individual wealth are not to be confused with ways of increasing the wealth of a nation. Within a country, an individual may get richer and richer the more material goods he appropriates at the expense of others. But for the country as a whole (if population remains constant) the amount of material goods at the disposal of the community can only increase to the extent that technical knowledge increases. For an industrial nation, wealth is not a stock of material goods (which only represent the external expression of it) – it is a stock of technical knowledge. The less some countries have of this type of wealth the less is also at the disposal of others; and the more some people know, the easier it becomes for others to know as well.[19]

It may be consoling to think that the wealth brought to us by the industrial age is a much more favourable type of wealth, than the old one, to relations among people and nations. For, if, in the pre-industrial world, the main way for a country to increase its wealth was to dominate and exploit its neighbours, today it has become to emulate them and do better. It is only a little less consoling to realise that, with all the new horizons open before us, we should so often let ourselves be prisoners of the old concepts and fall short of our actual possibilities, not because of objective difficulties, but because of the persistence of old ideas, which accomplish the rare combination of being both unfavourable and obsolete.

18 Paradoxically enough, the wave of wealth that has recently flown to the oil producing countries is of this type – it is a wealth of 'the old type', coming from the endowment of a natural resource. Thus, whatever its importance (a considerable importance indeed in this case), its effects are not permanent. It will have effects lasting beyond the period of exhaustion of the resource only to the extent that it is being used to acquire the other type of wealth, the 'industrial' wealth associated with technical knowledge.

19 I should like to add the important warning that this *should not* be taken as a basis for claiming that international exploitation does not take place. Unfortunately, international exploitation has taken place in the past and is taking place today in many guises. The simple point that is made here is that no exploitation is necessarily implied by the mere fact that better technical knowledge enables a particular country to achieve higher levels of per capita incomes than are obtained in other countries.

Index

utility, 11, 11n, 71, 139; *see also* marginal
　utility

value, theory of: in terms of labour
　equivalent, 42, 153, 179, 245 ff.; in terms
　of labour: *see* pure labour theory of
　value
variables vs. unknowns, 77–9; *see also*
　constants vs. data
vertically hyper-integrated: sectors, 147,
　148; labour coefficients, 102, 132, 148,
　198, 207, rates of change of, 103–4, 172
vertically integrated: labour coefficients,
　29, 112; capital/output ratios, 113;
　productive capacity, 29, 36; sectors, xii,
　29, 110, 112, favourable to dynamic
　analysis, 115–17, compared with
　input–output industries, 110–17, and
　empirical data, 112–14

viability conditions, 45, 45n, 94n
von Neumann, John, 17n, 59n, 119–23; his
　typically classical approach, 17–18n

wage rate, 39, 137, 192, 246; 'real', 98, a
　macro-economic concept, 136–8, its time
　path 142–3; and rate of profit
　(asymmetry), 142–3, 199; irrelevant to
　choice of technique, 192–7; in
　international comparisons, 246 ff.;
　exogenously given in classical
　economics, 40
wages (total), 143–4; as a 'surplus', 144; vs.
　total consumption 146–8
Walras, Léon, 9n, 12n, 18n, 110
wealth, concept of, 5, 275
Wicksell, Knut, 15n, 180, 192, 230
Wold, Herman O. A., 70n